T·U·L·S·A
The Great American City

Produced in partnership with the Metropolitan Tulsa Chamber of Commerce

Photo by Don Sibley.

T·U·L·S·A
The Great American City

Written by JOHN HAMILL
Corporate Profiles by CHRIS METCALF & BARRETT WALLER
Featuring the Photography of DON WHEELER

The Metropolitan Tulsa Chamber of Commerce and Community Communications, Inc.,
would like to express our gratitude to the following companies for their leadership in the development of this book.

DOERNER, SAUNDERS,
DANIEL & ANDERSON, L.L.P.

T·U·L·S·A
The Great American City

Produced in partnership with the Metropolitan Tulsa Chamber of Commerce
Jay M. Clemons, President and CEO
616 South Boston Avenue, Suite 100
Tulsa, OK 74119-1298

By JOHN HAMILL
Corporate Profiles by CHRIS METCALF *and* BARRETT WALLER
Featuring the Photography of DON WHEELER
Additional Photographs by DON SIBLEY

Community Communications, Inc.
Publishers: Ronald P. Beers and James E. Turner

Staff for *Tulsa: The Great American City*

Acquisitions: HENRY S. BEERS
Publisher's Sales Associates: JOHN TEW AND ROBBIE WILLS
Executive Editor: JAMES E. TURNER
Senior Editors: MARY SHAW HUGHES AND WENDI LEWIS
Managing Editor: AMY NEWELL
Profile Editor: MARY CATHERINE RICHARDSON
Contributing Editor: MICHAEL HIGHTOWER
Design Director: SCOTT PHILLIPS
Designer: HOLLI T. HAWSEY
Photo Editors: HOLLI T. HAWSEY AND AMY NEWELL
Production Manager: JARROD STIFF
Editorial Assistant: AMANDA BURBANK
Contract Manager: CHRISTI STEVENS
Sales Coordinators: ANNETTE LOZIER AND SANDRA AKERS
Accounting Services: SARA ANN TURNER
Printing Production: GARY G. PULLIAM/D.C. GRAPHICS
Pre-Press and Separations: ARTCRAFT GRAPHIC PRODUCTIONS

CCI

Community Communications, Inc.
Montgomery, Alabama

James E. Turner, Chairman of the Board
Ronald P. Beers, President
Daniel S. Chambliss, Vice President

TABLE OF CONTENTS

Chapter One

TULSA NOW
Positioned For Prosperity

*O*il put Tulsa on the map and led to the creation of a classic American boomtown. Throughout the years, the city enjoyed good times, but its economy was held hostage to the price of oil. Thanks to the vision of business leaders and the development of a diversified economy, Tulsa's roller coaster ride came to an end in the 1980s.

Page 16

Chapter Two

THE EARLY DAYS
Typically Tulsan

*T*ulsa has a colorful history, and its roots trace back far before the days of oil. The area's first settlers, a band of Lochapoka Creeks, arrived after they were forced from tribal lands in the Southeast. The community later evolved into a frontier town, but the discovery of oil changed Tulsa's fortunes forever.

Page 40

Chapter Three

EDUCATION
Meeting of the Minds

*T*ulsa always has fostered excellence in education, as the area's many quality schools prove. But until recently, one dream went unrealized–the presence of a comprehensive, publicly supported university. The quest came to fruition with the creation of OSU-Tulsa in 1999.

Page 52

Chapter Four

HEALTH CARE
Caring Hearts & Hands

*T*he discovery of oil brought sudden growth, and the city needed health care to keep pace with the population boom. From the opening of Tulsa Hospital in 1906 to the University of Oklahoma's announcement in 1999 that it would open a medical research and training facility in midtown, Tulsans have always enjoyed first-rate medical services.

Page 62

Chapter Five

A CITY OF NEIGHBORHOODS
Diversity Abounds

*T*ulsa is a multi-faceted city whose neighborhoods reflect distinctive personalities. Some residents prefer to live near the bustle of downtown; others opt to join quiet suburban communities. Whatever their tastes, Tulsans can always find a great place to call home.

Page 74

Chapter Six

CULTURE
Living On Tulsa Time

*E*ver since the Opera House brought highbrow entertainment to the Oklahoma frontier, Tulsans have embraced culture. Times have changed, but Tulsa's commitment to the arts has never wavered. Simply put, Tulsa's wealth of cultural and artistic offerings gives residents and visitors alike plenty of opportunities for entertainment.

Page 88

Chapter Seven

RECREATION
On Your Own Time

*T*ulsa's first baseball team, the Oilers, hit the field in 1905–before Oklahoma even achieved statehood. Today, the Drillers continue the baseball tradition, and college sports offer many options for fans. Lush fairways await golfers, boating enthusiasts can find lakes and rivers within a short drive, and the Tulsa Zoo is one of America's finest. A variety of ethnic and seasonal festivals puts the finishing touches on Tulsa's recreational offerings.

Page 106

Chapter Eight

A CITY OF FAITHS
Religion & Community Service

*E*arly settlers arrived with deep moral and religious convictions, and churches, synagogues, and charitable organizations soon emerged as cornerstones of civic life. Today, Tulsans carry on the tradition of improving lives and helping the less fortunate.

Page 126

Chapter Nine

TULSA'S FUTURE
A New Century

*T*ulsans have always prided themselves on their entrepreneurial spirit and willingness to embrace challenges, and that same attitude is very much alive on the threshold of a new millennium. Blessed with a progressive outlook and distinct economic advantages, Tulsa is truly poised for an era of prosperity.

Page 142

Photos by Don Wheeler.

FOREWORD

ulsa: The Great American City
offers a glimpse into a community whose thriving business environment is complemented by urban amenities and rich cultural experiences.

Whether you're interested in Native American pageantry, top-notch art collections, or state-of-the-art technology, Tulsa has what you're looking for. It's a cosmopolitan place where Art Deco architecture from the 1920s stands side-by-side with telecommunications centers. It's a city of entrepreneurs and Fortune 500 executives. And as locals will tell you, it's a community with the body of a large city, but the heart and soul of a small town.

When wildcatters struck "black gold" and launched the age of petroleum, Tulsa earned distinction as the "Oil Capital of the World." Empires were built overnight, and oilmen-turned-philanthropists used their good fortune for the benefit of the entire city. World-class museums, hospitals, and educational institutions stand as testimonies to their generosity and serve as examples to later generations of the vision that lies at the core of any strong community.

Oil, though still an important feature of Tulsa's economic landscape, has made way for industries ranging from telecommunications to aerospace. Diversification has brought an end to the boom-and-bust cycles inherent in a one-industry economy and ushered in an era of unprecedented opportunity. Tulsa-based companies generate more than 60 percent of Oklahoma's exports and continue to capture market share overseas. Thanks to workforce development programs that serve as models throughout the country, companies whose employment bases are expanding can count on a pool of qualified workers to help them grow. Public-private partnerships are energizing all sectors of our community and contributing in myriad ways to Tulsa's quality of life.

Tulsa has always had a unique and remarkable story to tell. These pages capture the essence of that story. From its founding by a tiny band of Creek Indians in the early 19th century to the present day, Tulsa has always been a city of surprises and a city of treasures. Entrepreneurial start-ups and multinational corporations alike have found Tulsa to be fertile ground for economic growth and innovation. And if past is prologue, we can look forward to more of the same in the years to come.

Jay M. Clemens
President & CEO
Metropolitan Tulsa Chamber of Commerce

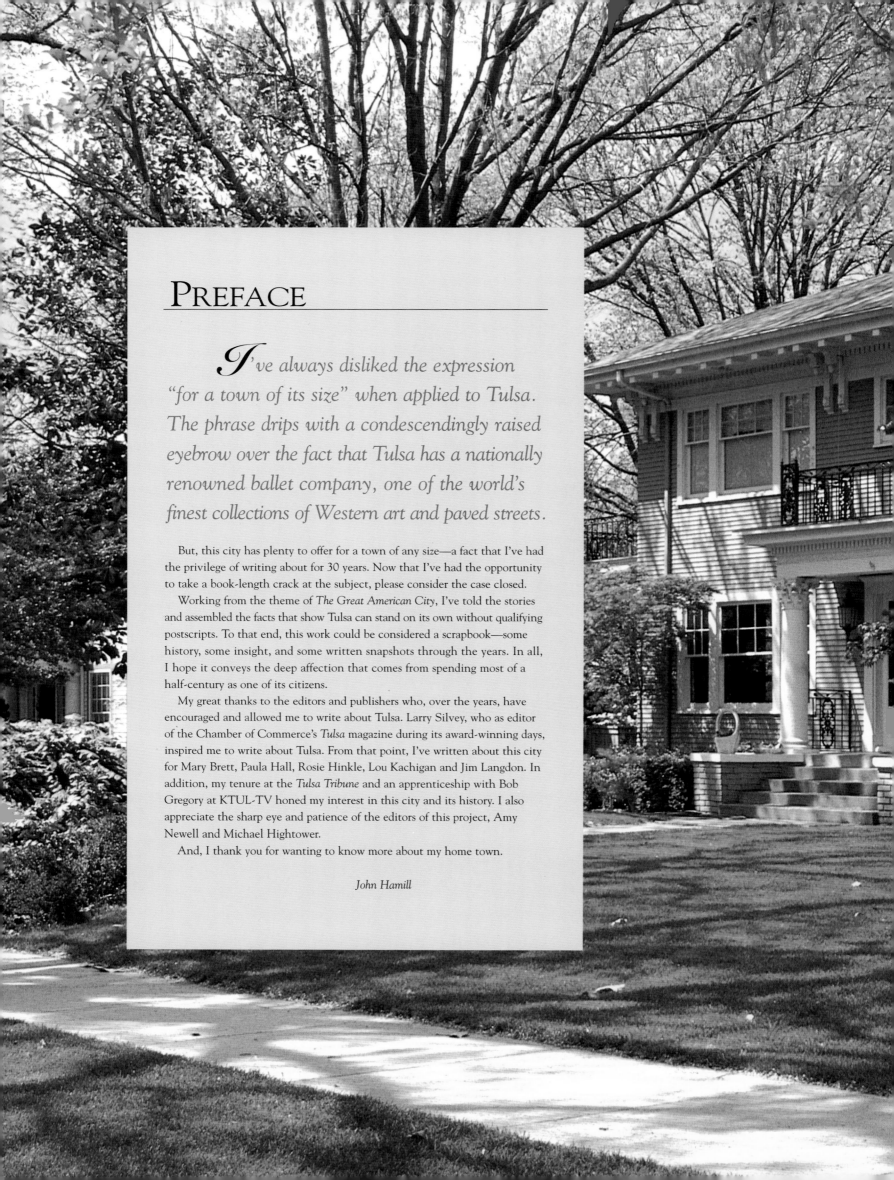

PREFACE

*I've always disliked the expression
"for a town of its size" when applied to Tulsa.
The phrase drips with a condescendingly raised
eyebrow over the fact that Tulsa has a nationally
renowned ballet company, one of the world's
finest collections of Western art and paved streets.*

But, this city has plenty to offer for a town of any size—a fact that I've had
the privilege of writing about for 30 years. Now that I've had the opportunity
to take a book-length crack at the subject, please consider the case closed.

Working from the theme of *The Great American City*, I've told the stories
and assembled the facts that show Tulsa can stand on its own without qualifying
postscripts. To that end, this work could be considered a scrapbook—some
history, some insight, and some written snapshots through the years. In all,
I hope it conveys the deep affection that comes from spending most of a
half-century as one of its citizens.

My great thanks to the editors and publishers who, over the years, have
encouraged and allowed me to write about Tulsa. Larry Silvey, who as editor
of the Chamber of Commerce's *Tulsa* magazine during its award-winning days,
inspired me to write about Tulsa. From that point, I've written about this city
for Mary Brett, Paula Hall, Rosie Hinkle, Lou Kachigan and Jim Langdon. In
addition, my tenure at the *Tulsa Tribune* and an apprenticeship with Bob
Gregory at KTUL-TV honed my interest in this city and its history. I also
appreciate the sharp eye and patience of the editors of this project, Amy
Newell and Michael Hightower.

And, I thank you for wanting to know more about my home town.

John Hamill

1

Part One

1
Chapter One

TULSA NOW

Positioned For Prosperity

Photo by Don Wheeler

*W*ill Rogers, Oklahoma's favorite son and an astute observer of the goings-on in his home state, once remarked, "Even if you're on the right track, you'll get run over if you just sit there."

Oklahoma was a young state when Will was making his timeless observations. Nevertheless, the state's main vulnerability was already coming into focus: Every time Oklahomans seemed to be on the right track, something came along to run them over. The chief culprit? Oil. It was a blessing during the good times and a curse when prices headed south. As long as Oklahomans were held hostage to the price of oil, there was no way out of the boom-and-bust economy.

Early on, oil was hailed as an unqualified blessing. Tulsa was just a dot on the map when, in 1882, the Frisco Railroad made its way into the heart of the Creek Nation. Some saw great opportunity with the arrival of the steel rails. But it wasn't until 1901 when oil was discovered across the Arkansas River, and then again in 1905 when drillers made an historic strike a little farther south, that Tulsa truly came into its own. Almost overnight, streets were paved and buildings dotted the landscape. Tulsa was on its way to becoming a classic American boomtown.

Oil remained the underpinning of Tulsa's economy for the next half-century. *Collier's* magazine, one of the most popular publications of its time, paid tribute to Tulsa's commercial and industrial reputation in a two-page spread in its February 5, 1949, edition. " . . . Tulsa can call itself the 'Oil Capital of the World'," claimed the author. "It's an honest boast based on plain fact."

The author of the *Collier's* piece proceeded to describe Tulsa as the primary production, manufacturing, and distribution center for the

nation's petroleum industry. The city was home to such petroleum giants as The Texas Company, Sinclair, Shell and Gulf, all of which contributed to a vibrant urban culture and a quality of life that was already earning Tulsa a reputation as America's most livable community.

With 20/20 hindsight, we know better than to take the author's next claim at face value. Tulsa, he wrote, "is a wise town, too—smart enough not to become stale with specialization." The secret to Tulsa's economic diversification in 1949 was its "more than 600 factories making everything from oil field machinery to sulfuric acid, mattresses, prefabricated houses, plastics and boats."

Was Tulsa at mid-century, then, a mature town sophisticated enough to take rank with the Eastern metropolises? Was its economy diversified enough to weather the ups and downs that bedeviled one-industry towns such as Detroit and Pittsburgh? Or would its oil-based economy prove to be its Achilles heel?

Educational opportunities, always excellent in Tulsa, were further enhanced by the creation of Oklahoma State University's Tulsa campus. Photo by Don Sibley.

Thirty years later, the jury was still out. *The Tulsa Spirit*, a handsome book sponsored by the Metropolitan Tulsa Chamber of Commerce, made the bold claim that oil had loosened its grip on northeast Oklahoma. "Tulsa, of course, is no longer completely dependent upon the oil industry," asserted the author. "Other industries make for a well-rounded, diversified economy; among them are data processing, metal fabrication and distribution, aviation-aerospace, the manufacturing of fishing tackle, winches, industrial heaters and the world's largest fork lift truck and two-axle vehicle."

Optimists seemed to be vindicated during the boom times of the late '70s and early '80s. Oil prices went through the stratosphere, and signs of prosperity were everywhere. Advertising executives were buying drilling rigs, a filter company purchased an oil field equipment manufacturing concern, and swigging champagne out of a cowboy boot became a rite of passage for the *nouveau riche*. Everybody wanted in on the act, and many had the brand new Mercedes in the garage as evidence of their own good fortune. As they say down in New Orleans, *laissez les bons temps rouler!*

But a funny thing happened on the way to the bank. Oil never quite hit its anticipated price of $80 a barrel. Not even close. Much to Tulsa's chagrin, the bottom fell out. The boom had turned to bust, and oilmen and their dependents were running for cover. Seems that much of the data being processed was for energy companies, and fabricated metal was going to the oil fields. Tulsa's number one customer for manufacturers and data processors was closed for business.

In 18 months, Tulsa lost 40,000 jobs.

But Oklahomans are a resilient lot. Rather than post signs requesting that the last one leaving turn out the lights, city leaders seized the mid-1980s bust as an opportunity to tackle once and for all the issue of economic diversification. They set a goal of creating 36,000 new jobs by the early 1990s. Why 36,000 rather than 40,000? Mainly because Tulsa's economy was showing signs of recovery on its own.

The plan worked. By the late 1980s, more than 10,000 jobs had been created by companies that had relocated to Tulsa. Another 24,000 were created through expansion of existing businesses, and 4,000 emerged in home-grown entrepreneurial ventures.

Best of all, the new jobs represented a wide range of industries. One company with an oil field heritage transformed itself into the manufacturer of a fitness machine. Insurance, a paper company, an appliance manufacturer—businesses were lining up to take advantage of Tulsa's lost cost of living and highly qualified labor force.

Meanwhile, Tulsa-based companies were reinventing themselves. Take, for example, a company with roots dating back to 1908. Two brothers, Miller and David Williams, had considerable experience in concrete construction. They knew little about pipelines, but when they won a contract to build one, they put their entrepreneurial skills to work and set about hiring people who did. The money flowed in, and by 1915, their aptly named Williams Brothers Company was constructing cross-country pipelines. During World War II, the company solidified its leadership in the pipeline construction business by building the "Big Inch" and "Little Inch" pipelines for the war effort.

A new generation of the Williams family assumed leadership of the company at mid-century. They embarked on a path of diversification

Ford Glass is among a host of companies that have established operations in the Tulsa area.
Photo by Don Wheeler.

In 1995, Whirlpool selected Tulsa as the site of a major plant. Today, the appliance maker pumps more than $25 million into the city's economy.
Photo by Don Wheeler.

(Opposite page) In the late 1990s, TV Guide joined Tulsa's growing roster of high-tech communications companies.
Photo by Don Wheeler.

to mitigate the "boom-and-bust" cycles inherent in pipeline construction and smooth out the company's erratic earnings performance. In a deal that rocked Wall Street as the largest cash-for-assets transaction to date in U.S. history, the Williams Brothers Company purchased Great Lakes Pipeline Company for $287.6 million. The company was now under the direction of two brothers, Charles P. and John H. Williams, and a cousin, David R. Williams Jr., son of an original founder. Williams Brothers Company had total assets of $30 million, and on the day of the purchase, John Williams signed his name 2,000 times to make the deal official. Clearly, the minnow had swallowed the whale, and Williams Brothers Company was poised for growth.

The company's management found striking similarities between pipeline construction and operations. The new Williams Brothers Pipe Line Company resembled a utility in the predictability of its earnings, whereas the construction end of the business was far more volatile. Operating within the confines of a highly regulated industry, managers came to the realization that their growth would follow a predictable trajectory—too predictable, perhaps, for a bunch of Oklahoma entrepreneurs.

Under the leadership of John Williams, the company continued to diversify into LP-gas marketing, discount and auto parts stores, insurance, steel manufacturing, and fertilizer processing and marketing. By the late 1970s, the company proudly advertised itself as The Williams Companies. By this time, its pipeline construction business had been sold to a group of management employees.

But the Williams brothers were by no means finished with their diversification. A new management team was put into place. Joe Williams, John and Charles's cousin and David's younger brother, maintained the family tradition. Keith Bailey, a high-powered executive who had joined the company in 1974, joined him at the top of the corporate ladder. Under their leadership, the company entered the brave new world of communications. The cornerstone of their strategy was to couple acquisitions of pipeline systems in the Northwest and mid-continent with usage of decommissioned pipelines to develop housing for fiber optic cables, a new mode of communications transmission that promised speed as well as almost limitless capacity.

Soon after selling its interests in metals and fertilizer, The Williams Companies created the largest volume system of interstate natural gas pipelines in the United States. When a suitor from Mississippi, LDDS, showed up in 1994 with an unsolicited offer, Williams decided to sell Wil Tel, the network portion of the telecommunications business, for $2.5 billion. LDDS subsequently reorganized as LDDS-WorldCom and bought MCI and became MCI WorldCom. In the following years, MCI WorldCom increased its employment base in Tulsa.

The Williams Companies retained several of its telecommunications units, and following the expiration of a non-compete period, reentered the market with the ambitious goal of creating a billion-dollar business.

Meanwhile, the company expanded its energy interests with the

acquisition of Tulsa-based MAPCO, a company that owned a pipeline system originally built by none other than the Williams Brothers Company—the original Mid-America Pipeline Company. A darling of Wall Street, the company now known simply as Williams has grown from assets of nearly $486 million in 1970 to more than $19 billion as a new century begins.

Williams serves as a textbook example of a company willing to redeploy its assets, to expand upon its strengths, and to strategically diversify—a company much like the city it calls home.

Tulsa's assets, obvious enough to the people who live here, are marketed day in and day out to the movers and shakers of American industry. In terms of educational resources, Tulsans are fortunate to rely on public and private universities committed to public-private partnerships. Public education and a strong contingent of private schools continue to be a source of pride. Transportation needs are well served by the Tulsa Port of Catoosa, the nation's most inland port with access to New Orleans and the Gulf of Mexico. Interstate highways and railways crisscross the heartland and allow easy access to all points of the compass, and air service gives Tulsans contact with major centers of national and international commerce.

Visitors to Tulsa are sometimes pleasantly surprised to find two symphony orchestras, a nationally recognized ballet company, an internationally acclaimed opera company, first-rate theater, and two museums whose collections are remarkable by any standard. Thousands of miles of shoreline await boating enthusiasts only minutes

Tulsa's parks offer residents many ways to enjoy recreation and relaxation.
Photo by Don Wheeler.

from downtown, and a host of sporting opportunities are available for participants and spectators alike. A thriving two-party political system and a strong mayor/city council system support economic initiatives, and the state constitution requires a balanced budget and provides tax incentives for corporate newcomers. It all adds up to a diversified economy and a cosmopolitan culture that stand as bulwarks against recession.

Tulsans were put to the test in the mid-'90s when the price of oil once again hit bottom. Only this time, plummeting oil prices failed to bring the economy to its knees. There were no dire headlines, no gnashing of teeth, and no wringing of hands. True, there were some energy-related layoffs as companies were forced to make cuts. But the economy held its own; those who were displaced were quickly absorbed into the workforce, and many wound up launching their own ventures.

Diversification has bred more of the same. Avis, Kimberly-Clark, Blue Bell Creameries, Ford Glass, Metropolitan Life, Citgo Petroleum, Dollar Rent A Car Systems, the John Zink Company, TV Guide, and Whirlpool are among the firms that have either expanded their market share or relocated to the Tulsa area. Whirlpool, a major manufacturer of household appliances that pumps some $25 million annually into the city's economy, illustrates the benefits of public-private cooperation. Moreover, Whirlpool's successful move to Tulsa has not gone unnoticed by other companies. Many economic development inquiries have originated with executives interested in Whirlpool's multimillion-dollar decision to build a major plant at Tulsa's Cherokee Industrial Park.

One of the challenges facing business leaders today is to ensure a steady stream of qualified workers for expanding companies. Efforts to maintain a strong labor pool are evidenced by cutting-edge workforce development programs as well as Tulsa's highly respected vocational and technical schools. Businesses are more conscious than ever of the need to build stronger ties between education and the workplace, and many have chosen to participate in the Metropolitan Tulsa Chamber of Commerce's Adopt-A-School program. Tulsa Community College, one of the nation's most respected community college systems, has also played a key role in providing job seekers with the educational background they need to qualify for high-wage employment. And, in one of the most significant developments in recent history, Oklahoma State University has made a commitment to its Tulsa campus that promises to transform higher education in the metropolitan area. School officials anticipate an enrollment of 20,000 within less than 25 years. None of these developments comes a moment too soon. With job creation clipping along at nearly 14,000 new jobs annually, workforce development and broad-based educational opportunities will decide the city's future.

Nobody weaned on the prescient wit of Will Rogers would be willing to bet the ranch on a future of unlimited growth. But Tulsans, accustomed to tales of dry holes, have good reason to be optimistic, as long as their optimism is tempered by a healthy dose of realism. Strategic planning has replaced wildcatting as the topic of conversation in executive suites, and diversification has become more than a slogan. Perhaps it's safe to say that Tulsans are on the right track—as long as they remember to keep looking over their shoulders. ❖

A wide range of festivals take place throughout the year in Tulsa. Mayfest, held in the downtown area, features food, music, and arts and crafts. Photo by Don Wheeler.

THE BAMA COMPANIES

*P*aula Marshall-Chapman, a dynamic leader, who inspires growth in Bama, its employees, and the Tulsa area, heads The Bama Companies. She understands the value of Bama's more than 600 Tulsa-area employees, as she lives by the company's vision statement "People Helping People Be Successful."

The company has seen amazing success, starting in 1927 with one woman selling homemade pies to a near-by restaurant, now selling millions of baked and ready-to-bake goods a day, to such companies as McDonald's. Bama's success has impacted Tulsa, the site of its world headquarters. From the Bama/United Way Golf Tournament to the Bama Volunteers' program to the "Pie Land, USA" sign, Bama has changed the face of Tulsa, forever.

Tulsa once relied almost solely on the oil industry, but today's economic strength comes from diverse sources.
Photo by Don Wheeler.

BLUE CROSS AND BLUE SHIELD OF OKLAHOMA

*B*ecause a group of civic and medical leaders in Oklahoma saw the need for prepaid hospital plans, Blue Cross and Blue Shield can boast 60 years in Oklahoma, now insuring nearly 20 percent of the state's population.

The insurance company has truly embraced Tulsa and its people, employing more than 1,000, committing to keeping the cost of benefits down, and developing a number of programs to benefit the community's total health. These additional services include the Caring Program for Children, Mobile Health Screening Unit, and Caring Van, all dedicated to helping Tulsans live healthier lives.

DOERNER, SAUNDERS, DANIEL & ANDERSON, L.L.P.

*D*oerner, Saunders, Daniel & Anderson, L.L.P., is Oklahoma's oldest and one of its most respected law firms. Throughout the history of the state, Doerner Saunders' attorneys have played an important role in the growth and expansion of Oklahoma's economy by representing the legal needs of its clients in virtually every form of transaction and every kind of litigation.

For more than a century, Doerner Saunders has given creative legal advice and been an active partner with its clients in solving problems and capitalizing on opportunities in Tulsa, throughout Oklahoma, around the nation, and abroad. With this experience, the firm has and will continue to provide its clients with the expertise, versatility, and imagination needed to successfully meet the future.

HILLCREST HEALTHCARE SYSTEM

*H*illcrest HealthCare System (HHS) is Oklahoma's largest nonprofit, nonsectarian health system, employing over 7,000 and offering a myriad of services in eastern Oklahoma. From Hillcrest Medical Center, Tulsa's oldest established hospital, to Tulsa Regional Medical Center, the state's only osteopathic teaching hospital, to Hillcrest Medical Group, the area's largest physician group, and to AirEvac, Oklahoma's first air and ground intensive care service, HHS meets healthcare needs.

Hillcrest HealthCare System is supported by hundreds of dedicated hospital volunteers; in return hospital employees volunteer in a wide variety of community projects, working to improve the community's health status and quality of life. Hillcrest HealthCare System's relationship to eastern Oklahoma is a mutual commitment to compassion through service.

HILTI, INC.

*H*ilti is a world leading manufacturer and supplier of quality, innovative and specialized tools and fastening systems for the construction industry—with a presence in more than 100 countries. In the United States, Hilti, Inc. has 700 highly-trained Hilti field representatives throughout the country, with an additional 500 Hilti employees at the Tulsa, Oklahoma headquarters. Hilti expertise covers the areas of powder-actuated fastening, drilling and demolition, diamond coring and cutting, firestopping, screw fastening, adhesive and mechanical anchoring, laser positioning and measuring, and strut and hanger systems. Professionals in the construction, electrical, plumbing, and building maintenance industries look to Hilti for the highest quality and value-added tools and consumable. We meet and exceed customers' needs by offering an uncompromising level of customer service and product knowledge, on-time delivery, and continuous research and development. Hilti adds expertise ... In every case—to professionals.

Photo by
Don Wheeler.

Honeywell Aerospace Services, Tulsa Heat Transfer Operations

*H*oneywell Aerospace is the world's largest supplier of aircraft engines, equipment, systems, and services. And Tulsa Heat Transfer Operations is proud to be located in the Cherokee Industrial Park in north Tulsa.

With nearly 25 years of experience, the company is able to provide solutions for all of their customers' heat transfer needs, even if that involves researching and developing new products. Honeywell is confident in its quality work, so much that satisfaction is always guaranteed. This company has a world-renown reputation for excellence, and is a fine example of the kind of businesses Tulsa fosters.

MANHATTAN CONSTRUCTION COMPANY

*M*anhattan Construction Company has been building Oklahoma since 1896, 11 years before statehood. It is responsible for many Tulsa landmarks including the original State Capitol Building.

This family business, founded in Oklahoma by L.H. Rooney, employs over 1,200 people internationally, serving clients from Washington D.C to Mexico City. It has grown substantially over the years, due to strong leadership, skilled workers, and progressive philosophy. But its roots are still in Tulsa, and Manhattan maintains its human resources, accounting, and IS departments for the entire company in its hometown.

Adding to its extensive construction experience and state-of-the-art technology, Manhattan is poised to help Tulsa build a prosperous future.

Youngsters enjoy the super-size sandbox in the Kidzone at Mayfest.
Photo by Don Wheeler.

NORDAM

*N*ORDAM, a world-class aviation service company with a true dedication to superior service, is headquartered in Tulsa. NORDAM, employing 2,500 people worldwide, supports Tulsa not only through the jobs it provides and the special educational opportunities for employees through "NORDAM University" but also through community service.

CEO Ray Siegfried gives credit to NORDAM's employees, which it calls stakeholders, for the substantial growth the company has experienced. He especially praises the strong work ethic of Oklahomans, and is thankful for the dedication of Oklahoma's people who have risen to meet the high standards and challenges set by the company. NORDAM is pleased to be a part of the Tulsa community.

The "Golden Driller," located at Expo Square, pays tribute to the countless workers who labored in area oil fields. Photo by Don Sibley.

PARAGON FILMS, INC.

Paragon Films, Inc., located in Broken Arrow has produced a series of innovative products and has a growing customer base that views them as the technological leader in the industry. The company was established by William E. Baab, Chairman of the Board of Paragon Films, Inc. and his son Michael J. Baab, President and CEO.

Paragon finds the Tulsa area the ideal location for its operations. Baab points out that Tulsa's central location works extremely well for his company. He counts the Tulsa-area workers among the company's greatest assets. "We have superior people throughout the organization," says Baab. "We provide them with training, research, equipment, and authority to do their jobs. In turn, they continuously perform at a level which has made Paragon a leader in our industry."

T.D. WILLIAMSON, INC.

In 1920, T.D. Williamson, an enterprising engineer, launched the Petroleum Electric Company in Tulsa, to serve the emerging petroleum industry's needs for electrical power. Later, during World War II, realizing that no company had specialized in engineered pipeline maintenance tools, T.D. Williamson and his son, T.D. Williamson, Jr., stepped boldly into the void, changing the company name to T.D. Williamson, Inc.

Sixty years later, the company is an industry leader, with a myriad of technological innovations and patents to its credit. Despite immense worldwide success, T.D. Williamson, Inc. has not forgotten its roots. It's still a family business, now led by the founder's grandson, R.B. Williamson, and is still a strong Tulsa enterprise.

THE TULSA WORLD

*A*s editor and publisher of the *Tulsa World* for more than 30 years, Eugene Lorton helped build a city as well as a newspaper. Lorton fought the Ku Klux Klan, politicians, and others who stood in the way of Tulsa's growth and prosperity. Through his efforts, Tulsa ensured its future by obtaining an adequate water supply from Lake Spavinaw.

Now led by Lorton's grandson and great-grandson, the *World* is much more than a family business. It is a national leader in applying state-of-the-art printing technology and a regional leader in economic, educational, and civic affairs. The *World* serves Tulsa not only by providing information, but also by generous giving, volunteerism, and sponsoring major charity and community events.

The BNSF Rail Yard provides Tulsa industries with a vital transportation link.
Photo by Don Wheeler.

THE UNIVERSITY OF OKLAHOMA

$\mathscr{T}$his exceptional institution has been educating Tulsans since before Oklahoma's statehood and will continue to offer progressive, quality education into the new millennium.

OU serves Tulsa in many ways, assisting local businesses through energy research and providing health care for thousands of Tulsa residents through the OU Health Sciences Center-Tulsa and the OU College of Medicine—which produces many of Oklahoma's physicians. It cares for victims of child abuse through The Children's Justice Center.

As OU is becoming more well-known and respected, it has not forgotten Tulsa. There are plans for a number of innovative programs to expand OU's involvement in teaching, healing, and discovering in the Tulsa area.

WILLBROS GROUP, INC.

As a leading independent contractor, Willbros provides services to energy customers worldwide. Constructing and engineering pipelines and facilities in some of the most remote areas of the globe, Willbros has maneuvered through challenging terrain ranging from mountains to the Sahara desert to swamps. Innovation and tenacity have become the Company's hallmarks, as it rises to meet each client's needs.

With Tulsa roots dating back over 90 years, Willbros has evolved into one of the city's major employers. Regardless of which developing country or extreme environment Willbros is working in, its roots and heritage will always be in Tulsa.

WILLIAMS

*W*illiams, an international leader in energy and communications, has experienced enormous growth since its founding in 1908 as a small construction business. This profitable and continuously expanding group of companies, with assets of about $20 billion at the end of 1999, was a primary driver of the revitalization of downtown Tulsa.

By choosing to stick with Tulsa, no longer the "Oil Capital of the World," Williams proved its dedication to the city and its people. Through building projects such as the Williams Center/Performing Arts Center and the 52-story downtown headquarters, tireless and generous community service, and impeccable corporate stewardship, Williams has continued to stand behind the city of Tulsa.

2
Chapter Two

THE EARLY DAYS
Typically Tulsan

The discovery of oil ushered in a new era for Tulsa. The city staked its fortunes on oil money, and agrarian interests lost prominence. Photo courtesy of Tulsa Historical Society.

American history is replete with stories of great cities founded on a single industry. In Pittsburgh, steel was the backbone of the economy. Chicago sprouted on the prairie as a rail center, and Detroit gave birth to the automobile industry. Tulsa, of course, was long known as the "Oil Capital of the World."

And for good reason. Tulsa was home to the giants of the petroleum business, and their companies helped lay the foundation for an industrial empire that has transformed the globe. But, like other one-industry towns, Tulsa had a rich and colorful history that predated its rise to greatness in the industrial age. Its roots can be traced back to the early nineteenth century, when America's European settlers found Indian lands in the Southeast too hard to resist. Native Americans, powerless to defend against white encroachment, were uprooted and forced to settle in the western wilderness of what is today Oklahoma. Their homes were to be secure, according to treaties long since abrogated, "as long as the grass shall grow and the waters shall run."

The land that oilmen flocked to in the early days of the 20th century was the end of the trail for a band of the Lochapoka Creeks. Forced by the U.S. government between 1828 and 1836 to leave their ancestral land in Alabama, these Native Americans brought to their new home the ashes from their last council fire. They rekindled the ashes on a hill overlooking the Arkansas River. Town chief Archee Yahola presided at the ceremony under a sturdy oak tree that still stands today near Eighteenth and Cheyenne as a symbol of Tulsa's beginnings.

Tallahassee, as the town was known to its Creek founders, became a crossroads for ranchers, farmers, traders, merchants and a considerable number of outlaws. Fortunately, the community was declared a "safe haven" from early on, and outlaws did much of their mischief elsewhere. Over the years, Tallahassee evolved into Tallasi, Tulsey Town and Tulsi, and finally Tulsa. All were derivations of the Creek word connoting, appropriately enough, "old town."

The first post office was established at Perryman's Store in 1879. Two decades later, a contingency of citizens rode to Muskogee—a larger and more prosperous town some 40 miles to the southeast—to receive the city's charter. Tulsa was incorporated as a town on January 18, 1898. Cattle ranchers ruled, and businesses that supported them prospered. Merchants such as J.M. Hall and Tate Brady found pretty much everything they needed in a town with a Main Street of mud when it rained and dust when it didn't.

Tulsa was incorporated as a town in 1898. Whenever it rained, the city's dusty Main Street was transformed into a sea of mud. Photo courtesy of Metro Tulsa Chamber of Commerce.

Ranching's days as the area's main industry were numbered when, just before midnight on June 24, 1901, a gusher came in at Red Fork, four miles west of Tulsa. Drilled by doctors Fred S. Clinton and J.C.W. Bland and known as the Sue Bland, the well was the first of many in Indian Territory. It was a low producer and failed to open up a new oil field. Nevertheless, the boom was on. Tulsa's era as a sleepy cow town was fast drawing to a close.

On November 22, 1905, drillers hit the jackpot on Ida Glenn's farm some twelve miles south of Tulsa. Unlike the Sue Bland, the Ida Glenn #1 turned out to be a major strike. Oil became a serious business, and there was a population boom to show it. Tulsa's population grew from 3,000 people prior to the oil strikes to 7,000 in 1907, the year Oklahoma was admitted into the Union. By the roaring twenties, the city boasted a population of 72,000.

It was in this world that Tulsa's oil giants made their mark. The twin towers located on the northeast corner of Fifteenth and Boulder represent a small part of their legacy. The tower closest to the corner was once called the Skelly Building in honor of the man who built it: W.G. "Bill" Skelly.

The Skelly Building is a landmark for a man who came to Tulsa by way of the oil fields of Pennsylvania. Unlike some of his contemporaries, Bill Skelly stayed. Such was his stature that newsman Alex Drier, a man who had once been sponsored by Skelly Oil Company, reported his death on network news. "From the NBC newsroom in Chicago," began the nationwide newscast. "The date: April 12, 1957. W.G. Skelly, one of the few remaining pioneers of the oil industry, died yesterday afternoon."

A quarter of a century later, when merger mania hit the oil patch, Skelly's name was replaced by the name of a man who founded a company, made his fortune, and left: J. Paul Getty. A second tower was built, and out of respect and in keeping with sound architectural principles, it matched the original.

Getty's signage was short-lived. Texaco acquired Getty, and its trademark star went atop the building. Eventually, Texaco moved its operations and sold the building, and the star came down. Today, the twin buildings are known rather anonymously as Boulder Towers. Yet Bill Skelly has been commemorated as the namesake for the drive that parallels Interstate 44 through the heart of the city he called home.

Others on the roster of pioneer oilmen include Josh Cosden, Harry Sinclair, Tom Slick, Waite Phillips and Thomas Gilcrease. The latter two left behind elegant homes that nowadays rank among the country's most prestigious museums: Philbrook Art Center and the Gilcrease Museum of Art.

In the glory days of the 1930s and 1940s, the Hotel Tulsa—depicted quite accurately, by most accounts, in the Robert Preston/Susan Hayward motion picture *Tulsa*—was the site of many a multimillion-dollar deal. Back then, research and development amounted to buying a new rig, strategic planning involved little more than hiring a geologist, and

(Above) **The Phillips brothers, from left, Fred, Waite, Ed, L.E., and Frank, pose for a family photo at a Tulsa gathering.** Photo courtesy of Tulsa Historical Society.

Oil baron Waite Phillips and his wife, Genevieve, could sometimes be found in country duds at Philbrook. Photo courtesy of Philbrook Museum of Art.

implementing a strategic plan was what happened when you followed the geologist's advice. Kings of the oil patch insisted they could "smell" oil thousands of feet below the surface. And who's to say they couldn't?

With the exception of Skelly, Phillips and Gilcrease, most of the pioneer oilmen are all but forgotten—except for one remarkable man who turned to philanthropy for the benefit of future generations: Franklin Edwards Bernsen. His is the only name left on a building—the Bernsen Community Life Center, a former Masonic Temple across the street from First Presbyterian Church. Bernsen's generosity lives on through his foundation that has contributed more than $14 million to his adopted community.

Franklin Bernsen never gained the notoriety accorded to Getty, Skelly, or Phillips. He was born in 1893, just months before 30-year-old Henry Ford's first automobile rolled off the assembly line. Automobiles were well on their way to usurping horsepower when Bernsen graduated from Williams College and relocated from the East Coast to California in 1915. He worked for Western Electric Company and appeared as an extra in silent pictures starring Charlie Chaplin. Meanwhile, on the other side of the country, Henry Ford was cranking out a Model N that sold for around $600. By the time Bernsen returned from 18 months of service in World War I and relocated to the oil fields of Oklahoma, Ford's mass production techniques had made the Model T available to anyone with $290. Oil, of course, was indispensable to the new mode of transportation.

There were plenty of skeptics who questioned assumptions that the newfangled horseless carriage would one day conquer the world. A story, perhaps apocryphal, has been handed down of Bill Skelly's conversation with a New York City banker.

"Mr. Skelly," said the banker, "we hear the future of oil is not too good."
Skelly replied, "Sir, how did you come to work this morning?"
"The way I always do." answered the banker. "My chauffeur drove me."
"Did you see any horse manure in the streets?" Skelly asked.
"No," he said.
"Well," said Skelly, "until you do, oil has a great future."

In 1995, First Presbyterian Church opened a community life center, which is named for benefactors Franklin and Grace Bernsen. Photo by Don Wheeler.

Franklin Bernsen started his career as a salesman in the Oklahoma oil fields. In coming years, he would amass a fortune and become well-known for his philanthropic efforts. Photo courtesy of Bernsen Foundation.

Waite Phillips's success as a pioneer oilman made him one of Oklahoma's wealthiest citizens. Photo courtesy of Philbrook Museum of Art.

As oil pumped money into Tulsa's economy, the city experienced rapid growth. Photo courtesy of Metro Tulsa Chamber of Commerce.

Thomas Gilcrease, namesake of the Gilcrease Museum, enjoyed careers as a farmer, a banker, a storekeeper, and an oil speculator. Photo courtesy of Gilcrease Museum.

Equipped with a college education, Bernsen moved quickly from early jobs on the factory floor to a position as a salesman in the Oklahoma oil fields. During his early career as a drilling-rig salesman, he worked out of the ninth floor of the Mayo Building at Fifth and Main. The people he met—Sinclairs, Skellys, Cosdens, and Gettys— were busy making deals in the lobby of the Hotel Tulsa, and their exploits made them household names. Bernsen and others like him who occupied the oil service sector spent their days in the oil fields to considerably less acclaim. Nevertheless, Bernsen was well-positioned to build a network among the movers and shakers. His contacts eventually took him to Oklahoma City, where he was destined to make his fortune.

The state's capital did not cash in on the oil boom until 1928. Like Tulsa, Oklahoma City prohibited drilling within its city limits. At the urging of Phillips Petroleum and a young attorney by the name of Robert S. Kerr, Oklahoma City's citizens were convinced that repeal of the prohibition would be in their best interests.

There was, however, a holdout: the KATY Railroad. Discoveries near the KATY maintenance yard in Oklahoma City convinced oilmen that oil would be found in abundance beneath the roundhouse. Yet railroad officials adamantly opposed drilling on the property.

As the story goes, Franklin Bernsen had a problem of his own. He had a drilling rig that wasn't drilling. In oil field lingo, it was "stacked"—a waste of assets. As a rig salesman, Bernsen was deeply troubled at the sight of an idle rig. A friend agreed to buy the rig from Bernsen and operate it as a joint venture if Bernsen could find a drilling site.

Bernsen's first stop was at Barnsdall Oil Company, where he asked the president if his refinery could produce diesel fuel. The president answered in the affirmative, as long as a steady supply of crude oil could be matched with a continuous demand for diesel.

Bernsen then met with a KATY executive and learned how much the railroad was paying for diesel fuel. Bernsen explained that he could deliver diesel fuel to KATY at a lower price if he could obtain leasing rights to the acreage then occupied by the KATY maintenance yard in Oklahoma City. KATY agreed, and Bernsen had a deal.

Later, Barnsdall used its own stock to purchase Bernsen's interest in the KATY maintenance yard. Barnsdall was subsequently acquired by the Sunray Company, which in turn merged with the DX Oil Company. Finally, the combined Sunray-DX Company was purchased by Sun Oil Company. By then, Bernsen was one of the largest share-holders of Sunray-DX preferred stock.

The 1920s were exhilarating times in Bernsen's new home of Tulsa. As the decade ended, some $1 million a month was being spent on downtown construction. An abundance of land eliminated the need for skyscrapers, but Tulsans didn't want to be left out of the 20th century obsession with high-rises.

Bernsen led a rich social life. He and his wife, Grace, spent the summer of 1929 traveling through Europe, and memberships back home included Indian Hills Country Club, the Tulsa Club and the University Club. He became a Shriner Mason, voted Republican, and lived in a stately, two-story home at 2819 South Cincinnati. His office at 224 East Brady was in the warehouse district near other oil field equipment and supply companies.

Shortly after his European sojourn, disaster struck. After years of unprecedented gains founded on speculation, the stock market fell through the floor. At first, the oil patch seemed immune from the economic tailspin affecting the rest of the country. Some even had time to combine pleasure with business. In 1932, Bernsen hooked up with a friend he had met years before in the oil fields and had once employed as a roughneck on a rig in Texas—Wiley Post, the famed

(Opposite page) **One of Tulsa's early schools, Lincoln Elementary, was located in the Cherry Street district. Today the former school property is known as Lincoln Plaza and is home to popular shops and restaurants.** Photo by Don Wheeler.

The city enjoyed a thriving economy in the 1920s, and construction boomed. Photo courtesy of Tulsa Historical Society.

aviator and pilot of the *Winnie Mae.* During a trip to Los Angeles with Bernsen and other oilmen to attend the Summer Olympics, Post investigated a plant that was in receivership. He subsequently reported to Bernsen that the plant carried a price tag of only $40,000. Bernsen declined a chance to buy it. In later years, he told his friends, "I walked away from an opportunity to buy Lockheed Aircraft."

In 1933, as the price of crude oil plummeted to 25 cents per barrel, Oklahoma oilmen realized there was no escaping the effects of the Great Depression. Bernsen was constantly on the go; business trips took him to Oklahoma City; St. Paul, Minnesota; Chicago; and Pittsburgh. Not surprisingly, his marriage began to suffer, as did his attention span. Years later, he admitted leaving at least one Sunday service at First Presbyterian Church with no recollection whatsoever of the sermon. Business problems had become all-consuming.

Yet Bernsen was tenacious, and he proved himself adept at networking with his contacts in the oil business. He invested in other companies as well as other oilmen's drilling programs, and he then sold them the oil field equipment and supplies they needed. In 1934, he felt sufficiently secure to move uptown to the eighth floor of the Genet Building at 910 South Boston. The building had been vacant for the previous four years, but Tulsa's economy was on the mend. The Genet Building had become known as the Tradesman Building, and its basement and seven of twelve floors were occupied.

Three years later, in 1937, Bernsen relocated once again, this time to the First National Bank Building. His company now went under the name of Lucey Products Company. Bernsen's knack for networking led to his involvement in two drilling companies that occupied neighboring office space—Hugh Hodges' Mid-Union Drilling, and Falcon Seaboard Drilling Co. It's likely that other neighbors figured prominently on his buyers' list.

Meanwhile, Bernsen kept up his interest in aviation. According to a newspaper account in 1937, Bernsen owned a $20,000 Spartan that cruised at slightly more than 200 miles an hour with a range of 1,500 miles. When he wasn't making oil deals, Bernsen found time to serve as chairman of the Chamber of Commerce's Aviation Committee from 1939 to 1942.

Bernsen now lived in a graceful home at 2126 East Thirtieth Street. The *Tulsa Tribune* described a beautifully grilled fretwork iron balcony

that had been an outstanding feature of Jefferson Davis' home in New Orleans.

As the Depression and World War II faded into memory, Bernsen was able to turn his attention to philanthropy. In 1948, he and his wife launched the first of many charitable endeavors by establishing a milk bank at St. John Hospital. "Being without children," ran a newspaper account, "their interest turned to the plight of premature babies." When baby formula rendered milk banks obsolete, the Bernsens donated equipment for premature babies to St. John Hospital.

In the early 1950s, Bernsen joined a trade mission to Japan to explore ways to assist in the county's post-war recovery through purchases of steel pipe. During 1952 and 1953, pipe imports to Bernsen's company exceeded $1 million a month for 18 consecutive months.

Though many oilmen felt just as comfortable on the floor of a drilling rig as they did in their executive offices, they never shed their Eastern heritage. Bernsen's idea of casual was a bolo tie and a cardigan sweater on weekends, and photos survive of him fishing with a properly knotted tie. Such deportment carried into a passion for the arts. Bernsen, no stranger to the arts, recalled in a 1981 interview the founding of the Tulsa Philharmonic. "Mr. Whitehill, Mr. Mayo and I organized the symphony here in Tulsa," he said simply.

His philanthropy extended to his church, St. John Hospital and the legacy of his former colleague in the oil fields, the Philbrook Museum of Art. He and his wife formalized their philanthropy in the late 1960s by creating the Franklin E. and Grace W. Bernsen Foundation. In 1995, the Bernsen Foundation enabled the First Presbyterian Church to purchase the nearby Masonic Temple. The church then designated the renovated building as the Bernsen Community Life Center.

Grace Bernsen died in April 1982. Her husband followed her in 1984, less than a month short of his 91st birthday. His death marked the end of the line for a generation of oilmen who transformed their adopted city from a boomtown into a modern metropolis. ✦

Oil baron Thomas Gilcrease, a Native American, acquired an extensive collection of art from the old West. These treasures now are housed in the Gilcrease Museum. Photo by Don Wheeler.

Native American culture has played an important role in Tulsa's heritage. The city's name is derived from the Creek word "Tallahassee," which means "old town." Photo by Don Wheeler.

3

Chapter Three

EDUCATION

Meeting of the Minds

**Oklahoma State University-Tulsa, established in 1999,
is the city's first comprehensive, publicly supported university.
In the foreground is the Greenwood Cultural Center, home of
the Oklahoma Jazz Hall of Fame.** Photo by Don Wheeler.

*P*retend for a moment that you've been transported to the waning days of the 21st century. You're sitting quietly in some future library, surrounded by high-tech gadgetry that we can scarcely imagine, reading Tulsa's bicentennial history.

The author has identified key events and developments that shaped the city's growth. The usual suspects are there: the arrival of the Creeks and the rekindling of their sacred flame beneath an oak tree that would one day symbolize Tulsa's native American legacy, the discovery of oil, the building of bridges to span the Arkansas River, and construction of the McClellan-Kerr Waterway that linked northeast Oklahoma to the sea. Our historian of the future emphasizes the vision that was required to carve a new city out of the prairie, and entire chapters are dedicated to the men and women who made their dreams come true.

Midway through the book, you reach a chapter on education and learn about the whirlwind of events that captivated the attention of Tulsans during the fall and winter of 1998 and culminated with the establishment of Oklahoma State University-Tulsa on January 1, 1999. Twenty years after that auspicious date, the school known by most as OSU-Tulsa boasted an enrollment of 20,000. Three thousand students were living in private housing near campus, 800 members of the faculty were residing in the area, and approximately $80 million worth of research was being performed annually.

Sound like fantasy? Maybe. But maybe not. The emergence of a top-notch, comprehensive, state-supported university in Tulsa wouldn't be the first development to be dismissed in its early stages as a pipe dream. In fact, proponents of higher education appear closer than ever to bringing the university described in our fictional history within reach.

Yet establishing the university was no easy task. For much of the 20th century, Tulsa was the largest metropolitan area in the United States without comprehensive public higher education. Not that colleges in Oklahoma are hard to find. Fact is, you can't find an area of the state that isn't home to a junior or four-year college. Tulsa has been

the glaring exception, and to understand why, you need to delve into the state's populist roots and appreciate the historic distrust that rural legislators have felt toward urban areas. Most Oklahoma lawmakers have been supportive of higher education, as long as schools were located in their districts. Not surprisingly in a state where urban legislators have always been outgunned by their rural counterparts, colleges and universities have been situated far from big cities. It wasn't until the U.S. Supreme Court issued its historic "one-man, one-vote" ruling that rural domination of Oklahoma politics was finally broken.

Even with the high court's ruling, Tulsans in the late 1960s could do no better than wrest enough funding from state coffers to establish a junior college. Tulsa Junior College opened its doors in 1970 to wide acclaim, but it was a far cry from the four-year institution so desperately needed.

The frustration among Tulsans was exacerbated by the University of Oklahoma's proximity to Oklahoma City. Legislators in central Oklahoma had the best of both worlds: OU was easily accessible to voters in Oklahoma City, and its location in Norman reinforced their popularity among the rural electorate.

At the same time, Tulsans were to some extent victims of their own success. With some 4,500 students and more than 80 undergraduate and graduate degree programs, the University of Tulsa was then and remains among the most highly rated universities in the country. Higher education in Tulsa received a boost when, in the mid-'60s, internationally known evangelist Oral Roberts founded Oral Roberts University. His ability to blend evangelical Christianity with rigorous academics attracted a first-rate faculty and substantial funding. ORU earned its accreditation in record time, and highly qualified students

from around the world flocked to the modernistic campus in south Tulsa. A branch of the University of Oklahoma's medical school, together with Oklahoma State University's College of Osteopathic Medicine, enabled students to receive first-rate medical training in Tulsa. Oklahoma City University, Southern Nazarene University, Bartlesville Wesleyan College, and the University of Phoenix completed the mosaic of higher education opportunities in Tulsa.

All of these schools added grist to the opposition's mill.

In the mid-1960s, evangelist **Oral Roberts** founded **Oral Roberts University. The Prayer Tower is a landmark on the school's modernistic, south Tulsa campus.** Photo by Don Sibley.

Why, some asked, did Tulsa need another school? If anything, Oklahoma needed fewer, not more colleges. Other justifications for opposing yet another institution of higher learning bordered on paranoia; one state legislator voiced concern that a "Tulsa State University" would send a football team down the Turner Turnpike and beat OU on the gridiron.

Tulsans adopted a practical approach and poured resources into Tulsa Junior College, since renamed Tulsa Community College. TCC has evolved into one of the most respected community colleges in the country, and it now ranks 26th out of 1,200 community colleges in the number of annual graduates. Today, some 20,000 students are enrolled at four campuses throughout the city.

Still, Tulsans were determined to bring a comprehensive, publicly supported institution into their midst. The standoff appeared to be broken when four state universities—OU, OSU, Langston, and Northeastern State—came together at a new campus in the historic Greenwood district just north of downtown to form a consortium known as the University Center at Tulsa. UCT, or "UCAT," as it was affectionately known, was granted institutional status and soon flexed its muscles by merging with a community college in nearby Claremore and renaming itself Rogers University.

No sooner had the paint dried on the new signage at Rogers University than controversy erupted. One contingency insisted that Rogers University retain its independent status and outsource its

By the year 2020, OSU's enrollment is expected to reach 20,000 students.
Photo by Don Wheeler.

needs to the participating universities. Others warned that such a makeshift compromise would never work. Letters to the editor flooded into the *Tulsa World*, and the race was on to see which side would prevail in the quest to bring some semblance of order to the cobbled-together university on North Greenwood.

Representatives of the Tulsa business community deserve much of the credit for leading the way out of the impasse. Under the leadership of Metropolitan Tulsa Chamber of Commerce Chairman Ed Keller, serious negotiations were held between business people, Tulsa's legislative delegation, and the state's higher education establishment. It is no exaggeration to say that their discussions gave birth to a new era in Tulsa's higher education. The cornerstone of their plan was to establish

an urban campus of Oklahoma State University. With characteristic eloquence, OSU President Dr. James E. Halligan summed it up best when he described OSU-Tulsa as "one university, two sites."

Tulsa's success in its decades-long quest to improve education is reflected by an impressive statistic: Nearly one-fourth of the city's residents hold a bachelor's or even higher degree.

Higher education is complemented by Tulsa County's public school system that boasts an enrollment of 90,000 students. More than 40,000 of those students are enrolled in Tulsa Public Schools—the state's largest school district, and the city's second-largest employer. These schools offer courses ranging from the fine arts and engineering to foreign language immersion programs. Nearly half of the instructors

in Tulsa's public schools hold advanced degrees, and more than half have acquired at least 10 years of teaching experience. An Adopt-A-School program provides vital links between business and education, and the Metropolitan Tulsa Chamber of Commerce's workforce development initiatives allow students to get a head start on careers of the 21st century.

With its four campuses and three satellite-training locations, Tulsa Technology Center serves more than 32,000 high school and adult students and offers custom-designed programs for private industry.

In addition to its public schools, Tulsa offers some of the finest private school opportunities in the United States. Universities nationwide recruit college-bound students from both public and private education, but for those who choose to stay close to home, the opportunities have never been brighter.

Our historian of the 21st century was perceptive to recognize January 1, 1999, as a milestone in the development of higher education in Tulsa. Complemented by a strong public school system and a wide range of institutions that offer specialized training, OSU-Tulsa is poised to become an anchor for Tulsans in search of a comprehensive education. ✦

Youngsters enrolled in Tulsa Public Schools receive an excellent educational start. Pupils at Eliot Elementary School find fun ways to sharpen their skills in the science room, right, and computer lab, above. Photos by Don Wheeler.

❧ **Holland Hall School**, a college preparatory school in south Tulsa affiliated with the Episcopal Diocese of Oklahoma, provides a first-rate education for students from early childhood through grade 12.
Photo by Don Wheeler.

❧ (Following page) **Tulsa Community College**, with four campuses throughout the city, is among the nation's most highly rated community colleges. **TCC Metro's** new activity center has become a favorite gathering place
Photo by Don Wheeler.

4

Chapter Four

HEALTH CARE

Caring Hearts & Hands

St. Francis Hospital's critical-care transport system, established in 1979, has helped thousands of patients to reach expert medical help quickly.
Photo by Don Wheeler.

*T*he discovery of oil in the early 1900s brought prosperity, but the financial boom also left the burgeoning city in dire need. Oil money replaced Tulsa's agricultural economy, and the growing population required services to suit city life.

It is certain that oil's windfall brought advances in health care to Tulsa. The expanding city was ready for a large-scale medical facility—one with services more sophisticated than rural medical practitioners could offer.

In November 1906, this need was met when Tulsa Hospital opened on Fifth Street. The facility offered state-of-the-art care, and Tulsa quickly gained a regional reputation for its medical services.

In 1916, Hillcrest Hospital began admitting patients, and a decade later, the Sisters of Sorrowful Mercy opened St. John Hospital. Tulsa was making significant medical improvements by 1926, but a void still remained; the city's poor children lacked adequate health care. That

year, the Junior League of Tulsa established Children's Medical Center to serve Tulsa's less-fortunate youngsters.

In 1940, support grew for establishment of a prepaid hospitalization plan in both Tulsa and Oklahoma City. The two cities decided to hold a contest; the first city to raise $5,000 would earn the headquarters of Group Hospital Service, now known as Blue Cross and Blue Shield of Oklahoma. Tulsa won, and it remains the organization's home.

In 1960, a major philanthropic medical effort was launched-the creation of the Saint Francis Health System by oilman W.K. Warren and his wife, Natalie. Over the years, Saint Francis has grown into a large medical complex that now includes Laureate Clinic and

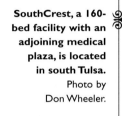

SouthCrest, a 160-bed facility with an adjoining medical plaza, is located in south Tulsa.
Photo by Don Wheeler.

Psychiatric Hospital, Warren Clinic and Broken Arrow Medical Center. Its 897-bed regional medical center was the site of Tulsa's first heart transplant in 1993 and is recognized for recent advances in treatment of abnormal heart rhythms.

Three of the area's early hospitals also continue to serve Tulsa residents. The Hillcrest HealthCare System plays a leading role among the city's medical providers, and St. John Hospital runs a network of hospitals in the area. And today, Children's Hospital is a Hillcrest-affiliated facility that serves 10,000 children a year. Its mission of community service goes on; dedicated volunteers donate 27,000 hours of their time to the hospital each year.

Also contributing to medical excellence in Tulsa are two medical schools—the University of Oklahoma College of Medicine-Tulsa and the Oklahoma State University College of Osteopathic Medicine. Top medical experts serve as instructors at both institutions, and graduates often establish their medical practices in the Tulsa area.

Tulsa's medical facilities have made a significant contribution to the city's economic health. Nearly 10 percent of Tulsa's employees work in medical positions or related industries, and Saint Francis, St. John, and Hillcrest are among the city's top 20 employers. Joining that top 20 is another health-care giant—Blue Cross and Blue Shield of Oklahoma.

Preventative health care has gained popularity in recent years, and city hospitals are keeping pace with that trend. The St. John Siegfried Health Club and the Saint Francis Health Zone both offer programs to help Tulsa residents stay healthy. The Saint Francis facility also fosters a spirit of involvement by sponsoring the annual Corporate Challenge, the nation's largest communitywide wellness event.

Tulsa's health-care systems often work together to achieve common goals. A prime example is the creation of CommunityCare Managed Care Plans of Oklahoma, which was organized by St. John Health System, Saint Francis, and two Oklahoma City hospitals. It is the state's first provider-owned health maintenance organization.

As in the past, private cooperation still is a mainstay in many areas of health care. Tulsa's local Lung Association, Heart Association, Arthritis Foundation, and other organizations provide vital dollars and volunteers for both care and research. Tulsa's annual Heart Ball, for example, consistently ranks among the nation's top 10 fundraisers for Heart Association groups. Also playing a key role in the community is the Tulsa affiliate of the Red Cross. This well-respected organization served as host for the 1995 Red Cross national convention, and 1,500 delegates traveled to Tulsa for the event.

As the new century begins, Tulsa's medical services continue to grow with the addition of SouthCrest, a 160-bed facility with an

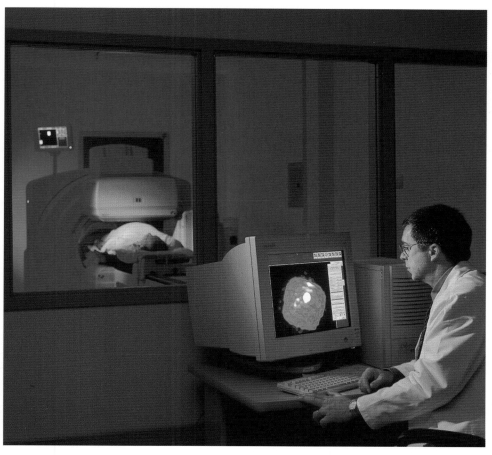

The Cancer Treatment Center provides its patients with state-of-the-art care. Photo by Don Wheeler.

adjoining Medical Plaza. The complex is strategically located in south Tulsa, and a large percentage of city residents live nearby. SouthCrest is a joint venture between two health-care leaders—Columbia/HCA Healthcare and Hillcrest HeathCare System. Hillcrest also has expanded on other fronts through the acquisition of Tulsa Regional Medical Center, Doctors Hospital, and Specialty Hospital of Tulsa.

Tulsa's reputation as a medical center was secured when, on December 8, 1999, the University of Oklahoma Regents announced their plan to purchase BP-Amoco's Tulsa Technology Center at 41st and South Yale Avenue and establish the Tulsa Campus of the OU Health Sciences Center. The new campus provides OU and the northeast Oklahoma medical community with an infrastructure for developing a world-class knowledge cluster, enhancing the quality of medical training, and attracting biomedical research dollars to Tulsa.

The presence of quality medical care provides both physical and economic benefits. And, in both these regards, Tulsa's health providers contribute greatly to the city's well-being. ✦

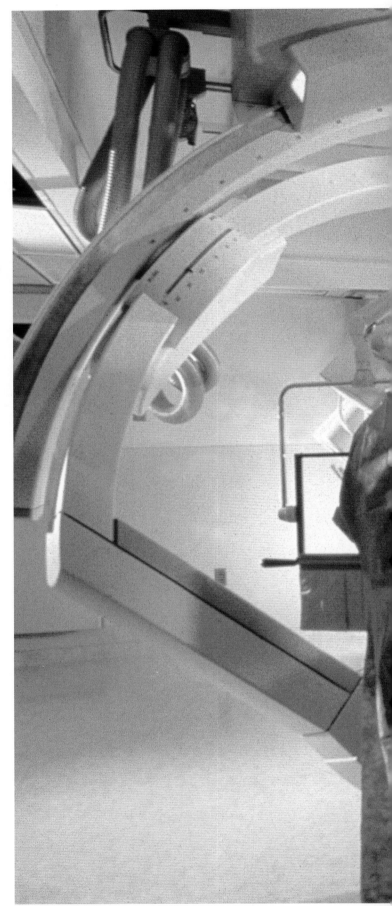

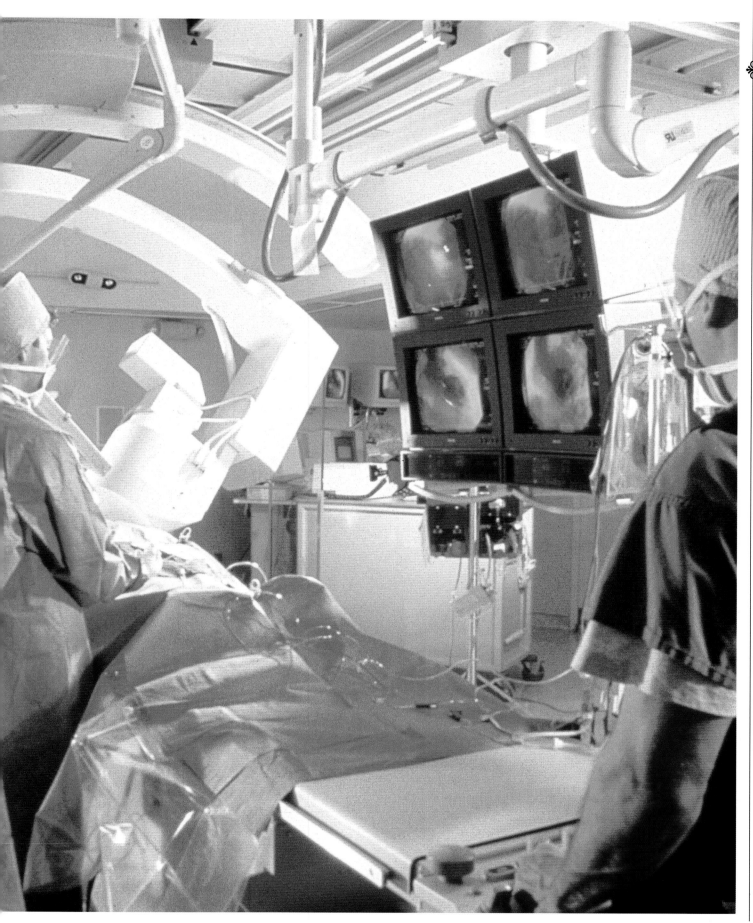

Hillcrest Hospital, part of the Hillcrest HealthCare System, maintains a tradition of outstanding medical care. Photo courtesy of Hillcrest.

The St. John's
Siegfried Health
Club offers
members a wide
range of activities
to stay fit.
Photo by
Don Wheeler.

Blue Cross And Blue Shield of Oklahoma has its headquarters in Tulsa and is one of the city's top employers. Photo by Don Wheeler.

Volunteers lend a hand at Red Cross headquarters during the annual United Way Day of Caring. The agency is one of many that helps Tulsa residents in times of need. Photo by Don Wheeler.

(Following page) Tulsa's annual Corporate Challenge is the nation's largest community wellness event. Every year, hundreds of participants compete in a variety of fitness events that require both teamwork and stamina. Photo by Don Wheeler.

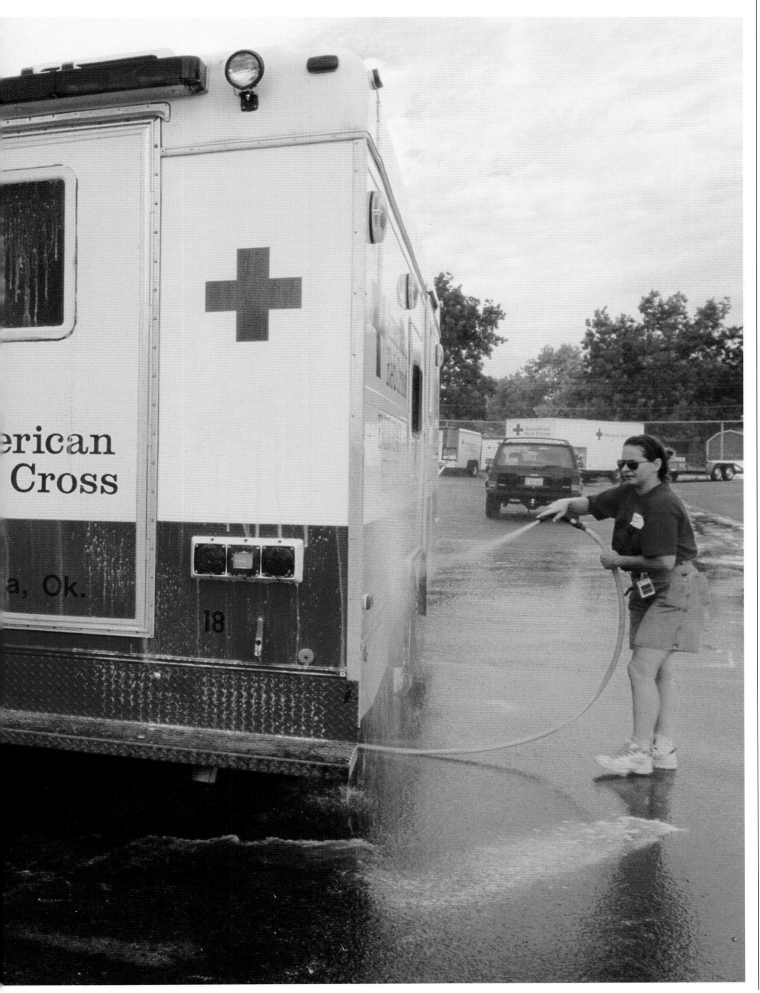

5
Chapter Five

A CITY OF NEIGHBORHOODS

Diversity Abounds

**As springtime begins, the Maple Ridge
area is awash in colorful blooms.**
Photo by Don Wheeler.

Tulsa's neighborhoods are a mixture of historic and modern, palatial and quaint, urban and suburban. And, although the city of Tulsa provides a common link between communities, all maintain distinctive personalities.

The two "mini-downtowns" of Tulsa—Cherry Street and Brookside—provide perfect examples. Although neither neighborhood is located downtown, both closely resemble Norman Rockwell portraits of Main Street America. And retail business booms in the charming Cherry Street and Brookside areas.

In its early days, the Cherry Street district was anchored by Lincoln Elementary School. Before he achieved movie fame as "Hopalong Cassidy," William Boyd attended Lincoln. Another former student, Tony Randall, went on to television stardom as Felix Unger in *The Odd Couple*. Tulsa's resident jazz genius, Sonny Gray, also spent his early school days at Lincoln Elementary.

Today, as Lincoln Plaza, the building anchors a thriving commercial district of antique shops, boutiques, flower emporiums, interior designer studios, a CD "warehouse," bookstores, nightclubs, trendy restaurants, and neighborhood bistros.

Cherry Street was once home to one of Tulsa's most venerable bars—Arnie's, where every day was greeted with the gusto of Saint Patrick's. Sadly, Arnie passed away. In mid-1999, his bar was completely remodeled and is now home to the decidedly upscale Drake's Tavern.

Even though the ambiance has changed, chances are that the new establishment will continue to lure Saint Paddy's Day revelers and anybody else in search of a good time.

Tulsa's other "downtown" center runs along Peoria Avenue. Here is located the Brookside branch of the Bank of Oklahoma, formerly known as Brookside State Bank. A wide array of restaurants can be found throughout the area, in addition to quaint shops, grocery stores, a bartending school, coffee shops, and popular nightspots—including one that attracts a remarkable collection of Harleys each evening. This eclectic blend creates one of Tulsa's most interesting neighborhoods.

Traffic often is light in Brookside because many patrons are neighborhood residents who simply stroll to their favorite spots. A walk through Brookside offers a tempting assortment of dining options. Among the many choices are a wonderful breakfast at Brookside by Day, an *al fresco* lunch of oysters on the half shell at S&J Seafood Cafe/Oyster Bar, and a gourmet feast at the Bistro on Brookside for dinner.

Nearby is Eliot Elementary, one of Tulsa's best-known grade schools, and a former dairy farm that today is an upscale, gated

Tulsa Garden Center's greenhouse is a year-round treat for visitors. Photo by Don Wheeler.

❦ **Woodland Hills Mall**, located in south Tulsa, attracts shoppers from throughout the region.
Photo by Don Wheeler.

The Greenwood
district, an area of
black-owned busi-
nesses, homes and
churches, was left
in ruins by the race
riot of 1921.
Greenwood's
determined and
resilient residents
rebuilt, and the
area has enjoyed a
renaissance.
*Photo courtesy of
Tulsa Historical Society.*

(Below)
Today, the
Greenwood area
thrives once again,
and many unique
shops can be found
in the district. The
newly established
Oklahoma State
Univeristy-Tulsa
makes its home on
North Greenwood
Avenue. Another
recent addition to
the neighborhood
is the Greenwood
Cultural Center,
which houses the
Oklahoma Jazz
Hall of Fame.
*Photo by
Don Wheeler.*

(Opposite page)
Greenwood is one
of Tulsa's most
historic neighbor-
hoods. A memorial
near the entrance
to the Greenwood
Cultural Center
pays tribute to
African-American
entrepreneurs
who created the
"Black Wall Street
of America."
*Photo by
Don Wheeler.*

that many small colleges would envy. Another scenic site is located at Chandler Park, where bluffs offer a stunning view of the Arkansas River. On weekends, rock climbers flock to the park to test their skills on its sheer cliffs.

To the north is the home of Thomas Gilcrease, one of Tulsa's most famous oil barons. Gilcrease believed that "every man must leave a track," and he left a lasting impression on Tulsa. When he suffered a cash crunch in the early 1950s, Gilcrease offered to sell his collection of Western American art to the City of Tulsa. Thanks to a successful bond election, the city now owns one of the world's most extensive collections of Remingtons, Russells, and Morans. The museum is located on the grounds of the Gilcrease home.

Other historic Tulsa homes are located in Reservoir Hill, close to downtown. Through homeowners' dedication and hard work, stately mansions have been restored to their former glory. Neighbors enjoy Reservoir Hill's renewed beauty and its convenience to the business district.

Other communities can be found beyond the Tulsa city limits. Keystone offers lakeside living, and many recreational opportunities are available at Skiatook Lake. Sand Springs and Collinsville lie at the western and northern extremities of the urban area. The booming community of Owasso is duplicating the growth that marked Broken Arrow at the end of the century. And pocket communities such as Berryhill retain proud traditions and schools known for their excellence.

Variety is the hallmark of Tulsa neighborhoods; from fast-paced to laid-back, the city adapts to any lifestyle. With so many choices, Tulsa residents can always find the perfect place to call home. ❦

Utica Square, which opened in the 1950s, enjoys a reputation as the city's premier high-fashion center. Photo by Don Wheeler.

(Following page) **Brookside, located along Peoria Avenue, contains a wide array of shops, restaurants, and clubs. On the weekends, Harley enthusiasts gather at the Blue Rose Cafe.** Photo by Don Wheeler.

Charming shops greet visitors to the Cherry Street district.
Photo by Don Sibley.

A dusting of snow adds a surreal touch to the grounds of the **Philbrook Museum.**
Photo by Don Sibley.

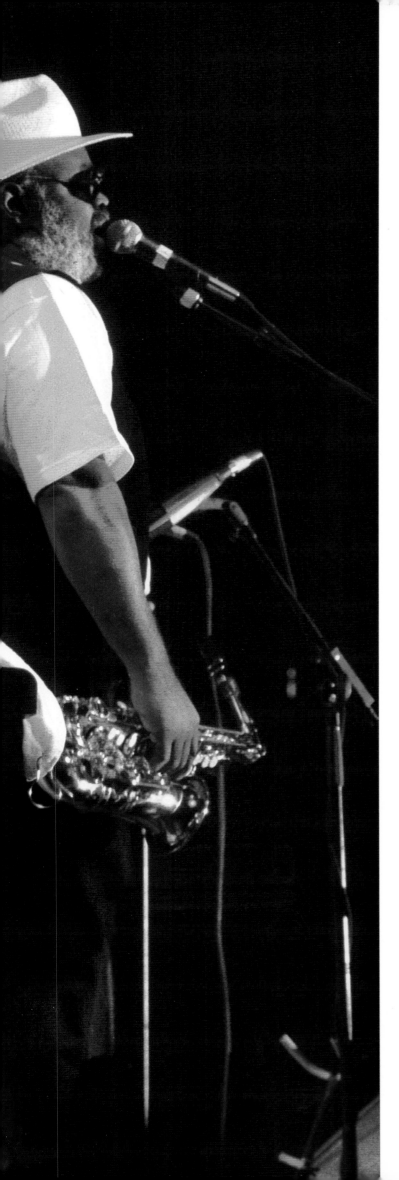

6
Chapter Six

CULTURE

Living On Tulsa Time

**Every August, music fans can see a wide range
of talented performers at the Bank of
Oklahoma/Williams Jazz on Greenwood Festival.**
Photo by Don Wheeler.

$\mathcal{C}$ount Basie, one of the world's most revered Big Band leaders, found his future in Tulsa.

The Opera House, which was constructed in 1906, brought Tulsa its first taste of culture.
Photo courtesy of Tulsa Historical Society.

The piano player from Red Bank, New Jersey, was in Tulsa with Gonzelle White and the Big Jazz Jamboree at Greenwood's Dreamland Theatre. The year was 1927. One night after the show, young Bill Basie was looking for some after-hours entertainment. He met a local man-about-town known as Pencil, who took Basie down an alley and to a house. Among Basie's memories of that evening was his first taste of Choc, short for Choctaw beer, an Oklahoma brew that packs a wallop when consumed in excess.

A few too many glasses of Choc were no doubt to blame for young Bill's befuddlement the next morning when loud music roused him from his bed at the Red Wing Hotel. At first, he thought he was listening to a recording. But, as the fog cleared, Basie realized that a band was playing in the street below to promote an appearance that night in Tulsa. And it wasn't just any band. It was the famed Oklahoma Blue Devils from Oklahoma City, led by bass player Walter Page. As Basie recalls in the opening pages of his autobiography, "After all these years I still have not forgotten how the Blue Devils sounded that morning in Tulsa. I had never heard anything like that in my life. I forgot all about my hangover and about catching up on my sleep. I just wanted to hear those guys play some more."

Among the guys he heard that morning was legendary blues singer Jimmy Rushing, an Oklahoma City native who would later earn acclaim as a singer in Basie's own band. As he lay on his bed, recovering from his encounter with Choc the night before, the young piano player from New Jersey could not have known that his future was coming into focus. He dreamed of playing in a band like Page's Blue Devils. In his case, dreams came true.

Grand Opera House, Tulsa, Okla.

It's no surprise that the man who would become known as Count Basie would have a life-changing musical experience in the Tulsa's Greenwood district. Tulsa was one of the places that embraced the Big Band jazz that Page's Blue Devils were playing. Other band leaders, including Tulsans Ernie Fields and Clarence Love, would also launch successful careers from the nightspots and after-hours clubs that made Greenwood fertile ground for ace musicians.

Tulsans' appreciation for art and culture dates back to the city's early days. America's first oil discoveries were in the fields of

The Adkar Theatre opened in 1925 and was billed as "Oklahoma's Most Beautiful Playhouse."
Photo courtesy of Tulsa Historical Society.

Pennsylvania. When more of the same was found in Oklahoma, oilmen packed their households and headed for the frontier. Oil they found, and in such quantities as to dwarf their discoveries in the East. It was culture that was lacking. So, with a determination to bring refinement to their prairie home, Tulsa's founders set about making sure that their families had the same cultural amenities in Oklahoma that they had enjoyed "back East." The Opera House was constructed in 1906; other projects were completed in rapid succession. Priorities were clear: There were no sewers, no paved streets, and no sidewalks—but there was an opera house.

Whatever the impetus, it is clear that Tulsa residents, both black and white, were a ready audience for imported culture. Nearly every major performer graced Tulsa's stages, from Paderewski to Pavlova, Walter Damrosch to Fats Domino, and Eddie Cantor to Enrico Caruso.

Bringing refinement to the frontier was not always smooth sailing. An icon of Tulsa's cultural attractions, known today as the "Old Lady of Brady," stands at the corner of Brady and Boulder. According to city lore, thoughtful leaders directed construction of the theater in 1914 to provide a proper setting for the arts. In reality, the structure was built as a convention hall because the city was losing business to nearby

Muskogee. When the building proved to be ill-suited for conventions, it was converted for use as a theater and was known simply as Tulsa's Municipal Theatre. As fate would have it, theatrical performances fared no better than conventions; Carol Channing, performing "Hello, Dolly" in the 1960s, stood on the stage and referred to the building as "this relic, this antique."

According the style of the day, the stage was "raked," or tilted forward to improve the audience's view. Unknowing performers found dancing uphill to be tiresome, only to accelerate as they maneuvered upstage. In the late 1920s, Ignace Jan Paderewski felt compelled to have the south end of his piano jacked up when he noticed its starboard list during a rehearsal.

In 1925, the Akdar Theatre opened at Third and Boulder. In its heyday, the theater was billed as "Oklahoma's Most Beautiful Playhouse." It was home to teenage dances during the 1950s, and performers included Ronnie Hawkins and the Hawks. The Akdar fell to the wrecking ball in 1973.

The lack of first-class facilities failed to dampen the enthusiasm of Tulsa's artistic community. The Tulsa Philharmonic was launched in 1948, and the following year, the Tulsa Opera held its opening

The Performing Arts Center provides a focal point for many cultural events in Tulsa, including theatrical and musical performances. Photo by Don Wheeler.

performance. The Tulsa Ballet made its debut in 1956. The Tulsa
Little Symphony, which began in 1978 as a small classical music
company, evolved into the Oklahoma Sinfonia and finally into the
Sinfonia. Each of these organizations has earned distinction as an
integral component of Tulsa's cultural repertoire.

Meanwhile, Tulsa's theatrical groups were busy staking their claims.
Tulsa Little Theatre, established in 1922 and equipped with its own
playhouse near 15th and Delaware, became one of the oldest continuing
community theater groups in the country. It is known today as
Theatre Tulsa. Thespians continued to assert their independence
when, in 1970, graduates of the University of Tulsa's Theater
Department decided to keep their talents at home rather than strike
out for Broadway. Since then, the American Theatre Company has
evolved into a successful professional community theater. Nationally
acclaimed actors from Tulsa include William Boyd (Hopalong
Cassidy), Jennifer Jones, Tony Randall and Gailard Sartain.

Success stories notwithstanding, the absence of a building to serve
as a focal point for the arts continued to rankle. Carol Channing had
bruised some egos with her unflattering remark, but nothing had been
done. Bond issues were proposed and rejected for a variety of reasons.
It wasn't until one of Tulsa's corporate citizens took the bull by the
horns that plans were made to build what has since become the city's
cultural trademark—the Tulsa Performing Arts Center.

The company that served as a catalyst for one of the city's most
ambitious construction projects to date was none other than the
Williams Companies. Under the leadership of John H. and Joseph H.
Williams, the company that was their namesake had achieved remarkable
success. There was only one problem: employees were scattered
throughout several downtown buildings. After exploring the possibility
of relocation, the company's management decided to stay put and
build a central headquarters in downtown Tulsa.

A nine-square-block tract of urban renewal land was selected, and
the architects and planners went to work. Original plans called for
two 32-story buildings on opposite sides of Boston Avenue. As the
story goes, John Williams picked up models of the buildings, stacked
them one on top of the other, and planted them on Boston Avenue.
The result was the 52-story Bank of Oklahoma Tower.

Never one to shrink from innovation, John Williams came up with
an idea for using space that had been made available during construction
of the BOK Tower. He shared his vision with Leta M. Chapman.
Together, they proposed putting up $7 million for construction of a new
performing arts center. Their plan called for an additional $7 million that
the city would raise through a bond election. It was, as Bill Donaldson
of the *Tulsa Tribune* wrote, "a proposition it (Tulsa) can't refuse."

Characteristically, Tulsans rose to the occasion. When inflation
drove up the cost, Williams raised another $3 million, and the city
agreed to tap sales tax dollars. On March 19, 1977, jazz legend Ella
Fitzgerald opened the Tulsa Performing Arts Center—and opened a
new chapter in Oklahoma's cultural history.

Of course, a vibrant urban culture doesn't need to restrict itself to
highbrow entertainment. Only a few blocks north and one block west
of the Performing Arts Center stands a building that has become a
shrine for aficionados of a musical style known as Western Swing.
It was once a lowly garage prior to its rebirth as a dance academy.

Whimsical costumes add a colorful touch to "Beauty and the Beast" at the Performing Arts Center. Photo by Don Wheeler.

For decades, Cain's Ballroom has been a popular spot with musicians and fans alike.
Photo by Don Wheeler.

And in its glory days as Cain's Ballroom, the modest structure at 423 North Main was the home of Bob Wills and his Texas Playboys, where the sound of hillbilly music's steel guitars and fiddles merged with the Big Band sounds of brass and reeds.

Though he came to Tulsa from Texas, the man who engineered this musical mixture drew upon two traditions indigenous to his adopted home: the sounds of the Big Bands, and hillbilly music with its folk and country roots. The first Western Swing broadcast aired on September 23, 1934, on Tulsa's KVOO radio station, whose strong signal carried the music nearly coast to coast. Cain's Ballroom became a mecca for this exciting new sound, and Bob Wills, whose poster hangs to this day behind the stage, went on to become one of the country's highest-paid Big Band leaders and a star in motion pictures. There are plenty of folks around today who recall with nostalgia the days when the "King of Western Swing" made it nearly impossible to resist a whirl around the spring-loaded dance floor. After he left Tulsa for greener pastures, his brother, Johnnie Lee, carried on the Western Swing legacy. Contemporary artists from Jerry Lee Lewis to Janna Jae continue to perform at Cain's Ballroom, surrounded by portraits of the singing cowboys who contributed an important chapter to America's musical history.

Artists such as Ernie Fields and Bob Wills were followed by other musical successes. Patti Page, David Gates, Dwight Twilly, Leon Russell, the GAP Band and a host of others have presented their own versions of the "Tulsa Sound" with music ranging from pop to rock, country and classical. The variety of musical styles is reflected in the number of songs that celebrate Tulsa, of which "Living on Tulsa Time," "Twenty-four Hours from Tulsa," and "Take Me Back to Tulsa" are perhaps the most notable. In addition to homegrown talent, national stars have always found an enthusiastic audience in Oklahoma. Elvis Presley, the Beach Boys, Lawrence Welk, The Oak Ridge Boys, Natalie Cole, and Kenny G. are just a few of the major league performers who have graced Tulsa's stages.

Cain's Ballroom has survived, even though modern-day performances bear little resemblance to the rhythmic cadence of days gone by. Another musical landmark was not so fortunate.

A piano-playing graduate of Central High School opened the Rubiot in a strip center near 51st and Harvard in 1959. The jazz club quickly became known for its sophistication and coolness, and before long it was relocated to a more expansive facility near 61st and Peoria where it opened as a dinner club. Its owner, Sonny Gray, led a quartet that accompanied a fetching singer named Suzan Gray. As club owner and host, Sonny Gray welcomed to his small stage such legends as Teddy Wilson, Cal Tjader, Terry Gibbs and Bill Evans.

Those were the days when the state allowed alcohol sales only at liquor stores; the law prohibited so-called "liquor by the drink." Yet patrons were free to bring their own bottles into a private club. Gray tried the brown bag approach but was frustrated by Oklahoma's antiquated and restrictive liquor laws. The Rubiot closed its doors in the late 1960s, the victim of a law that never made much sense and has since been repealed.

The spirit of the Rubiot lives on in the Greenwood district's annual Juneteenth Celebration. Likewise, the Bank of Oklahoma/Williams Jazz on Greenwood Festival in August features music from the free

Dreamland Stage near Greenwood and Archer. Performers have included jazz greats such as Nancy Wilson, Natalie Cole, Lou Rawls, and Royal Crown Revue. Sonny Gray of Rubiot fame leads an annual contingent of local jazz luminaries that typically includes Grady Nichols, Earl Clark, Rick Fortner and Tuxedo Junction.

Musical haunts have come and gone: Ziegfield's and its Las Vegas-style venue, the Apollo Delman, Little Joe's, Magician's Theatre, Joey's, and Sunset Grill all had their day in the limelight. But culture is never static. For every club that's gone by the wayside, there's a Tulsa City Limits, a Blue Rose Cafe or Caz's ready to fill the breach.

Visual and literary artists have also played a role in shaping Tulsa's cultural identity. P.S. Gordon, an artist whose "surreal realism" brings a bold approach to still-life paintings and landscapes, is recognized nationally as a fresh talent. Independent publishers based in Tulsa have provided a literary outlet for writers frustrated by the crushing power of publishing conglomerates. Some of the area's authors—most notably Jay Cronley, Darcy O'Brien, S.E. Hinton, Michael Wallis, and Clifton Taulbert—have enjoyed the notoriety that comes with East Coast publishing, but have preferred to remain in the city that has inspired their best works.

From Cain's Ballroom on North Main to the Performing Arts Center in the heart of downtown, Tulsa's culture is as varied as the people who call the city their home. Young Bill Basie may have been one of the first to find inspiration for his artistic career in the streets of Tulsa, but he has plenty of company, and it's a safe bet that others are waiting to be discovered. ✦

(Following page) **The Bank of Oklahoma/Williams Jazz on Greenwood Festival, held every August, features music from the free Dreamland Stage near Greenwood and Archer.** Photo by Don Wheeler.

In its glory days, Cain's Ballroom was the home of Bob Wills and his Texas Playboys, who popularized Western Swing. Photo courtesy of Tulsa Historical Society.

TWO OF TULSA'S ARTISTIC VIEWS

In both style and substance, two of Tulsa's museums are worlds apart. While the Philbrook Museum of Art features treasures from the Old World, the Gilcrease Museum displays brilliant New World works.

Waite Phillips's success in the Oklahoma oil fields led him to purchase 23 acres of land near the city. On that site, he built an Italian Renaissance villa with formal gardens—a place of classic style and beauty. Friends say that Villa Philbrook was designed as a place for Waite and Genevieve Phillips' children to enjoy. So, after the youngsters were grown, Phillips and his wife decided that Philbrook needed a new purpose. Phillips, who said, "All things should be put to their best possible use," donated the mansion as an art museum in 1938.

Villa Philbrook's stately design complements its most impressive exhibition, the Samuel H. Kress Collection of Italian Renaissance Paintings and Sculpture. Other notable exhibits include contemporary, ancient, and Oriental pieces.

The Gilcrease Museum reflects the Native American heritage of its namesake, Thomas Gilcrease. In contrast to Villa Philbrook, the Gilcrease home is an unpretentious stone structure that shares the museum grounds. The original museum was built in the style of an Indian Longhouse, and the art displayed is distinctly New World. The artwork of Frederic Remington, including three-fourths of his bronzes, can be found at the Gilcrease. In addition, the museum also houses works by Charles M. Russell, George Catlin, Albert Bierstadt, and Thomas Moran.

When Gilcrease needed to pay off debts in the 1950s, he offered to sell his extensive collection to the City of Tulsa. The city raised the necessary funds, and today the museum is enjoyed by thousands of visitors each year. In his book "Oil in Oklahoma," author Bob Gregory best summed up the legacy of Thomas Gilcrease: "With very few exceptions, Oklahoma oil money was never used more wisely, nor for the educational common good of more people" ✦

THE AMERICAN WEST
Perception & Reality

7

Chapter Seven

RECREATION

On Your Own Time

❧

**Tulsans have a wide variety of ways to
have fun and stay fit.** Photo by Don Wheeler.

Western lore resonates with stories of bored cowhands charging into town after a long day in the saddle, firing their pistols into the air and causing everyone in their paths to run for cover. But the more civilization came to grace the frontier, the more such activities were frowned upon by irate citizens and law enforcement officials. Inevitably, the raucous hell-raising of the Old West gave way to more refined recreation that the whole family could enjoy—without getting shot or mowed down by an errant horse.

Like nearly all Americans, Tulsans early on developed a love affair with America's favorite pastime: baseball. Oklahoma's entry into the Union as the 46th state was still on the horizon when, in 1905, a team dubbed the "Oilers" participated in founding the Missouri Valley League with a game against Vinita. According to a notice in the local newspaper, "All business houses will close from 3 to 5 on Monday afternoon in order that the clerks and all others who wish may attend." Tulsa was destined to win Western League Championships from McNulty Park and field future major leaguers like Joe Adcock and Johnny Temple at Texas League Park.

Baseball fans survived a scare when the team was almost moved to Albuquerque. When the Oilers actually packed their gear and left town, entertainer Roy Clark and businessman Bill Rollings teamed up to launch the Drillers, and baseball was here to stay. Today's winning team plays from Driller Stadium, one of the finest Double A stadiums in the country.

Basketball, whose season was once endured as an unwelcome hiatus sandwiched between football and baseball, captured the city's imagination when Nolan Richardson, a tough-minded coach from a Texas junior college, accepted a position as head coach at the University of Tulsa. Richardson led his team to an N.I.T. championship, and fans came to expect NCAA playoff appearances practically as their birthright. South of TU, the Golden Eagles of Oral Roberts University were coming into their own as a nationally ranked team. Fans forgave them for a slump in the mid-1990s, and a revived program led to conference championships and unforgettable games at ORU's Maybee Center.

When soccer finally came to town in a big way, sports fans were overjoyed that Tulsa had shed its provincialism and entered into the arena of global sports. The object of their affection was the Tulsa Roughnecks, a team that won the North American Soccer League championship and found itself featured in *Sports Illustrated*. Unfortunately, the league folded. Similarly, dreams of establishing a

Golfers can tee off at a wide range of courses in Tulsa, including the Page Belcher Golf Course.
Photo by Don Wheeler.

presence in professional football were dashed when another major league team, the Oklahoma Outlaws, failed to draw sufficient crowds. Its doom was sealed when the fledgling United States Football League foundered.

Disappointed with professional sports, football fans have latched on to the University of Tulsa's Golden Hurricane. Under the able leadership of Coach Glenn Dobbs, Jerry Rhome and Howard Twilley dazzled spectators with their passing game. And who can forget Coach Dave Rader's stunning victory over the University of Oklahoma? Although low attendance and occasional probations have dampened spirits from time to time, Skelly Stadium is still the place to enjoy some good football on crisp autumn afternoons.

Perhaps nothing dispels Oklahoma's image as a dusty and treeless expanse as effectively as Tulsa's lush golf courses. One of Tulsa's most renowned courses, Southern Hills Country Club, is rated among the top 25 in the nation by none other than *Golf Digest*. Volunteers come out in droves to support U.S. Opens, PGA Championships and other tournaments. Thanks to extensive television coverage of marquee golfing events, it's a safe bet that many golfers around the country associate Tulsa with camera shots of a crisp downtown skyline peeking above the trees on the first fairway of Southern Hills.

There are three ways to secure a tee time at Southern Hills—you can purchase a membership, become best friends with a member, or qualify for a major championship. Most Tulsans take the path of least resistance and head for one of the city's remarkable public courses and less exclusive private clubs. Tulsa Country Club, one of the city's oldest private clubs, and newer ones such as Meadowbrook, where $1.4 million was spent to upgrade greens and tee boxes, offer challenging holes lined with majestic trees. Those who play the municipal course at Mohawk Park can enjoy a taste of the exotic. It's close enough to the Tulsa Zoo so that golfers can tee off to the sound of roaring lions.

For some, recreation isn't all about chasing, whacking, throwing, or bouncing a ball. Boating options, including skiing, fishing, or simply lounging on an inner tube, are available only a short drive from the heart of the city. Lake Keystone is closest to town, and Grand Lake, home to handsome estates and first-rate vacation facilities, is only 90 minutes to the northeast. Those with a penchant for the ponies will find a haven during racing season at Fair Meadow Downs in Expo Square. Simulcasts from tracks throughout the country are available even when the ponies at Fair Meadows are taking a break. Nearby, Bell's Amusement Park combines the pizzazz of Coney Island with rides for the little ones.

The Drillers baseball team plays from one of the finest Double A stadiums in the country.
Photo by Don Wheeler.

One of Tulsa's most popular attractions is the Tulsa Zoo. Opened in 1928 with 35 animals in traditional cages, the Tulsa Zoo today features nearly 1,500 animals in 70 acres of natural settings. Popular financial support facilitated construction of the Chimpanzee Connection, where only a glass barrier stands between chimps and human viewers. Other intriguing exhibits include the Elephant Encounter, a shark aquarium, the jaguar enclosure, a tropical rain forest habitat, a renovated polar bear exhibit, a cheetah exhibit, and an improved children's zoo. Every year, the Waltz on the Wild Side party draws a crowd and helps fund ongoing enhancements. In the late 1990s, Tulsans supported bond issues and fund-raisers to generate more than $10 million for the zoo.

Shoppers with even the most discriminating tastes are rarely disappointed in Tulsa's stores. From the fashionable Utica Square in midtown to Woodland Hills Mall to the south, shoppers from a four-state region flock to Tulsa for necessities as well as specialty items.

Everyday attractions are complemented by a plethora of festivals that offer a glimpse into Tulsa's ethnic and religious heritage. From Oktoberfest and the Asian Festival to Greek and Scottish festivals, Tulsa is home to events that celebrate the American melting pot. Mayfest is a rite of spring that provides a venue for regional artists. An annual chili cook-off draws attention to homegrown culinary arts, and bluegrass music has become a staple of downtown entertainment. Seems like there's always an opportunity for celebration, no matter what your ethnic identity or favorite food.

Some say that Tulsa plays second fiddle to America's metropolitan centers. True, it's tough to compete with the likes of New York and Los Angeles, and even nearby Dallas offers recreation that you'd be hard-pressed to find in a mid-size city. But on the whole, Tulsa has come a long way from the days when shooting out the streetlights was some cowboy's idea of a good time. Whether you're looking for an action-packed ball game or the serenity of a quiet cove on the lake, Tulsa and its environs have a little something for everybody. ✦

Visitors find a world of exhibits at the Tulsa Zoo.
Photo by Don Wheeler.

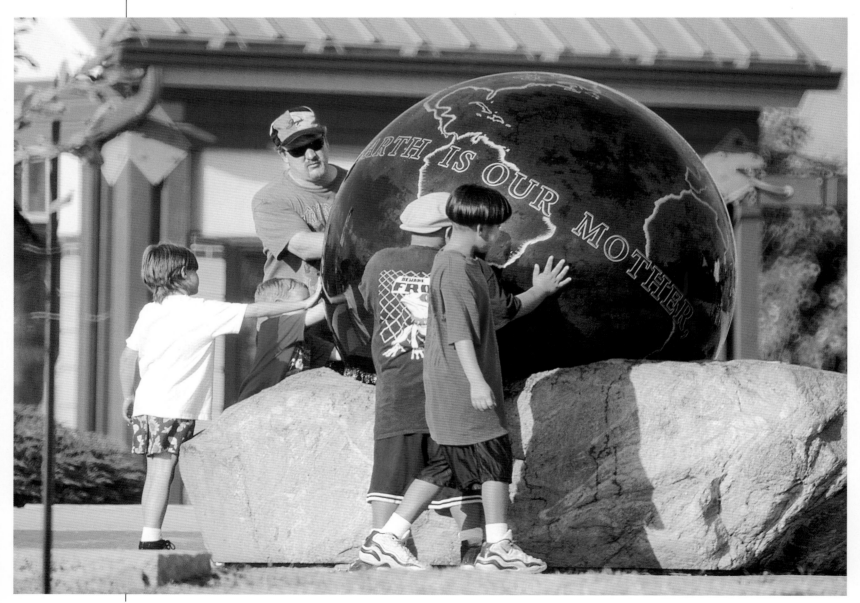

Children enjoy up-close encounters at the Petting Zoo. Photo by Don Wheeler.

Keystone Lake provides a perfect place for boaters to set sail.
Photos by Don Wheeler.

(Pages 114-115)
The roller coaster at Bell's Amusement Park brings thrills to the brave at heart.
Photo by Don Wheeler.

(Pages 116-117)
Every fall, the Tulsa State Fair features two weeks of big-name entertainment, midway food and fun, and livestock events.
Photo by Don Wheeler.

Tulsa is home to a wide variety of cultural festivals. Among these yearly events are the **Greek Festival**, and the **Scottish Festival**, below.
Photos by Don Wheeler.

The Pow wow at Mohawk Park celebrates Tulsa's American Indian heritage.
Photo by Don Wheeler.

Dancers twirl to the music at the annual Hispanic Festival in downtown Tulsa.
Photo by Don Wheeler.

(Following page) Jockeys get ready to race at Fair Meadow Downs in Expo Square.
Photo by Don Wheeler.

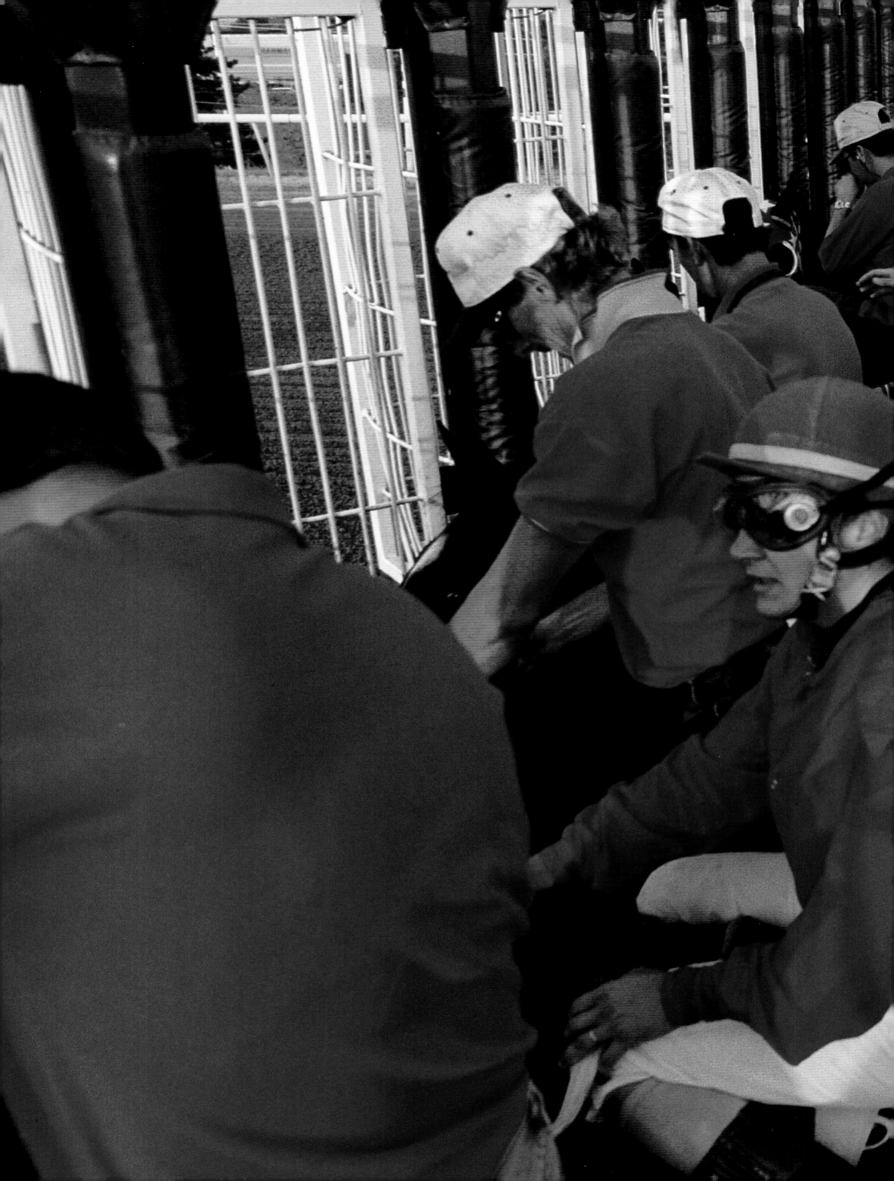

The Gatesway Balloon Fest, held every August, brings more than 70 hot air balloons to Tulsa. After the traditional "glow," balloonists take flight, filling the sky with color. Photos by Don Wheeler.

(Following page) The Tulsa Zoo is a scenic spot to spend a carefree afternoon. Photo by Don Wheeler.

8

Chapter Eight

A CITY OF FAITHS

Religion &
Community Service

**First United Methodist Church, located in
downtown Tulsa, is one of the denomination's
leading churches.** Photo by Don Wheeler.

Tulsa's early days were far from tame. The closest place to find justice in Indian Territory was Arkansas—a fact well known to scoundrels on the prowl for "easy money."

Most citizens, however, made a living without resorting to gambling or robbery. Law and order were lacking, but settlers were determined to establish moral order as a first step in creating a wholesome place to raise their families.

By the closing decades of the 19th century, religious communities were beginning to carve out a niche on the Oklahoma frontier. In 1883, residents joined forces to organize the Union Sunday School, and this multi-denominational group served all Protestant citizens for a while. Denominations then began to regroup, and First Presbyterian Church established Tulsa's first house of worship in October of 1885. First Methodist Episcopal Church followed suit in December of 1886.

Tulsa's early religious crusaders faced a tough job, but they adapted to the unruly environment. City lore has it that a pastor's wife stood at the door of the First Methodist Church on Sundays with her apron open, asking for firearms in exchange for forgiveness.

Churches were still in their infancy when oil put Tulsa on the map. Derricks dotted the prairie, and fortunes were made overnight. Yet Tulsa's newfound wealth came with a price tag. Oil field workers found themselves unable to afford adequate housing for their families, and schools became too crowded to accept more students. Social problems were the inevitable by-product of rapid growth, and in keeping with America's time-honored concern for the plight of the less fortunate, churches became a refuge for workers stuck at the bottom rung of the socio-economic ladder.

The religious community found allies among Tulsa businessmen anxious to mitigate the consequences of runaway growth. A group came together in 1909 to found the city's first YMCA. The organization began campaigns to eliminate housing shortages and school overcrowding. The YMCA and newly formed Boy Scouts also aimed to curb juvenile delinquency by providing youth with recreational facilities. Before long, several more agencies joined the battle against Tulsa's social ills.

In 1924, the city's Chamber of Commerce formed the Tulsa Community Fund, an alliance of local charitable groups. Charter agencies were the YMCA, the YWCA, the Red Cross, the Tulsa Boys Home, the Tulsa County Public Health Association, the Federation of Jewish Charities, the Girl Scouts, the Boy Scouts, Day Nursery, the Frances Willard Home for Girls, and The Confidential Exchange.

To make better use of contributions to these agencies, Tulsa at mid-century organized the Community Service Council. The council aimed to "do good better," and it began to research community problems and coordinate relief efforts. As a result, Tulsa's social agencies became much more efficient.

Over the years, Tulsans have generously given to help less fortunate residents, and that tradition continues. In the 1999 United Way Campaign, Tulsans gave $21.5 million—by far, the largest donation that year in the state.

Among Tulsa's religious groups, community service also remains a mission. Tulsa Metropolitan Ministry has brought religious creeds together to promote tolerance and to address social issues, including the plight of the homeless. Another influential organization is the

National Conference, formerly the National Conference of Christians and Jews. This group has become a major force in celebrating Tulsa's religious and cultural diversity.

Another high-profile religious presence in Tulsa is evangelist Oral Roberts. When Roberts moved from tent revivals to television specials, millions of viewers became familiar with his Tulsa address and the university he founded.

The Universalist-Unitarian movement is perhaps less visible, but it is an important part of Tulsa's religious spectrum. Tulsa's All Souls Church stands as one of the denomination's largest, most vital churches.

In some cities, congregations have abandoned their downtown churches, and once-vibrant places of worship have become empty historic sites. Tulsa's downtown area, however, remains home to an abundance of active churches, and thousands of dedicated members

flock to the city's center on Sundays to attend worship services. Among these churches is Boston Avenue United Methodist Church, an Art Deco masterpiece located at the corner of Thirteenth and Boston. Its 8,100-member congregation is one of the largest in United Methodism. Only blocks away is the impressive First Methodist Church, another of the denomination's leading churches.

Many other denominations maintain thriving churches downtown. One corner of Eleventh and Boulder, next to First Methodist, is the site of Cathedral Square. Tulsa's First Christian Church and First Church of Christ Scientist occupy two more corners at this intersection. Another block north on Boulder is the Catholic Church's stately Holy Family Cathedral.

Boston Avenue is the site of First Presbyterian, the city's first established church, which continues to grow. The congregation recently expanded

United Way's Day of Caring draws thousands of volunteers each year. These dedicated individuals spend the day helping others throughout the community.
Photo by Don Wheeler.

across Boston Avenue by acquiring the former downtown Masonic building, now home to the church's family life center. Further east and a little north is the impressive architecture of Trinity Episcopal Church. First Baptist Church, with yet another large downtown congregation, is located one block north. Grace Lutheran Church on East Fifth Place completes the downtown religious registry.

Downtown Tulsa also was the site of the Jewish community's first religious services in 1914. Two years later, Congregation B'nai Emmanau took its place among downtown houses of worship. Later, the congregation moved to Nineteenth and Peoria.

These houses of worship have played a key role in Tulsa's religious life. Once they became established downtown, these denominations inspired the formation of suburban churches and paved the way for a kaleidoscope of religious expression. Today, vibrant groups of nearly every faith—Islam, Greek Orthodoxy, Buddhism, and Hinduism—contribute to Tulsa's rich religious tapestry.

Both religious and charitable organizations persevere in their mission to serve Tulsa's citizens. These groups share bonds of hope and help—bonds that will always strengthen the spirit of Tulsa's people. ←

Sprucing up the Camp Fire Girls' headquarters is one of many missions during United Way's Day of Caring. Photo by Don Wheeler.

(Following page) **Athletes from throughout Tulsa participate in the annual United Way Sand Blazer Run.** Photo by Don Wheeler.

The spire of
**Boston Avenue
Baptist Church has
been a familiar sight
for generations
of Tulsans.**
Photo courtesy of
Tulsa Historical Society.
(Right) Photo by
Don Wheeler.

All Souls Unitarian Church plays a vital role in the Universalist-Unitarian movement.
Photo by Don Wheeler.

Rhema Bible
Church of Broken
Arrow spreads its
message on a Tulsa
Transit bus, shown
here in front of
MTTA's new bus
station in down-
town Tulsa.
Photo by Don Sibley.

(Left)
First Presbyterian
Church was
established in
1885 as the city's
first church.
Photo by
Don Wheeler.

9

Chapter Nine

TULSA'S FUTURE

A New Century

**As the new century dawns, Tulsa
prepares for the challenges ahead.**
Photo by Don Wheeler.

Tulsans are to be forgiven for cultivating a pride in their city that borders on hubris. Historically, Tulsans have perceived themselves—with considerable justification—as independent and self-sustaining. Theirs is a city founded on a spirit of entrepreneurship and dedicated to the principles of free enterprise. It is also a city steeped in cultural and ethnic diversity. After all, Tulsa has always been home to people from a wide range of backgrounds, from Native Americans, African Americans and Europeans of every nationality in Oklahoma's early days to Asians and Hispanics in more recent times. And it's a safe bet that Tulsa will mirror American society's increasing diversity in the years ahead.

Today, Tulsans are poised at a crossroads, and they will need to summon every bit of their entrepreneurial spirit if they are to make a successful transition to the emerging social and economic paradigm. E-commerce and telecommunications are transforming the world as we know it, and cities unable to adapt to change will find themselves at a serious disadvantage. Tulsa's challenges on the threshold of a new century will be to find its way in a world of constant change and to embrace the diversity of its people as a source of strength and optimism.

Fortunately, Tulsa enters the new economy with some distinct advantages. The cost of doing business in Tulsa remains far below the national average. Even comparable cities such as Dallas, Wichita, Little Rock and St. Louis report a somewhat higher cost of doing business. If you're looking for an affordable place to hang your shingle, urban centers like New York and Los Angeles aren't even in the running.

Tulsa is also below average in other areas where it's perfectly all right to come in behind the pack. Labor, energy, state and local taxes, and office costs all put Tulsa in a favorable light in comparison to other cities. Moreover, the area's moderate cost of living means that shoppers and homebuyers can get a bigger bang for their bucks in Tulsa.

Like the rest of America, Tulsans in the late 1990s woke up to the realization that full employment can be a double-edged sword. It's hard to complain about an economy that offers nearly everyone a job unless, of course, you happen to be an employer. In that case, your biggest problem might well be your inability to attract skilled workers.

A dearth of qualified employees and rapidly expanding markets worldwide have catapulted workforce development to the top of most cities' agendas, and Tulsa is no exception. Welfare reform was still on the horizon when, in 1992, the Metropolitan Tulsa Chamber of Commerce stepped up to the plate to form IndEx (an acronym for Industrial Exchange), a non-profit corporation whose goal was to train welfare moms and others on public assistance to manufacture light industrial goods under contract with area companies. Today, IndEx is both a model for other cities paralyzed by an inadequate or poorly trained workforce and home to out-of-school youth, non-violent offenders and others looking for a second chance. IndEx is complemented by the Chamber's cutting edge school-to-career programs and vocational and technical schools that are second to none nationwide.

Relatively low taxes, together with a functioning governmental structure that inspires widespread participation, have proven to be seductive lures to companies considering relocation. Ten years ago, Tulsa voters abandoned their century-old city commission form of government in favor of a strong mayor/city council system. As a result, residents have more opportunity than ever to influence municipal politics. City charter reform has inspired vigorous city council races. Today, councilors represent their districts without losing sight of the city's overall economic well-being.

In the realm of politics, perhaps no accomplishment in the late 1990s looms larger than the formation of Oklahoma State University-Tulsa.

Effective and persistent lobbying on the part of the Chamber and its key business partners brought the benefits of comprehensive, state-supported higher education to Tulsa. Another milestone was reached in late 1999 when the University of Oklahoma Board of Regents approved the purchase of the BP-Amoco Tulsa Technology Center in mid-town as a crucial step in establishing the Tulsa Campus of the OU Health Sciences Center. Few Tulsans were sorry to lose their city's distinction as the largest urban center in America without access to a comprehensive state university.

Much has been accomplished, but much remains to be done. At century's end, city leaders were busy soliciting citizen input for a plan to renovate tourism and convention facilities. Tourism ranks at the top of Tulsa's industries; conventions and visitors pump $1 billion annually into Tulsa's economy, provide $30 million in annual tax revenue, and guarantee jobs for some 24,000 people. But Tulsa's facilities have not kept pace with those in other parts of the country, and unless the issue is faced squarely and courageously, the city could experience a contraction in this vital economic sector.

Given Tulsa's progressive outlook, there are plenty of reasons for optimism. Perhaps nowhere is Tulsa's willingness to face up to its shortcomings more apparent than in its public inquiry into the darkest days of the city's history.

The year was 1921. A young black man was accused of assaulting a young white elevator operator in the Drexel Building downtown.

Tulsa is attracting many high-tech companies, including MCI WorldCom.
Photo by Don Wheeler.

Tulsa Technology Center helps provide northeast Oklahoma with a well-trained work force.
Photo by Don Wheeler.

What actually happened in that elevator will always be shrouded in uncertainty. In the end, it didn't really matter. Racial tensions in post-World War I America were at fever pitch, and in Tulsa, little more than a match was needed to ignite a conflagration.

Fanned by rumors and irrational hatred, a race riot erupted near the courthouse in downtown Tulsa. When the smoke finally cleared, dozens lay dead, and hundreds of structures were little more than smoldering ruins.

For generations, many Tulsans preferred the balm of denial to confrontation with the truth. The wall of silence was broken once and for all in 1999, when a commission was appointed to scrutinize every aspect of the 1921 race riot. Eyewitness accounts received front-page attention, and survivors were able at last to share their stories without fear of reprisal. Clearly, the truth was too long in coming. Yet come out it did. Perhaps Tulsa has reached a stage where its people can tear down the walls that divide them and work together to build a city that holds promise for all citizens.

Another affirmation of Tulsa's progressive outlook came in November of 1999, when voters overwhelmingly passed a $109 million bond issue to upgrade public schools. Included in that proposal was $25 million to build a new Booker T. Washington High School. With new facilities, students of all backgrounds and ethnicities will be able to set their sights on scholastic achievements that will carry them into the workplace of the new century.

Tulsans are accustomed to crossroads. They've enjoyed the booms and weathered the busts. They've welcomed new technologies without letting go of the qualities that enabled them to tame a prairie wilderness, and they've survived vicious storms with a resolve to rebuild. As changes continue to come barreling down the pike, they'll need to draw on their heritage and remind themselves of how far they've come in the span of a few generations. What was once touted as the "Tulsa Spirit" will serve them well as they determine what happens in the next hundred years. ⤶

American Airlines, one of Tulsa's largest employers, provides maintenance services for its aircraft in Hangar 6 at Tulsa International Airport.
Photo by Don Wheeler.

The Philtower is a colorful sight on Tulsa's skyline.
Photo by Don Wheeler.

Tulsa's thriving downtown district reflects the city's economic success.
Photo by
Don Wheeler.

Tulsa's Performing Arts Center provides an excellent venue for theatrical productions. Here, circus performers take the stage during a production of "Barnum."
Photo by Don Wheeler.

Youngsters are careful to sit still as face painters work their magic at the city's Mayfest celebration.
Photo by Don Wheeler.

The little red train is always ready to take visitors on a tour of the zoo.
Photo by Don Wheeler.

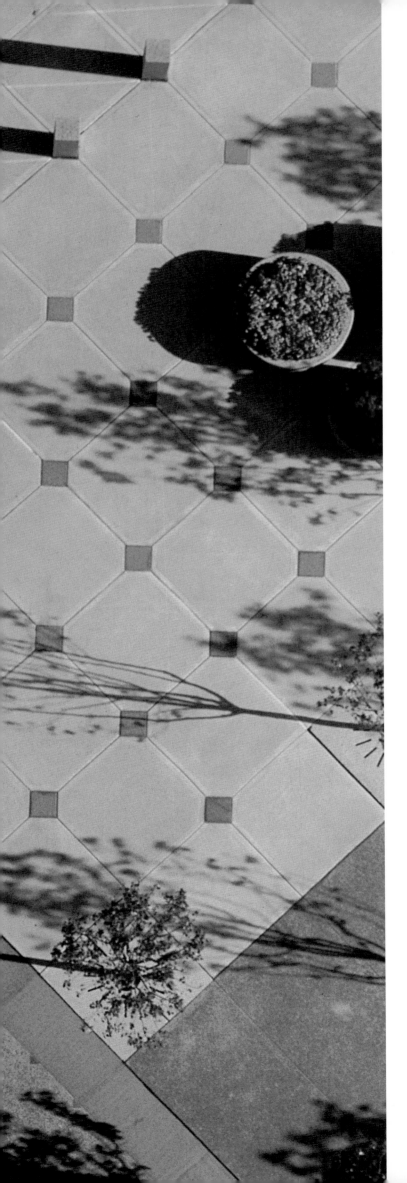

2

Part Two

10
Chapter Ten

NETWORKS

Photo by Don Wheeler.

THE *TULSA WORLD*

Eugene Lorton hit Tulsa on October 10, 1911, to edit a tottering little newspaper called the Tulsa World. Neither the World nor Tulsa was ever the same.

Eugene Lorton, left, is pictured in his office with his grandson, Robert E. Lorton, the current publisher, during the 1940s.

Today, at the start of a new millennium, Tulsa has grown from an oil boom town of 10,000 to a vibrant city of almost 400,000, with a diverse economy and people. The *World*, which will celebrate its centennial in 2005, now circulates throughout eastern Oklahoma and bordering states, reaching 400,000 adult readers daily, 500,000 on Sunday. It is still printed in downtown Tulsa.

An independent morning newspaper, the *World* has been owned by the Lorton family since 1917. Eugene's grandson, Robert E. Lorton is World Publishing Company chairman and publisher, and his great-grandson, Robert E. Lorton III, is president.

The *World* is a family operation in more ways than one. Some 800 employees work in the production, advertising, circulation, administration, and news departments. A number of those employees followed in their parents' footsteps when they joined the paper. In fact, the *World* engenders such loyalty that it is not uncommon for employees to retire with 30, 40, or even 50 years' service.

In addition to providing a comprehensive, attractive, and informative daily report on local, state, national, and international news, the newspaper is available online at its website. A telephone service, Tulsaline, offers a wide variety of information at 58-Tulsa. And the *World* publishes five weekly community news sections serving Broken Arrow-Coweta, south, midtown, east, and west Tulsa.

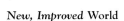

The newspaper is the recipient of numerous professional awards for reporting, editing, and photography. It is highly regarded throughout the region for its leadership in economic, educational, and civic affairs. Its editorial pages are known for their progressive and thought-provoking stances.

New, Improved World

The *World* recently embarked on a $60 million program to upgrade the newspaper production facility with new, state-of-the-art offset printing presses manufactured by Wifag in Switzerland. The first of two presses was installed in 1998. A second new press will be in place in 2000.

According to Robert E. Lorton III the new presses provide unmatched news page color and printing quality. Color photographs and advertising is available on almost every page. The Wifag units will produce as many as 72,000 copies an hour.

"We are the first newspaper in North America to have these presses," he said. "They will allow us to showcase the work of our photographers, artists, and designers, and also offer expanded color opportunities for advertisers."

Since 1995, the *World* has completed major renovations and expansion of almost every department. These included a new facade on the Boulder Avenue building, a new lobby entrance, new classified advertising, pre-press, display advertising, and circulation departments. The packaging and distribution department has been expanded.

The newspaper also has invested in a new pagination system which allows editors to assemble stories and pictures on a computer monitor and set an entire page in one operation. Photographers use computerized cameras to take pictures and store the images on floppy disks which can be read by other computers that transfer the images to the pagination computers.

From left: Robert E. Lorton, III, president, and Robert E. Lorton, chairman and publisher, in the *World* newsroom.

The computer photo system also allows all pictures to be stored on large capacity hard disks and compact disks in a computerized library system. Another computer system retains every story in a library that can be searched by key words.

History of the World

The *World* traces its roots to the *Indian Chief*, founded in 1884 at Third and Main streets. That publication later became the *Indian Republican*.

J.R. Brady and James McCoy published the first edition of the *Tulsa World* on September 14, 1905, in the back room of a store on West Third Street. It started as a four-page, six-column weekly paper. Just two months later, oil was discovered in the Glenn Pool oil field, and the *World* quickly became a daily paper.

Eugene Lorton arrived in Tulsa in 1911, to edit the newspaper. By 1917, he owned the newspaper outright, having brought it to profitability and bought out his last partner.

Before settling in Tulsa, Lorton had left Missouri to knock around the West as a printer's helper, telegrapher, fledgling actor, and newspaper editor and publisher. At age 42, he had a lot of experience in newspapering, but never had been fortunate enough to own a newspaper in a growing area.

In later years, Lorton expressed his views of newspapering: "There are two kinds of newspapers. One is an organ and the other an institution. The difference . . . is merely the degree in which they serve the public."

To become an institution, he said, a newspaper had to immerse itself in the life of a community and become part of its growth and prosperity. It had to advance policies that helped build the city.

Lorton opposed Prohibition, pushed for licensing drivers to operate those new-fangled automobiles, opposed Sunday Blue Laws, called for better state highways, backed Kendall College (now the University of Tulsa), and organized the forerunner of the Tulsa Chamber of Commerce.

A Crusading Editor

Lorton realized that the city's biggest problem was the lack of an adequate water supply. The Arkansas River was unusable, even for bathing. The city relied on wells and bottled water. By 1915, Lorton had written more than 600 editorials on the inadequacy of Tulsa water. On July 15, 1915, he first advocated going to Spavinaw Creek, 65 miles to the northeast, for water.

Many dismissed the idea as preposterous. But Lorton persisted. By the time water flowed to Tulsa from Spavinaw in 1924, he had written hundreds more editorials. Tulsans approved bond issues totaling $6.8 million and the proposal withstood lawsuits from opponents. The creation of an abundant water

supply ensured the growth of Tulsa into a major metropolitan and commercial center.

Very quickly after the tragic race riot of May 31, 1921, Eugene Lorton started a relief fund with his own money and pushed it on page one for days. Official Tulsa did not apologize for the riot, but Eugene Lorton did. In a page one editorial, he apologized for "proud, matchless Tulsa before the bar of Christian civilization" for that shameful event.

His big public fight was with the Ku Klux Klan. In 1923, Lorton wrote: "We do not believe there is a citizen of either the invisible empire or the visible republic who will question the statement that eventually the Ku Klux Klan will run its course and be disbanded. Organized for the announced purpose of saving the country from an imaginary peril, it has come to constitute the very greatest peril the republic faces . . . "

Lorton was a tough, hard-driving publisher who often expressed his views in pungent editorials. He once wrote of a local businessman: "The accident of wealth alone is all that prevented him from being a porch climber (burglar), a yegg (safecracker), and a low-down sneak thief."

About a governor of Oklahoma: "You are an egotistical, law-defying, self-centered bigot."

Two new state-of-the-art presses manufactured by Wifag in Switzerland are part of a $60 million effort to enhance the quality and efficiency of the newspaper.

The *Tulsa World* building, with its recently refurbished facade, in downtown Tulsa.

Lorton died in 1949 and control of the newspaper was assumed by his executives under the direction of his widow, Maud, who became publisher and chairman of the board. She later named general counsel and Vice President Byron V. Boone president and publisher. He held that position until 1968 when the Lortons' grandson, Robert E. Lorton, became president.

The *World* has had several homes but all within a block of each other. From 1907 until 1914, the paper was located at Third and Boulder, a site now occupied by one of the Williams Towers. The U.S. District Court was housed on the second floor of the *World* building at this location. The newspaper has been located at 315 South Boulder Avenue since 1918.

The *World* expanded across the alley with a new building to house its presses and newsroom in 1975. That building faces Main Mall and is connected to the Boulder building by walkway over the alley.

Some *Tulsa World* 'Firsts'

While supporting improvements for Tulsa, the newspaper has been a leader in technology and journalistic functions. It had the first oil page in the United States. It had the first local cartoons, the first photo engraving plant, and the first Sunday tabloid magazine section in the state. Another first was in obtaining the full leased wire service of the Associated Press in 1911.

The *World* also was among the first newspapers to join with a competitor in mechanical and distribution function. The business, advertising, circulation, and mechanical departments of the *World* and the *Tulsa Tribune* were merged and an agency called Newspaper Printing Corporation was created in 1941 as a method to cut rising labor and material costs for both newspapers.

Editorial operations of the two newspapers remained separate and fiercely competitive. The *Tribune* moved into the *World* building and dropped its Sunday edition. The idea of a joint operating agreement spread to competing morning and afternoon newspapers in other cities and several other similar agreements were made. Economics of the newspaper business changed and the *Tribune* folded in 1992.

In the last decade, the *World* was the first U.S. metropolitan daily newspaper to convert its photographic equipment to the digital camera. The newspaper also was among the first metropolitan newspapers to produce its pages through the computerized pagination process.

Community Support

In addition to serving readers and the business community, the *Tulsa World* sponsors a number of programs and activities that help enhance the academic, cultural, and social climate of our city.

Annually, the *World* donates more than $2 million in advertising space to a variety of community efforts. With the help of readers, the newspaper raises more than $150,000 annually to help support the Salvation Army's holiday programs for underprivileged children and their families.

And the World sponsors an annual golf tournament in which the $50,000 in proceeds go toward sight-saving programs at the Oklahoma Society to Prevent Blindness.

The paper also sponsors:

- Spelling bees for approximately 850 schools in 30 eastern Oklahoma counties. The winner of the state finals receives a week-long, expense-paid trip to Washington, D.C., to compete in the National Spelling Bee.

- Oklahoma FreeWheel, a week-long bicycle trek across the state during June that attracts 1,500 riders each year.

- The Tulsa Run, one of the top 15-kilometer foot races in the nation. Held in downtown Tulsa, the race also features a 15k wheel-chair race and a two-mile Fun Run. The annual event attracts nearly 10,000 participants from around the world.

The *World* is a longtime supporter of the University of Tulsa, Tulsa Area United Way, the Tulsa Zoo, the Nature Conservancy, the Tulsa Opera, the Tulsa Philharmonic, Philbrook and Gilcrease museums, and a host of other charities and worthy causes. ✦

 The *Tulsa World* has been published at 315 S. Boulder Ave. since 1917. This photo was taken in 1937. Photograph courtesy of Beryl Ford Collection.

MCI WorldCom

MCI WorldCom is a unique global telecommunications company. Operating in more than 65 countries, the company is a premier provider of facilities-based and fully integrated local, long distance, international, and Internet services. It is the second largest long distance provider in the U.S. with a 45,000-mile fiberoptic nationwide network. MCI WorldCom plays an active role in the daily lives of individuals, families, and businesses worldwide.

Each month Wholesale Customer Service and Support in Tulsa handles more than 54,000 inbound calls from customers. The department oversees ordering, provisioning, design, and installation and maintenance for the wholesale division's 1,000 customers on a 24-hour, seven-day-a-week basis.

A New Kind of Communications Company

MCI WorldCom is taking telecommunications to new levels. Following the 1998 merger of WorldCom and MCI, and following the announcement in 1999 of the merger with Sprint, this global communications company provides a full set of data, Internet, local, and international communications services over its own seamless "local-to-global-to-local" system to network customers around the world.

"MCI WorldCom is uniquely qualified to lead the industry in growth and to build on the tremendous value we have created for our shareholders," said Bernard J. Ebbers, president and chief executive officer of MCI WorldCom. "We have the right network—built for the explosive demand for high-speed data and Internet services—the right talent, and the right strategy at the right time. MCI WorldCom is out in front and sets the standard by which all other communications companies will be measured."

MCI WorldCom Tulsa Facility

The MCI WorldCom Tulsa facility is located in the Cherokee Industrial Park, seven miles north of Tulsa's downtown, between Highways 75 and 169. MCI WorldCom purchased a 320,000-square-foot building in 1995. That building was expanded to 660,000-square-feet to accommodate the company's explosive growth.

"Tulsa has some of the best telecommunications expertise in the country," said John Barnett, President of MCI WorldCom Wholesale Services. "That's in part to the commitment this area made several years ago to target this industry. In addition, the local educational facilities have provided a rich assortment of classes in this field so the Tulsa area can retain many of its brightest students. Not only was the area a perfect fit to expand our operations, but it also offers a lower cost of living and affordable housing. Once you have these kinds of infrastructures in place, all the other advantages are magnified ten-fold."

Tulsa a Vital Component of Company

MCI WorldCom has a substantial amount of capital and time invested in Tulsa. The Tulsa MCI WorldCom facility is a vital component of one of the world's largest telecommunications companies.

MCI WorldCom traces its involvement in the community to the early 1980s and its relationship with WilTel Network Services, which MCI WorldCom acquired in 1994.

One responsibility of the Network Operations Center in Tulsa is to "groom" the network's fiberoptic pathways for optimum efficiencies, assuring digital traffic is relayed as quickly as possible.

Tulsa is home to about 4,200 employees and accommodates the global headquarters of MCI WorldCom's Wholesale Services division.

Other divisions located in the facility include Information Services, Engineering, International Data Services, Network Operations, Enhanced Data Network Services, Commercial Customer Services-East, Corporate Facilities and Maintenance, Corporate Real Estate, Corporate Credit, Human Resources, Training, and Public Relations.

MCI WorldCom Tulsa employees service customers throughout the U.S. as well as globally. Customers from various business segments, including wholesale, commercial long distance, and data services, are serviced by MCI WorldCom professionals in Tulsa. Many of the corporation's intricate infrastructures, with their complicated levels, programs, and services, are maintained in Tulsa.

As the company experienced phenomenal growth, MCI WorldCom added a 260,000-square-foot facility. The MCI WorldCom Tulsa facilities feature the most modern amenities which afford employees the opportunity to conduct their work and take care of personal business. The facility features a distance learning center, health and fitness center, cafeteria, credit union, convenience store, flower and card shop, outdoor walking track, and more.

MCI WorldCom is committed to community involvement. In Tulsa, MCI WorldCom employees play an active role in supporting many nonprofit causes, such as the American Red Cross, the Tulsa Run, the MS 150 bike tour, and the United Way. Each year, the company invests more than $100 million into the Oklahoma economy

in payroll alone. MCI WorldCom continues to be a leader in Tulsa and globally.

Local-to-Global-to-Local

MCI WorldCom is a dominant provider of integrated voice, data, Internet, and communication services. The company serves millions of U.S. business and residential customers over a 45,000-mile, all-fiber high capacity nationwide network—enough fiber to stretch from San Francisco to Washington, D.C. 16 times.

UUNET supplements MCI WorldCom's Internet and technology operations, allowing businesses and consumers the ability to harness the full power of the Internet as well as leading networking and hosting solutions.

The company's domestic presence is complemented by the investment MCI WorldCom has made in the international arena. MCI WorldCom is partnered with U.K.'s Cable & Wireless in the ownership of Gemini, a transoceanic, fiberoptic cable between New York and the United Kingdom.

The company also establishes itself as a local, facilities-based competitor in 16 countries outside the U.S. with high capacity connectivity to the rest of the company's network via transcontinental and transoceanic cables.

The MCI WorldCom pan-European network links major commercial locations including London, Paris, Frankfurt, Brussels, Amsterdam, Stockholm, and Rotterdam. The company continues to strengthen its international service with the development of nationwide networks throughout U.K., France, and Germany.

MCI WorldCom also is well established in Latin America and Mexico and has a strong presence in the Pacific Rim and Australia.

"We offer products and services which allow companies to be more productive and ones that add some level of ease to people's lives," said Barnett. "We have staked our reputation on being one of the leading providers of communications products and network transmission services to our global customers.

"The list could go on ad infinitum, but the bottom line is this—we are committed to providing the best products and services available at a very competitive price." ↵

An MCI WorldCom employee checks the integrity of a section of fiberoptic cable. The company's 45,000-mile, all-fiber high-capacity network spans the nation.

Tulsa's Cherokee Industrial Park facility, opened in 1996, houses approximately 4,200 MCI WorldCom employees. The multi-building campus environment includes amenities such as a full service cafeteria, convenience store, flower and card shop, fitness center, credit union and more.

TV GUIDE

In a video editing room, a producer is hard at work editing an Insider segment with X-Files star David Duchovny. At a computer terminal, a programmer writes lines of code for an interactive program guide. At a workstation, a customer service representative takes a call from a cable operator in Mexico requesting programming changes.

Three very different tasks, but vital functions for the same company—Tulsa-based TV Guide.

The constant companion and entertainment "bible" for generations of television viewers, TV Guide has grown up, offering television guidance and entertainment information wherever there is a need, as well as a bevy of other services ranging from satellite distribution and data services to customer service and technology consulting. By investing in new technologies, TV Guide has parlayed the magazine's original audience into what *Advertising Age*[1] calls "one of the largest, if not the largest, mass audience of any media brand."

"TV Guide really epitomizes the breadth essential to compete in the media and communications industry," says Peter C. Boylan, III, president and chief operating officer of TV Guide. "Through leadership in our three key franchises—television guidance products and services, satellite superstation and programming services, and direct-to-home satellite services—we continue to offer the highest quality products, services, support, and innovation."

Stationed at the corner of 71st and Lewis, now officially TV Guide Plaza, TV Guide is a global diversified media and communications company, and a major player in the new digital world. Although its offices are spread across the country, TV Guide's major presence is in Tulsa, where two of its three primary business units and more than 1,200 employees are based. Other offices include New York, Los Angeles, Philadelphia, Chicago, Atlanta, Miami, Denver, and Detroit.

TV Guide Entertainment Group

The Tulsa-based TV Guide Entertainment Group delivers an array of entertainment-driven, technologically advanced guides: cable's *TV Guide Channel* available in 54 million homes[2]; the Internet's *TV Guide Online* with 2.8 million unique users per month[3]; and *TV Guide Interactive* targeted at the exploding digital cable market. No matter how viewers search for their favorite programs, TV Guide is there to guide them. The Entertainment Group leverages the brand internationally, reaching 3 million subscribers in more than 20 Latin American countries and Canada, while *Screen TV*, a unique network, showcases hi-tech consumer products and pay-per-view movies and events.

United Video Group

The United Video Group, also based in Tulsa, provides services ranging from satellite delivery of superstations and cable networks to customer service. The United Video Group includes *UVTV*, which markets and distributes Chicago superstation WGN to more than 47 million households[4]; *Superstar/Netlink Group*, which holds a 58 percent share in the direct-to-home C-Band satellite market; *SpaceCom*, distributor of satellite bandwidth; and *SSDS*, provider of information technology consulting. Also part of the United Video Group, *TV Guide Affiliate Sales* is the arm responsible for distribution of 15 prod-

ucts and services to 15,000 cable systems, with both figures projected to increase dramatically over the next decade.

TV Guide Magazine Group

Generations of television viewers have turned to *TV Guide* magazine to learn what's on—and turned it into a trusted American icon. TV Guide magazine is produced by the New York-based TV Guide Magazine Group. The Magazine Group also produces *TV Guide Ultimate Cable*, a weekly full-size magazine for the multi-channel universe; *TV Guide en Español*, America's first weekly Spanish language magazine; *Celebrity Dish*, a digest-sized monthly, featuring celebrities' favorite recipes, restaurants, and entertaining tips; *The Cable Guide*, a monthly magazine targeted to cable customers; and *See*, the official guide to DirecTV.

Because the industry undergoes constant change, TV Guide continually investigates new ways to remain an industry leader. The result is a host of innovations including TV Games Network, a 24-hour horse racing / interactive wagering network; extensive redesigns and upgrades of popular services like TV Guide Channel and TV Guide Interactive; and strategic alliances with other companies in the industry, such as a recent content agreement with America Online.

On October 4, 1999, TV Guide, Inc. and Gemstar International Group Limited announced their entrance into a definitive merger agreement under which TV Guide, Inc. will become a wholly owned subsidiary of Gemstar. This latest collaboration will strengthen TV Guide's position as a leader in media and communications on a worldwide scale.

Tulsa stands to share fully in the success and international celebrity of TV Guide, one of Oklahoma's most highly valued and progressive companies. In explaining the essential strength and growth of TV Guide, Boylan says, "We see significant opportunities for TV Guide with the explosion of digital television and rapid expansion of media worldwide. We remain more confident than ever in our ability to seize these opportunities."

In the video editing room, the producer makes final edits on the *Insider* segment and places it on air. A few hours later, the computer programmer saves final changes and uploads code that will make navigating through the multitude of channels on digital cable manageable.

At the same time, a customer service representative offers a solution to a Spanish-speaking cable operator, and a new programming list is inserted for air. All this to ensure the entertainment, information, and guidance needs of more than 100 million viewers worldwide are met. Just a typical day at TV Guide. ✦

[1] *Advertising Age, October 25, 1999*

[2] *Nielsen Media Research Universe Estimate, 1/00*

[3] *@plan, Winter 1999*

[4] *Nielsen Media Research Universe Estimate, 1/00*

Today, TV Guide's multimedia portfolio of products and services reaches more than 100 million viewers and readers worldwide.

TV Guide's newest service—TV Games Network—works closely with the National Thoroughbred Racing Association, and has exclusive long-term agreements with more than 20 premier U.S. racetracks.

With circulation of more than 11 million, *TV Guide* magazine is America's largest-selling weekly publication. An ever-expanding array of print guides, including *TV Guide Ultimate Cable, The Cable Guide* and *See*, meet ever-changing consumer needs.

PUBLIC SERVICE COMPANY OF OKLAHOMA

Public Service Company of Oklahoma (PSO) originated during Oklahoma's pre-statehood days as the Vinita Electric Light and Power Company, which was chartered in 1889 to provide electric service in Indian Territory. On May 29, 1913, PSO was incorporated in Oklahoma, consisting of the original Vinita firm combined with small electric companies at Atoka, Coalgate, Lehigh, Guthrie, and Tulsa, which became company headquarters.

PSO powers the city of Tulsa and some 230 communities in eastern and southwestern Oklahoma. In foreground is Riverside Station, situated along the Arkansas River south of Tulsa, near Jenks.

Louie the lightning Bug is the company's popular safety "spokesbug," informing young children how to be safe around electricity. Louie conveys his safety messages through live appearances in schools and parades as well as in television commercials.

It was a humble beginning. PSO officials revealed plans to provide electric service 24 hours a day. Growth came slowly in those early years. World War I delayed expansion.

During the prosperous 1920s, PSO bounded ahead. Power lines were extended to communities without electric service. Small existing electric systems were merged with PSO. By combining smaller systems into a single, integrated company, PSO was able to provide electric energy more efficiently and at a lower price.

Expansion continued during the 1930s and 1940s. By 1947, the 30,000-square-mile area currently served by PSO essentially had been established.

PSO today provides electric service to approximately one million people in eastern and southwestern Oklahoma. The company's electric generating capacity exceeds 3.7 million kilowatts, one-fourth provided by coal and three-fourths provided by natural gas. PSO is a wholly owned subsidiary of the Central and South West (CSW) Corporation, a global energy services provider based in Dallas, Texas. Included in CSW's portfolio of energy-related businesses are four U.S. electric utility companies which operate in four states in the Southwest.

Today, PSO and the other CSW electric utility companies are preparing to successfully operate in a dramatically restructured and highly competitive business environment. In Oklahoma, full retail competition commences July 1, 2002. In this new scenario, customers will be able to choose which provider generates their electricity. However, the delivery of that energy to homes and businesses will remain the responsibility of the local electric distribution company.

PSO's formula for success in the new, competitive marketplace is simple: continue to offer low prices (PSO's electric prices overall are 40 percent below the national average) and excellent service, including highly reliable electric service and convenient around-the-clock access by customers whenever they need to contact PSO.

PSO is an important force for community growth and development. In 1998, PSO and the other CSW electric utilities played key roles in attracting 155 companies to build or expand facilities in their service areas, providing $561 million in investments and nearly 11,000 new jobs.

PSO and the other CSW System electric companies have a long history of environmental stewardship including, in PSO's case, support for the Tallgrass Prairie Preserve, efforts to conserve and increase the population of threatened birds of prey, and promotion of non-polluting electric vehicles. Another environmental initiative is to protect and improve the urban forest in the communities PSO serves. By properly pruning trees, planting appropriate species, and educating the public, PSO works to both beautify its communities and reduce interference of tree limbs with power lines. In 1998, PSO was honored for the sixth time with the Treeline USA designation presented by the National Arbor Foundation for its tree management program.

The CSW System electric companies also are committed to using renewable and other forms of energy that have a minimal effect on the environment. In 1998, the companies announced plans to purchase 75,000 kilowatts of renewable energy from a wind generation facility in Texas. The companies also operate a 75-acre renewable energy demonstration project in Texas that includes wind turbines, solar arrays, and rooftop photovoltaic systems.

PSO is headquartered in the renovated historic building that for more than 60 years housed Tulsa's Central High School. This is appropriate, given the major role that PSO has played and continues to play in the economic history and development of Oklahoma. ❖

VoiceStream® Wireless

VoiceStream® Wireless may be one of the newest names in wireless digital technology, but chances are you already know something about it (it's the wireless phone actress Jamie Lee Curtis favors!), and you'll soon know a lot more about this system that is literally setting a new standard for the industry.

VoiceStream, spun off in 1999 from its parent Western Wireless Corporation of Bellevue, Washington, already has established a network in 15 mostly-western cities, Tulsa among them. It has been licensed to provide service in 13 more over a broad region that includes cities the size of Dallas, San Antonio, Chicago, St. Louis, and San Francisco.

The company counts on two elements to catapult it to the front of the market. One is the VoiceStream Wireless itself. Through the use of a special "smart card," VoiceStream makes possible levels of privacy, security, and service that are uncommon in the field. For example, the phone will not operate without insertion of the smart card, containing an imbedded programmable microchip, so its unauthorized use is virtually eliminated. The same card ensures that all calls are "digitally encrypted," which means eavesdropping or theft of phone or ID numbers is impossible.

The other key factor on which VoiceStream counts is its total dedication to the Global System for Mobile Communications (GSM), which has been adopted as the internationally accepted standard for wireless telecommunications. GSM started in Europe, and has now been selected by operators in 133 countries. Approximately 160 million subscribers already use GSM-based systems in the U.S., Europe, Asia, Africa, the Middle East, Australia, New Zealand, India, China, and several other regions.

VoiceStream is not the only North American carrier using GSM technology, but another recent development suggests it may become one of the largest. In June 1999 VoiceStream and Omnipoint Corporation boards of directors approved a merger of the two companies.

In a June 25, 1999 article, the *Wall Street Journal* described the merger as the creation of "a national wireless empire that could challenge AT&T Corporation and Sprint Corporation." It pointed out that both VoiceStream and Omnipoint utilize GSM. The writer of the article hinted that the combined companies, with licenses covering 17 of the nation's top 25 markets, is in a position to create "a national behemoth."

Certainly, VoiceStream has expansion in mind. Its motivation is not to become a national behemoth, but rather to distinguish its service to its customers by making possible a broad range of ancillary services, world-wide roaming, and the ability through GSM and the smart card to make and receive calls while visiting in almost any foreign country, and most importantly, to do it with the greatest voice clarity and quality of service possible. ⤸

Jamie Lee Curtis, VoiceStream spokesperson.

ONEOK, INC.

For most Tulsans, and indeed most Oklahomans, the "gas company" is Oklahoma Natural Gas. But the well-known Oklahoma Natural brand is part of a much larger organization that has a growing footprint in the natural gas business extending from the wellhead to the burner tip. That organization is ONEOK, Inc. and it is more than just a gas company.

ONEOK, through its marketing company, ONEOK Gas Marketing, sells gas to cities, utilities, and industrial customers in 28 states in the mid-continent region.

ONEOK may not be as well known as its Oklahoma Natural Gas utility division, but its impact on Tulsa has been significant. Oklahoma Natural Gas Company was established in 1906, a year before statehood. That's when a forward-looking group of pioneers recognized energy would fuel the growth of this land, which would soon become the 46th state.

The pioneer vision came to life with the construction of a 100-mile pipeline from just west of Tulsa to provide natural gas service to a brick plant in Oklahoma City. Today, that utility provides gas service to more than 750,000 customers in the Sooner state.

The company, with about 900 employees in the Tulsa area, is a major player in the production of gas and oil, and it processes gas to "clean it up" for use by its customers. The processing segment of ONEOK extracts liquids from the gas (i.e. propane, butane) which are sold as separate products.

ONEOK also stores gas in its five Oklahoma underground storages, located in depleted natural gas fields, for use during peak winter periods. The firm also transports gas to cities and towns and large industrial users throughout Oklahoma. And, it markets gas to cities, utilities, and industrial customers in the growing gas markets of the nation's mid-continent region.

ONEOK's growth took a giant step in 1997, when it acquired the natural gas utility of Western Resources in Kansas. Kansas Gas Service, also a division of ONEOK, serves approximately 660,000 customers in Kansas.

In 1998, ONEOK's vision of converging gas and electric service became a reality when it formed ONEOK Power Marketing, a company that uses natural gas to produce electricity to meet wholesale customers peak power needs.

As we enter the next millennium, the vision continues with an eye on growth. This includes a strategy of acquiring properties that support ONEOK's goal of extracting value along the natural gas chain of custody from the wellhead to the burner tip. This growth plan is directed at solidifying the company's financial strength.

ONEOK's financial health, coupled with its commitment to community improvement activities, has enhanced the quality of life in Tulsa and all the cities and towns in its service areas.

ONEOK works closely with local officials and business leaders in Tulsa to ensure the community will always have the vital energy it needs to sustain its economic growth and maintain its position as one of America's most livable cities. Through its contributions and the volunteer activities of its Tulsa employees, ONEOK gives back to the community it is privileged to serve every day.

ONEOK. A Tulsa energy company that you know and one you'll be hearing more about.

It is more than just a gas company. ✦

The corporate headquarters for ONEOK is, of course, ONEOK Plaza, located in downtown Tulsa.

MIRATECH CONSULTING GROUP

President and CEO David Grosse founded MiraTech in 1994 on the philosophy that every customer's problem is an opportunity for the company to provide solutions.

MiraTech's impressive growth is a testament to this simple philosophy. MiraTech clients are more than customers, they are long-term relationships, friendships, and the company's best word-of-mouth referrals.

MiraTech has grown into a thriving, multi-million-dollar information-technology company by providing a myriad of products and services to customers in Tulsa and throughout the region. MiraTech is proud to assist hundreds of small-to-medium-sized business clients with a full range of computer services. Customers, including the banking, manufacturing, and energy industries, as well as others, utilize MiraTech's range of services to define and implement solutions. Whether customer needs involve software development, consulting, project management, recruiting, or computer hardware, MiraTech can provide solutions.

A comprehensive blend of products and services allows MiraTech to offer expertise in nearly every aspect of a customer's computer technology needs. By providing solutions, MiraTech has become the choice of business customers.

Perhaps the most telling aspect of MiraTech's dedication to impeccable sales and service is the fact that the company's growth has occurred despite having no direct sales force. David Grosse and MiraTech Vice President Virgil Shelton, who trace their professional relationship back more than a decade, espouse the dynamic belief that the company's employees, consultants, recruits, and customers are the best sales force. MiraTech's belief is that by doing the best job possible, they can help increase their client's profitability, which will result in MiraTech's long term success.

Software development is a rapidly expanding division. By developing proprietary software packages and partnering with other software companies, MiraTech is establishing an impressive track record of success. MiraTech's goal is to further enhance its position as a premier software company that offers a variety of products for a multitude of markets.

MiraTech technical recruiters meet customer-staffing needs in computer-related positions. MiraTech hardware sales and technical service professionals assist clients with the purchase and installation of new computer systems. And MiraTech consultants and programmers aid clients with development and integration of software packages. Providing these comprehensive services has set MiraTech apart and positioned the company for continued impressive growth in the future.

MiraTech's newest business division is a wholesale computer parts distributorship. MiraTech stocks thousands of computer products and custom orders special products needed by resale or corporate customers. Expert service and timely delivery are earning MiraTech the reputation as a wholesale computer parts leader.

Everyday, MiraTech is a partner in the growth of Tulsa-based businesses and companies throughout the region. MiraTech prides itself on its diversity and flexibility in meeting the needs of every client. MiraTech—there is not a better company to turn to for computer consulting, programming, staffing, or hardware needs. ❖

 MiraTech was founded in 1994. Left: Virgil Shelton, Vice President Right: David Grosse, President / CEO.

MiraTech provides a full range of computer services including hardware, software, recruiting, and technical consulting.

11
Chapter Eleven

MANUFACTURING & DISTRIBUTION

Photo by Don Wheeler.

THE NORDAM GROUP

When Ray Siegfried II, CEO of the NORDAM Group, talks of the world-class aviation service company he has headed for 30 years, he speaks with a thousand voices—well, actually, 2,500 voices. Those are the 2,500 employees who are responsible, Siegfried insists, for NORDAM's emergence as an international business success story.

The NORDAM Transparency Division produces its own brands of stretched and cast acrylic materials, which are used in the manufacture and repair of aircraft windows, windshields, wing tip lenses, flight simulator screens, and more.

"NORDAM is a company that climbed to where it is by thinking and acting differently," Siegfried observes. "Although we're described as a manufacturing and repair, and overhaul company, we are a service company. It's not just a company that makes parts—it's a people-driven service." He illustrates this point by his definition of "service." Only about five percent of the people in a company actually come into contact with customers, he points out. So the real service happens between people in the company—between the different departments.

Siegfried insists on sharing with his associates the credit for the company's growth and ascendance in its industry. NORDAM is twice the size of its closest competitor. "Management moves with the stakeholders (his term for employees)," he says, "encouraging them to always improve and achieve and allowing them the authority and the opportunity to become successful."

But there was no one sharing the load with Siegfried when he made the decision to take on the management of the firm. As a representative of the family insurance business delivering a policy to NORDAM, Siegfried discovered the building locked. Looking for a way in, he found some idlers at the rear door that told him he'd need to go to the bankruptcy court for information.

Siegfried did go to the court, found out a little about NORDAM, and three days later acquired the firm's assets at bankruptcy sale. With eight employees he set out in 1969 (somewhat unsteadily, he admits) to manufacture anything for domestic commercial aircraft.

In 1999, NORDAM had international sales of $400 million. Its company network now includes marketing and sales offices in Mexico,

Peru, Brazil, the Netherlands, France, Germany, England, China, Australia, Singapore, and the Middle East. And in the next three or four years, the employment base is expected to top 3,000.

Though senior management controls the corporate financial capital, the "intellectual capital," as Ray Siegfried describes it, is represented by the stakeholders. "They are the ones that service the customer, they are the ones that answer the phone calls and get up at night and render service to a customer who is needing attention from us. They are the ones who deliver the invoices on time—with accuracy—and they are the ones that provide an unprecedented quality of product that continues to improve every single day," he explains.

"Our service must be 'world-class'—that's when a customer doesn't want to do business with anyone else but NORDAM," Siegfried said.

Serving a Growing Aviation Industry

Compared to its original narrow area of service, NORDAM has

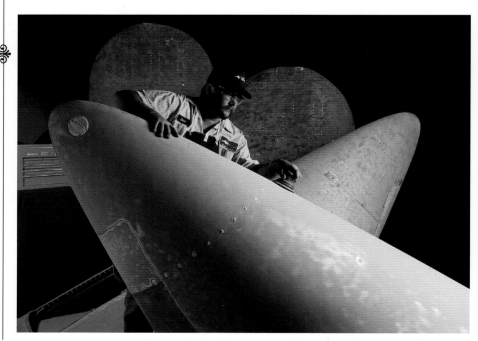

NORDAM has a long record of service to military organizations—offering comprehensive repair and overhaul services for components ranging from tail-cones to radomes for fighter jets and AWACS aircraft.

become one of the world's largest caterers to the aviation industry. The products of its Manufacturing Divisions alone could easily be mistaken as a build-it-yourself airplane kit if they were laid out in one place. The Manufacturing group has three parts: Interiors & Structures Division, Nacelle/Thrust Reverser Systems Division, and PRISM Division. Collectively, the group coordinates the design, engineering, tooling, and fabrication of metallic and composite structures; interiors and structural components; corporate aircraft nacelle and thrust reverser systems; repair of exhaust system components; and design, certification and manufacture of hush kits.

NORDAM's Repair Division includes airframe, engine, nacelle, and reverser product centers, along with spare parts.

The NORDAM Transparency Division manufactures, repairs, and overhauls a complete line of acrylics, polycarbonates, glass, and laminates for aircraft windows and lenses.

NORDAM-Texas manufactures, repairs and services radomes, wastewater tanks, flight control surfaces, doors, interior panels, and a broad selection of other aircraft components.

NORDAM's market for all these services and components includes 150 airlines, representing all the major air carriers around the world. Entire sections of its service are also dedicated to business aircraft.

About 40 percent of NORDAM's revenue comes from the international marketing efforts coordinated by World Aviation Associates, an affiliate with over a dozen offices stationed around the globe. Although this market has recently slowed, primarily due to the economic downturn in Asia, Siegfried believes the international trend is due for a turnaround, and the company is positioning itself on that assumption.

The company looks for substantial new business to develop along the Pacific Rim, which will be served by the Singapore facility, where an 80,000-square-foot addition is planned for the 40,000 square feet the company already has in place there. The company also plans a 50,000-square-foot plant in France (it already has a 100,000-square-foot facility in Wales).

Expected growth, and the need for facilities to handle it, is not exclusively in the foreign market, however. In Tulsa, NORDAM operates from its headquarters downtown, but in keeping with the plans to sell that complex, it will build an 80,000-square-foot main office, a PRISM products building of 100,000 square feet, and a 400,000-square-foot interiors and structures facility in the Cherokee Industrial District north of Tulsa. The company already has structures of 120,000 square feet and 250,000 square feet in the Cherokee Industrial Park. Near the

airport, NORDAM Repair Division added a 165,000 square-foot expansion to its primary facility to give the division 830,000 square-feet of worldwide component repair capability. The estimated cost of all this new construction is $50 million.

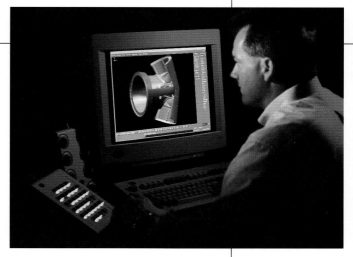

Making Quality a Way of Life

Unlike many rapidly growing organizations, NORDAM has not achieved its expansion by the acquisition of other companies. "The growth is coming in everything we do," Siegfried says. "There is nothing we have now that is not growing." Although NORDAM buys a small firm on occasion, "if it's not a growing business we get out of it," Siegfried explains.

"Our tradition has been to acquire very small businesses or products of businesses that are failing and convert the technology through our understanding of the market and our precise examination of the market's potential," according to Siegfried. "Being a market-driven company, the market tells us what we are going to do, when we are going to do it, how we are going to do it, and how much of it we're going to do. We do not exist for ourselves, but for the marketplace."

This philosophy has been the driving force for management, the stakeholders, and the company. In 1987, NORDAM introduced the process of Continuous Quality Improvement and a system of

NORDAM manu-facturing and repair services are backed by teams of top-flight engineers with expertise ranging from acoustics to ther-modynamics—all equipped with engineering tools that define the state-of-the-art.

This new 250,000 square-foot facility in the Cherokee Industrial Park serves as the location for the NORDAM Nacelle/Thrust Reverser Systems Division.

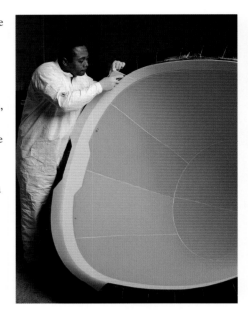

NORDAM-Texas, located in Fort Worth, offers comprehensive repair and overhaul services for regional aircraft fleets.

(Top, right) The WeatherMASTER™ Radome, available only from NORDAM, uses a revolutionary PVC foam core material to create a moisture-proof, longer lasting, better-performing radome, with 45 percent more impact resistance than conventional units.

Electronic testing to determine the extent of radar-inhibiting moisture infiltration is the first step in the radome repair process at NORDAM-Texas.

Performance Evaluation. "The heart and soul of a company is that it must have a performance-based system in which people are held accountable and responsible," says Siegfried. "If employees understand how to be accountable, if they are held to measures, and if they know how to improve, utilizing the CQI process, then they have a chance to meet their potential. Without it they cannot."

Siegfried's insistence on understanding and commitment from the stakeholders is a product of his own aversion to losing to a competitor in business. "I often wake up in a cold sweat, thinking that some competitor is going to out-service us for customers," Siegfried admits. "I never want to be in a position where my customers want to go somewhere else, some other company, because we are not servicing them properly."

Such an unthinkable lapse might be due to stakeholders who don't understand—or don't care, or the company being geographically dislocated so that there is a need to have a plant more strategically located, such as a new plant in France, he explains. "We cannot bear to think of losing business to a competitor."

Harnessing Oklahoma's Work Ethic

NORDAM has set high standards, and successfully challenges employees to meet them, by providing the environment for people to be successful. That includes working to hire the very best of the employee pool, says Siegfried. And he has tremendous confidence in the workers of northeast Oklahoma to live up to the company's expectations.

"It's not difficult to find people with a good work ethic in Tulsa and the surrounding area," Siegfried says. He credits it to the fact that Oklahoma was, until not many years ago, an agrarian and oil-based economy, and its people still remember how their grandfathers, their fathers, or even themselves in some cases worked on a farm, doing the chores that start early and end late and don't allow much rest in between.

In addition to Tulsa residents, NORDAM employees come from Skiatook, Sperry, Owasso, Foyil, Claremore, Pryor, Jay, and Coweta. "And I don't want to leave out Kellyville, Sapulpa, Beggs, and a lot of other good communities in our region," Siegfried hastens to add. "We didn't create the work ethic these people possess; that's just Oklahoma."

The opportunity to learn and grow with NORDAM is provided for every employee. The company offers a program called "NORDAM University," in which everyone in the company, 2,000-plus, averages 40 hours of education annually for the benefit of themselves and the company. It is not necessarily technical training in the employee's job specialty, but can cover anything that will improve career development, skill improvement, managerial improvement, or enlargement of intellectual capacity. Some even take college courses that are approved by the company as a source of learning that will help them in their work, and if successfully concluded the cost is reimbursed by the company.

"When an individual is able to reach his potential because of some way the company has assisted, and when that accomplishment also serves to meet the needs of the company, the results are awesome," says Siegfried.

Reaching Out to the Community

NORDAM and its stakeholders are of a like mind on another matter, too: the support of the community.

In the most recent campaign drive of the Tulsa Area United Way, NORDAM and its employees contributed over $1,000,000—the largest amount raised by a privately-held company in Tulsa. The company has been honored with several prestigious national awards for their United Way support. Almost 600 NORDAM employees gave $500 or more to the United Way—and the company matched every dollar.

When NORDAM reached its 30th anniversary, a committee organized from within the employees of the NORDAM Group was selected to undertake several appropriate observance projects. The first project was the construction of a house for Habitat for Humanity, with the company providing $30,000 for materials and NORDAM

employees providing the labor. "I have little skill in the area of home-building, but I was out there anyway," Siegfried assures.

As another part of the observance, every NORDAM facility held an open house for families of employees to see where their husbands, wives, mothers, and fathers work.

The pride of being an important part of NORDAM, and of the system that has allowed NORDAM to grow and prosper, are made clear in Siegfried's comment:

"This country's cost-effective manufacturing has been reborn and I'm proud to say that The NORDAM Group is at the head of the class. We have invested in our people, our technology, facilities, production equipment, education, and most important, in our ability to effect change." ✦

NORDAM's Integrated Interior Solutions℠ concept offers fit-checked ready-to-install executive aircraft interiors and cabin furnishings including galleys, entertainment centers, closets, tables, vanities, dividers, and side ledges.

HILTI, INC.

𝒱irtually anywhere in the world construction is taking place you will find Hilti. And in Tulsa, you will find nearly 800 Hilti employees. The legendary red Hilti tool case and other distinctive products can be found on construction and building maintenance sites around the world. Hilti is the world's leading manufacturer and supplier of specialized tools and fastening systems for the construction industry, with a presence in more than 100 countries.

Hilti's first European-based headquarters, circa 1941.

Professionals in the construction, electrical, plumbing, and building maintenance industries look to Hilti for the highest quality value-added tools and products. Hilti meets and exceeds their needs by offering an uncompromising level of customer service and product knowledge, on-time delivery, and continuous research and development.

Since its founding in 1941 by brothers Martin and Eugen Hilti, the Hilti Group has experienced impressive growth by remaining dedicated to the core values and areas of competence that set it apart from others.

Hilti North America

In 1979, Hilti established its North American headquarters in Tulsa. Additionally, the company's Latin American operations are administered from Tulsa. The Tulsa operation is home to nearly 800 employees, and includes the manufacturing, training, testing, marketing, and customer service departments.

Hilti North America's 1,850 employees, including the field sales and service representatives, serve customers in every state. Hilti, Inc.'s sales representatives offer customers the full line of more than 6,000 Hilti products. They are backed by world-class support services, including delivery, supply, and repair services.

Two Decades in Tulsa

Hilti, Inc. celebrated 20 years in Tulsa in 1999. Since locating its US manufacturing, supply, administrative customer service, and training

One of 700 Territory Sales Representatives who service Hilti, Inc. customers throughout North America.

operations to Tulsa, the company has expanded virtually all areas of business. Hilti has, from its first days in Tulsa, been an active leader in the business community. Hilti has supported and held leadership positions with important community organizations such as the Tulsa Area United Way and Metropolitan Tulsa Chamber of Commerce.

To improve the area's workforce, Hilti was the founding force in the creation of Craftsmanship 2000, a three-year program which trains high school students in the necessary skills to become professional machinists. Craftsmanship 2000 is regarded as one of the finest workforce development programs in the nation. Hilti was also a founding partner in the IndEx program, which brings people from welfare to work by giving them valuable skills to compete in the workforce.

Hilti's community service also includes sponsoring the "Playground for Children of All Abilities" in Tulsa's River Parks, which offers accessibility to every child with disabilities. The playground is a natural extension of Hilti's long track record of accommodating and empowering disabled employees.

Hilti celebrated two decades in Tulsa by beginning construction of a 59,000-square-foot office building addition. The new facility will bring the company's customer service, credit, and e-commerce groups together in one central location and will allow room for later expansion.

Hilti Group

Headquartered in Schaan, in the Principality of Liechtenstein, the Hilti Group operates in more than 100 countries. Production plants are located in Tulsa, Europe, Latin America, and Asia. The Tulsa manufacturing plant produces high quality anchors, powder actuated fasteners, and drill bits. Research and development is carried out in Liechtenstein, Germany, and China.

The Hilti Difference

Hilti is different—from the unique design of Hilti products, to unsurpassed product knowledge, to a commitment to quality that has set a standard for the world. By remaining dedicated to a set of core values and a defined niche in the market, Hilti stays focused on customer needs and changes in the market, while offering customers the greatest value possible. Because of a unique relationship between Hilti's field sales representatives and their customers, Hilti receives constant feedback from professionals—in fact, there are some 70,000 daily direct customer contacts worldwide. Flexibility and innovation in Hilti's product development and manufacturing processes allow for faster product research and development and quicker new product turnaround. Hilti's stated goal is, "to give customers exactly the right product for the job, meeting the most exacting standards of quality, ease of use, durability, and precision."

Hilti prides itself on the quality of its tools and services. The latest quality systems are used to continually improve processes and procedures. In 1996, the Hilti Group was one of the first companies in the world awarded the ISO 9001 certificate for the entire quality system

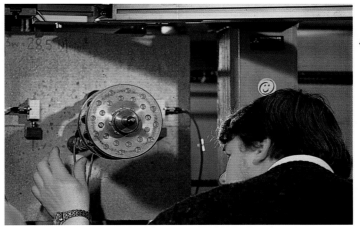

worldwide. Hilti's Tulsa Plant 5 was the first in Oklahoma and one of only a handful of organizations to receive the ISO 14001 certificate, which addresses environmental concerns. Hilti is also the recipient of the Oklahoma Quality Award for Achievement, which recognizes Hilti's commitment to strong leadership, customer satisfaction, and continuous quality improvements.

Products and Services

Hilti concentrates its efforts in the construction and building maintenance industries. Through a clear understanding of customers' various requirements, Hilti is able to offer products and services as a total system of solutions—simply the right products for the job.

In the areas of drilling and demolition, direct fastening, anchoring, diamond coring, construction chemicals, laser positioning, and installation systems, Hilti is a world leader.

Whether the job calls for hammer drills, chisels, cordless or electric screwdrivers, chemical adhesives, fasteners, or firestop systems, Hilti is the number one choice of professionals who demand the very best.

Hilti tools and products are repeatedly named products of the year by trade publications and industry professionals. Publications such as *Plant Engineering and Building Trends* have named Hilti products among the finest in recent publications.

Service is a Hilti hallmark. Sound advice, application training, technical support, comprehensive repair services, and environmentally sound disposal of Hilti products back up every customer's purchase. On-time delivery is an invaluable aspect of Hilti's customer satisfaction guarantee. Hilti's field sales representatives and field engineers spend

❧ Products are rigorously tested at the Tulsa-based North American headquarters of Hilti, Inc.

❧ Customers can order Hilti products and receive answers to technical questions through one of the nearly 130 experts in the Hilti, Inc. Customer Service Department.

Many products are produced locally in the Tulsa, Oklahoma manufacturing plant.

virtually every day at worksites around the world assisting customers with their changing needs, identifying new opportunities for customer success, and offering years of practical knowledge. Hilti North America's new e-commerce group is developing innovative new methods to meet customer needs over the Internet.

Every day, Hilti's sales, service, and customer service come into contact with more than 70,000 existing or potential customers— asking, analyzing, and updating Hilti's understanding of the building industry and the needs of the people working in it.

Hilti Centers

A growing portion of Hilti's operations are Hilti Centers. Today, Hilti Centers are becoming more and more popular with their comprehensive product offerings and service. In Tulsa, the Hilti Center is at the intersection of Highway 169 and 31st Street.

Customers can visit more than 86 Hilti Centers located across the US and throughout Canada to purchase any of the company's products and ask advice from specially-trained sales personnel. Customers have the opportunity to experience hands-on demonstrations in a clean, professional environment. Hilti Centers accentuate the more than 900 North American field sales representatives and managers. New Hilti Centers are being constructed in strategic locations throughout North America.

Champion 3C

Hilti's goal is to be the best, the leader, a champion. The Hilti Group has committed the resources, developed the strategy, and hired

Hilti expertise at work—worldwide.

people with the determination to achieve and maintain leadership throughout North America, the Western Hemisphere, and the world. Hilti developed the Champion 3C program to allow every one of Hilti's more than 13,000 employees worldwide the opportunity to be a part of the company's success. The three "C's" of Champion 3C are customer, competence, and concentration. Champion 3C commits

Hilti to a customer-driven approach, centered on core competencies and concentrating on products and markets in which leadership can be sustained.

By keeping Hilti's focus squarely on the customer, the company ensures that product development keeps pace with market requirements. This not only helps develop a better product, but a product that gets the job done better. Competence means understanding capabilities (what Hilti does best). Hilti's corporate values: responsiveness, innovation, efficiency, and integrity are part of this. Concentration is the difference between Hilti and competitors. Sustainable growth and added customer value come from concentration on truly innovative products.

The Future is Now

At Hilti, the future is now. Through constant research, development, practice, and evaluation, Hilti is able to work toward the future today. While manufacturing and supplying the world's finest construction tools is the company's goal, empowering people is the reason for Hilti's success. But at the core of Hilti's success are Hilti people. Their knowledge, skills, and dedication to quality sets the company apart and allow for future expansion. A committed team of employees all working toward the same goal will be the hallmark of Hilti's future, just as they have established the landmarks of our past. ↤

PARAGON FILMS, INC.

Paragon Films, Inc., does not operate from a sound stage making movies, as the name might imply. Instead, from its 130,000-square-foot manufacturing plant in Broken Arrow, the company has produced a series of innovative products and has a growing customer base that views them as the technological leader in the industry.

Paragon is one of a group of firms in northeast Oklahoma that provides 30 percent of all the plastic stretch film made in the United States. In fact, there are five plastic film producing plants in the Tulsa area, all of which were started by William E. Baab, Chairman of the Board of Paragon Films, Inc. alone, or in conjunction with his son Michael J. Baab, President and CEO.

After graduating from Oklahoma State University with a degree in mechanical engineering, Mike Baab spent a year managing a packaging room of a soap detergent plant owned and operated by Proctor & Gamble, a major American manufacturer of kitchen and household consumer products. Then in 1980, he joined his father at Linear Films, Inc., which became the second largest supplier of stretch film in this country. When Linear Films was sold in 1988, Mike resigned from his position as president, and along with his father and some former staff, founded Paragon Films, Inc.

Stretch Film Gets Rave Reviews

Paragon manufactures stretch film, which is an industrial packaging product. Paragon's film serves a broad industrial market, which is

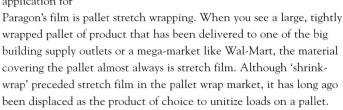

growing steadily. Its products range in size from a three inch, 1 pound roll (approximately the size of a standard roll of masking tape), to a roll of carpet wrap which can be as long as 100 inches and weigh in excess of 200 pounds.

The primary application for Paragon's film is pallet stretch wrapping. When you see a large, tightly wrapped pallet of product that has been delivered to one of the big building supply outlets or a mega-market like Wal-Mart, the material covering the pallet almost always is stretch film. Although 'shrink-wrap' preceded stretch film in the pallet wrap market, it has long ago been displaced as the product of choice to unitize loads on a pallet.

The advantages of stretch film are numerous. Shrink-wrap requires the application of heat to actually shrink the wrap so that it will firmly secure the products to the pallet. Stretch film, in contrast, is stretched around the product, firmly securing it to the pallet, without applying heat. The absence of a heat cycle and the yield gained by stretching film up to 300 percent results in substantial cost savings for the user. Also, the process of stretching film around a pallet of product imparts elastic load retention, assuring tighter packaging and less shifting of the product, with great resistance to punctures or tears.

Prior to the 1980s, companies shipping pallet loads of goods had choices such as metal strapping, plastic banding, or using containers made of corrugated cardboard secured with glue or tape. For a time, shrink-wrap was a popular innovation in the shipping industry. But as pallet shipping grew, the search for improved speed and lower costs took on a new urgency. Stretch film emerged to fill this need.

Every year, approximately 4.6 billion pallet loads of goods are shipped in the United States alone. Eighty percent of these pallet loads are unitized with stretch film, consuming 1.2 billion pounds of film per year. It takes less than a pound of film to wrap the average pallet, making stretch film extremely economical.

Paragon has become a major manufacturer and supplier in this market. "We started from scratch," says President, Mike Baab. "It took us a year to build the plant and get production up and running. Now, out of 30 film manufacturers, we are the sixth-largest producer of pallet wrapping film in America."

The company's film manufacturing capacity is growing rapidly to meet the needs of its customers. As new uses for stretch film emerge, Paragon stays one step ahead of its competition, with the operation of a full, on-site, Research and Development department. Paragon's lab personnel work in conjunction with the R&D group, testing new and existing products for key qualities such as cling, stretch, ultimate stretch, puncture resistance, clarity, and toughness.

"We continue to find new uses for stretch film," Baab explains. One new use is 'bundle' wrap, where products are bundled together and stretch wrapped without using a pallet. The consumer was introduced to this application in the packaging of firewood sold at grocery and convenience stores. "We are now getting into smaller and smaller bundles with the advent of computers and robotics. Consequently, stretch film continues to take market share from the shrink-wrap market." says Baab.

A Firm Grip on the Industry

From the standpoint of cost, the closest competitor to stretch film for securing products to a pallet is metal or plastic banding. The cost per load to use banding can exceed two dollars. Using stretch film, a similar pallet of product could be unitized for thirty cents. Stretch film has a lower cost of application than the alternative packaging

Pallet of stretch film depicting a vertical style, bulk package.

methods, including shrink-wrap.

Price is certainly one of the most important reasons for shippers to choose stretch film, but there are additional incentives. Stretch film provides superior protection for products. When properly applied, whether by special wrapping machine or manual hand application, it proves highly dust-proof and water-resistant—very important qualities when products are shipped by non-enclosed carriers or stored outside. Its strength is such that it is highly resistant to puncture, either from irregular or protruding angles of the product it covers, or from outside factors, such as rough handling. All these stretch film attributes work together to reduce product damage. The application of stretch film is a simple process that can easily be automated to further reduce manufacturing costs.

Stretch film allows the flexibility of securing pallet loads in three-dimensional planes. The flexibility of stretch wrap, in conjunction with its clinging quality, allows it to shape itself tightly to all contours of the product in such a way that the product is firmly stabilized. Movement during shipment is minimized or eliminated, thus reducing abrasion damage to the product.

The product's clarity can simplify shipments by eliminating additional application of bar codes or product identification to the external packing. The transparency of stretch film allows bar codes on the product within to be electronically scanned and allows contents to be visible for identification and warehousing. In other shipping applications, the film can be made opaque to block damage caused by the sun's rays or allow costly products to be stored or shipped confidentially. While industrial users are pleased with Paragon's stretch film, and have elevated the company to the top rank of film manufacturers, the concerns an average citizen might have regarding the environmental impact of stretch film can be dispelled. The manufacturing of stretch film is a very clean process. There is no residue hauled to landfills and no toxic fumes emitted into the air. Resin, the primary raw material used in the manufacturing process, leaves the plant

Practical method of how to use hand wrap. Employee shown using hand dispenser.

Stretch film is loaded into trailers for shipment to customers.

"Our goal," says Baab, "is to continue to grow at 11 percent per year. That would put us at a production level of 200 million pounds of film by the year 2010. With those numbers, we will have a 10 percent market share." Paragon is also looking at other markets to ensure company growth. "We plan to expand and diversify," Baab explains. "We are looking at making tape, shrink-wrap, food-wrap, and general films, with a goal of capturing a fair share of those markets."

Part of the strategy of Paragon's leadership is to keep a close eye on the "revolution" that Baab says is occurring in the plastic industry. "One of the things that makes us successful," he explains, "is that we have close relationships with three leading resin producers—Dow, Exxon, and Union Carbide. They sell 89 percent of the product used as raw material for producing stretch film."

In a recent survey among 200 top stretch film distributors in the marketplace, over 80 percent of the respondents named Paragon the best company for service, and named its Edge Stretch Film™ the best product. Paragon intends to use its sophisticated computer systems and

in the form of finished or converter products. All scraps that remain from a manufacturing run are reclaimed and reused in the next processing batch or shipped to a recycler for use in other plastic products.

Stretch film naturally decomposes into carbon dioxide and water. By special processing, stretch film can be made biodegradable or photodegradable, breaking down in a specified number of days through exposure to microorganisms and the sun's ultraviolet rays. For areas like Tulsa, with trash to energy plants, stretch film burns clean and has a higher BTU content than natural gas.

Skid of stretch film being machine wrapped.

Polyethylene (plastic) pellets are the raw material from which Paragon manufactures its film. The process starts with these pellets being fed through extruders, where they are melted and formed into thin sheets of plastic film with as many as five inseparable layers. The standard products in the industry have three-layer film structures. The film is cut to length and width, wound on cores, loaded on pallets, then wrapped—in stretch film, of course—to be shipped to the market.

Paragon sells its film, 70 million pounds a year, in all 50 states, and increasingly into the foreign markets. Foreign markets include Latin America, Europe, Australia, Mexico, and Canada.

A Growing Force in the Tulsa Area

The stretch film market is growing at a rate of 6 to 8 percent per year. Paragon has exceeded this with average annual growth of 14 percent since start-up. Founded in 1988, the company now has 130 employees.

Paragon just recently installed its seventh production line in its Broken Arrow plant. In addition to local manufacturing, Paragon has a 10,000-square-foot office building and four warehouses strategically located throughout the country. The company is now looking for a location in the Southeast to build its second manufacturing facility.

'industry leading technology' to ensure it meets its biggest challenge—to continue to deliver industry-leading customer service and quality, in an increasingly competitive environment.

Paragon finds the Tulsa area the ideal location for its operations. So ideal, in fact, that the company completed a $5 million expansion of its facilities in 1998, and $8 million expansion in 1999. Baab points out that Tulsa's central location works extremely well for a company that ships its products to national and global markets. He counts the Tulsa-area workers among the company's greatest assets. "We have superior people throughout the organization," says Baab. "We provide them with training, research, equipment, and authority to do their jobs. In turn, they continuously perform at a level which has made Paragon a leader in our industry." ⬳

Stretch film is available in a variety of sizes and colors.

Aerial view of Paragon Films before plant was doubled in size. The plant facility is the large blue building in the center, and the office is the gray brick building to its left.

THE BAMA COMPANIES

*P*aula Marshall-Chapman has a big, huge, audacious goal: to make The Bama Companies a part of every eating occasion worldwide. This goal might seem outrageous except for the fact that in 1927, her grandparents Henry and Alabama Marshall started the global company with a grand total of $1.67 with a wild goal of one day selling Bama Pies across the country.

It started one afternoon when Henry asked Alabama, who baked pies at a local restaurant, to bake him a few of her delicious pies so he could sell them to people in the neighborhood. Started in the kitchen of the family's rented home in Dallas, the Bama Pie Company, named after Alabama, grew steadily and soon kept every member of the family baking and selling pies. The business made quite a name for itself and gradually expanded into other communities.

In 1937, Paul Marshall and his wife Lilah came to Tulsa to carry on the family's business and expand into a new market. From a small shop at 11th Street and Delaware, where the company's world headquarters remain today, the business grew rapidly to become a supplier for restaurants and hotels throughout the region.

The company's fortunes changed forever when Paul Marshall paid an unannounced visit to the McDonald's world headquarters in 1965 and made a handshake deal to supply the growing restaurant chain with frozen pies. By 1968, the Hot Apple Pie was a popular item on McDonald's national menu. The operation grew by leaps and bounds to meet the needs of new customers across the nation. In the 1980s, McDonald's wanted to add biscuit items to their menu, and Bama soon found itself in the biscuit-making business.

Bama Pie continued its amazing growth under the direction of Paul Marshall until 1984 when Paula, the Marshall's youngest child, took over the company's helm. She continued her father's policy of meeting and exceeding all customer expectations while continuing to improve processes, which included upgrading technology and testing new markets. A decision was also made to increase the client base with additional

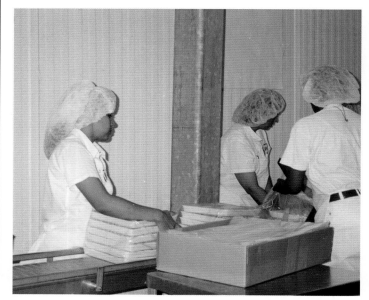

product lines. Baked and ready-to-bake or heat goods were supplied to the world's largest restaurant chains and food suppliers. Additional enterprises such as Bama Foods, Bama Frozen Dough, base, Inc., Bama Beijing, Bama Transportation, the Bama Cooking School, and the Bama Institute were established.

Along with continual expansion into new markets, the company developed a comprehensive program of quality improvement, continuing education, and employee empowerment. Employees helped create programs that improved customer service, streamlined distribution, and challenged individuals at every level to reach and exceed personal and professional goals.

For their creative programs, Bama and Paula Marshall-Chapman have received a number of quality awards. Marshall-Chapman was named the 1997 Entrepreneur of the year in the Principle-Centered Leadership category by Ernst & Young LLP.

The Bama Companies, and the more than 600 Tulsa-area employees, remain one of Tulsa's leading corporate citizens. Community involvement, whether in the form of volunteerism or philanthropic contributions, is a hallmark of The Bama Companies.

Bama is committed to its vision statement "People Helping People Be Successful." This is evident through the annual Bama/United Way

Golf Tournament. This fund-raiser, started in the hopes that Bama could better serve the community and helps raise funds for the Tulsa Area United Way, has become one of the company's most successful fund-raisers to date.

Bama is aware that as a leading corporate citizen in the community, it is able to make a difference in the Tulsa community, not only financially, but by assisting organizations and their need for volunteers. Bama created the Bama Volunteers' program to meet these community needs. The Bama Volunteers is an internal volunteer group comprising their most valuable assets—their employees. Any organization is welcome to request assistance through the program. Like every Bama Companies' success, it is the employees who make the difference and rise to the occasion, whether meeting company goals or helping those in need in the community.

Paula Marshall-Chapman believes there is no limit to what each person can achieve. Her inspiring and unconventional leadership have earned the respect of employees, customers, and fellow business leaders around the world. She puts her own special leadership skills to work for the Tulsa business community. In the year 2000, she will become

Chairman of the Metropolitan Tulsa Chamber of Commerce—only the second woman to lead the nearly 100-year-old organization.

Each day, The Bama Companies turn out more than 2 million biscuits, 1.5 million pies, and more than 300,000 pounds of frozen dough for pizza and breadsticks. Bama products are shipped to thousands of customers in the U.S. and around the world. Even though The Bama Companies do business globally, the heart and soul of the business remains in Tulsa. The company is built on more than 60 years of doing business from Tulsa. The Bama headquarters, with its distinctive "Pie Land, USA" sign, is a Tulsa landmark.

Paula Marshall-Chapman will be the first to tell you, the two most important things a person can have are family and goals. She learned these important lessons from her parents and grandparents. No goal is too big and family is not only your relatives, but the company you keep. The Bama Companies do have a grand, colossal goal to be a part of every eating occasion for families around the world. And if past achievement is any indication, the world better get ready for Bama at every meal. ✦

T. D. WILLIAMSON, INC.

Its name a byword for innovation the last 80 years, Tulsa's T.D. Williamson, Inc., has built an international reputation for manufacturing the world's most complete line of pipeline maintenance and service equipment for transmission, distribution, oil, and industrial piping applications.

T.D. Williamson (1886-1978) founded T.D. Williamson, Inc., in 1920. Directed the Tulsa-based company's worldwide operations and impressive growth until his retirement in 1978.

TDW specializes in providing products and services as dynamic as the world's piping needs—from design, engineering, and manufacturing, to inspection and contract maintenance services for pipeline and plant piping systems.

"In every aspect in which TDW does business, you'll find a genuine dedication to fulfilling our customers' needs with integrity and efficiency," says R.B. Williamson, TDW's chairman and CEO, and grandson of the company's founder. "We work diligently to support our reputation for vigorous attention to these values on a global scale."

An American Success Story

T. D. Williamson, Inc., is a classic example of the 20th Century American success story—bright young adventurer starts bootstrap enterprise and nurtures and guides it until it becomes an international company, and he becomes a celebrated industrialist.

But in a simpler analogy, TDW is the saga of a man and his pig—but what an exceptional man, and what an extraordinary pig.

T.D. Williamson grew up on an Arkansas farm and graduated from the University of Arkansas in 1909 with a degree in electrical engineering. His first job was with General Electric in Schenectady, New York;

then he followed the path of GE's expansion—including designing the controls for the locks on the Panama Canal, which are still in use today.

His GE odyssey brought him, in 1917, to Tulsa to open the company's first local sales office. The Oklahoma oil boom was at its height, and GE sold more electric motors and generators than it believed possible. In 1920 with assistance from GE, Williamson launched the specialized Petroleum Electric Company to serve the emerging petroleum industry's needs for electrical power.

It was during World War II that Williamson's inventiveness generated the idea of a rubber disc for use on pipeline scraper tools. The war had just begun, and the War Emergency Pipeline System was urgently looking for ways to transport huge quantities of oil and gasoline from the oil patch to supply armed forces in Europe. Among the solutions were two large (20-inch and 24-inch) pipelines—but no scraper then existed to service lines of such size. Williamson's company was commissioned by the government to develop, manufacture, and supply most of the scrapers used in the "Big Inch" and "Little Big Inch" War Emergency Pipelines.

It marked the birth of "the pig," a unique combination of rubber sealing and driving cups (later combined with spring-mounted steel brushes), that has been for sixty years the most effective pipe maintenance equipment available. A pipeliner once said of the revolutionary tool: "It sounds like a pig rooting its way through the pipeline"—and the name stuck.

Realizing that no company was specializing in engineered pipeline maintenance tools, T.D. Williamson and his son T.D. Williamson, Jr. plunged into the void and chartered a new enterprise—T.D. Williamson, Inc.

The Leader in Pipeline Maintenance

For sixty years, TDW has led the industry in providing piping solutions (onshore and offshore) for crude oil products, gas transmission and

TDW Technicians complete the installation of two STOPPLE® Plugging Machines to isolate a section of 30 inch gas transmission line, while flow continues through a temporary bypass line.

gathering systems, refineries, petrochemical plants, water works, waste water, public utilities, steel mills, paper mills, mines, nuclear power plants, and gas distribution systems.

The company's world reputation has been built on five core technologies:

- high pressure hot tapping and plugging (providing a system for isolating a section of pressurized piping to make repairs, connections, and extensions without shutdown or interrupting the operation of lines),
- low pressure hot tapping and plugging equipment,
- pipeline pigging products and inspection surveys,
- polyethylene pipe fusion equipment, and
- gas leak detection equipment.

In addition to the corporate headquarters in Tulsa, TDW manages 13 plants and offices in the U.S. and Canada, and 18 overseas facilities in Central and South America, the Middle East, Europe, the

United Kingdom, Asia, and Australia. The company currently employs 650 persons worldwide, 415 of them in the United States.

With such a rich company history, TDW has had more than its share of technological breakthroughs and record-breaking operations. TDW made the world's deepest underwater tap at more than 660 feet in the Gulf of Mexico. It performed tapping operations for Russia above the Arctic Circle. And it introduced the world's largest pipeline pig (60 inches) and made the Western Hemisphere's biggest "hot tap" (102 inches).

These breakthroughs are made possible by TDW's emphasis on continuous technological innovations. Even though TDW has been the industry's premier developer of pigs since 1940, for example, the company continues to "re-invent" the pig with new materials, improved designs, and chemical cleaning services to expand its performance and capabilities. New products and services play just as important a role in the company's continued growth. One such operation with great potential is TDW's CentreFuse®, a system that fuses poly-ethylene pipe together for gas, water, waste water, mining, and many other applications. It has quickly become one of the company's fastest growing product lines and could be the starting point for a whole new set of worldwide records and industry breakthroughs.

As the world's piping needs continue to change and grow in the coming years, TDW is committed to anticipate and provide the solutions to meet these needs.

"We are gratified in having such a rich history of breakthroughs and record-breaking operations," says Chairman R.B. Williamson. "Our partnership with our customers and other leaders in the industry has been a critical element in our becoming a worldwide leader in providing piping products and services. We're looking to the future with enthusiasm, not only because of where we are today, but because of our people's vision of what will be needed tomorrow!" ❖

Certified TDW Services, Inc., technician using a SHORTSTOPP®II plugging Machine to stop the flow of natural gas in a six inch polyethylene main line.

TDW Pipeline Surveys Specialist launching a 28 inch KALIPER® Survey Tool to inspect the interior condition of a products pipeline.

HONEYWELL AEROSPACE SERVICES TULSA HEAT TRANSFER OPERATIONS

Tulsa Heat Transfer Operations is an integral part of Honeywell Aerospace, the world's leading source of aerospace products and services. Honeywell Tulsa Operations is the world's leader in the repair, remanufacture, and manufacture of aircraft heat exchangers and other environmental control system components for the commercial and military aircraft markets. With 240 employees, Honeywell Tulsa Operations is part of Honeywell Aerospace's global network of aerospace maintenance, repair, and overhaul facilities.

Tulsa Operations History

Honeywell Tulsa Heat Transfer Operations was originally founded as LORI in 1976 as an FAA repair station. The small operation, dedicated to servicing heat exchangers, oil coolers, and other heat transfer components, soon saw demand for the business to expand and the operation became a thriving entity. In 1980, LORI pioneered the process known as RECORE®, which takes heat exchanger units considered beyond repair and rebuilds components to exacting standards with a new core matrix. This development allowed LORI to create an entirely new market with unlimited potential. LORI became an industry leader and innovator of preventative maintenance programs. And in 1987, LORI presented the commercial aviation industry with a dynamic new concept in heat transfer equipment repair—service agreements. The program was incredibly popular and highly successful with service agreements established for customers worldwide.

Also in 1987, LORI completed construction of a new facility in the Cherokee Industrial Park in north Tulsa. The state-of-the-art 136,000-square-foot facility brought all Tulsa operations under one roof, combined manufacturing and repair, and allowed added emphasis on new product development.

Today, Tulsa Heat Transfer Operations main product lines are heat exchangers, precoolers, oil coolers, fuel heaters, and fuel cooled oil coolers. Additional capabilities include: ozone converters, valves, and water separators.

Asia

Asia Heat Transfer Operations was established in Singapore to serve the heat exchanger needs of Asia Pacific Region. The operations in Singapore provides the same exceptional service customers expect from Tulsa Heat Transfer Operations in the United States. The 26,000-square-foot facility provides a full range of services, from minor repairs to overhaul of units by U.S. factory-trained specialists. Singapore also offers customers a full range of testing capabilities to guarantee the quality of repair work.

Honeywell International, Inc.

LORI was acquired in 1996 by AlliedSignal Aerospace, a U.S. $7.5-billion unit of AlliedSignal Inc. In December of 1999 Honeywell and AlliedSignal, Inc. completed a merger and became Honeywell International, Inc. Honeywell Aerospace is the largest supplier of aircraft engines, equipment, systems, and services for commercial transport, regional, general aviation, and military aircraft. Honeywell is a U.S. $25-billion advanced technology and manufacturing company serving customers worldwide with aerospace products and services, automotive products, chemicals, fibers, plastics, and advanced materials. It is one of the 30 stocks that make up the Dow Jones Industrial Average and is also a component of the Standard & Poor's 500 Index. The company employs 125,000 people in some 120countries.

Commitment to Quality

Through nearly 25 years of growth, Tulsa Heat Transfer Operations has maintained the same commitment to customer service that earned early business partners. Quality service is an unconditional Tulsa Heat Transfer Operations guarantee, from individualized customer support to turntime and delivery commitments to Total Logistics Support. This commitment to quality has earned Tulsa Heat Transfer Operations the distinction of being a "first line vendor of choice" for many customers. Other Tulsa Heat Transfer

Operations certifications include ISO 9001/AS9000, FAA Designated Alteration Station (DAS), JAA, and CAAC certifications.

Comprehensive Repair Capabilities

Honeywell Tulsa Heat Transfer Operations fulfills heat transfer needs for both new and existing aircraft for major airlines worldwide, the United States military, and other manufacturing companies. Tulsa Heat Transfer Operations has repair/rebuild capabilities for more than 8,000 aircraft heat transfer components.

Tulsa Heat Transfer Operations cost-effective alternative to replacing heat transfer equipment categorizes each unit into three levels of repair. Category I—minor repair, Category II—major overhaul, and Category III—overhaul utilizing RECORE®. Units requiring Category III also receive Tulsa Heat Transfer Operations patented LORCOAT protective coating which is baked on in special ovens.

Tulsa Heat Transfer Operations also offers worldwide customers a variety of Total Logistics Support services, including inventory buy-back programs, rotable pools, and exchanges. Satisfaction is always guaranteed.

Engineering and Manufacturing

Tulsa Heat Transfer Operations is an aerospace products innovator with hundreds of products available to the market and under development. Tulsa Heat Transfer Operations relies on product research and development to establish and maintain exacting standards, from the design stage through the engineering and testing stages. With its self-contained testing facilities and FAA DAS authority, Tulsa Heat Transfer Operations is uniquely positioned to meet demanding customer requirements with product development cycles as short as four months. Tulsa Heat Transfer Operations manufacturing products span the aerospace industry, including one of the largest fin production lines in the country.

Providing Solutions

Tulsa Heat Transfer Operations has built its outstanding reputation on one simple fact—when customers have heat transfer needs, it provides the solution. Honeywell Aerospace Services, Tulsa Heat Transfer Operations is proud of the world-renowned reputation it has earned. With is global network of heat transfer operations, Tulsa Heat Transfer Operations serves the needs of commercial airlines, regional airlines, and the military from Tulsa. It is also proud to call Tulsa home and proud to play an important part in Tulsa's continuing growth, diversification, and success. ❖

AAON, INC.

*T*ulsa's manufacturing industry has seen its ups and downs over the last decade, but AAON, Inc. has been "above it all"—literally.

Since its incorporation in 1989, the Tulsa-based fabricator and builder of heavy-duty roof-top heating and cooling equipment has become a major player in the competitive heating, ventilation, and air conditioning (HVAC) industry, where a company's survival and success are dictated by creativity and the ability to introduce innovative new products and services.

AAON's lineage is deeply rooted in local business lore. Its incorporation was for the purpose of acquiring the heating, ventilation, and air-conditioning division of the venerable John Zink Company, a business that was started in Zink's garage and went on to become a world leader in its field.

Growth of the acquired Tulsa business has only continued to swell at a heady rate—exceeding the industry's annual average tenfold since its beginning. The 60,000-square-foot facility in which AAON began operations in 1989 now spreads over 800,000 square feet.

Norman H. Asbjornson, president of AAON, admits the company's rate of growth is pretty spectacular for a product hardly anyone ever sees, except, perhaps, low-flying pilots, balloonists, sky divers, and roof repairmen. This is because all of AAON's HVAC products are designed for roof installation on only commercial buildings. Because the buildings on which they're installed may be as high as 10 floors, they're virtually impossible to observe from ground level.

AAON's business is produced essentially in two distinctive markets—for installation in new, large commercial structures and for replacement of original equipment. Though the majority of sales traditionally have been produced in these two areas, a third target—foreign sales—has been getting increased attention since 1993. Exports are steadily growing and accounted for an appreciable percent of all sales in 1998.

"Our products and sales strategy focuses on a 'niche' market," Asbjornson explains. "This target market is customers, often replacement-buyers, seeking a product of better quality or with options not offered by standardized manufacturers."

The strategy has obviously worked. AAON sales were up 30 percent in 1998—for the second consecutive year. From its start with two customers ten years ago, AAON has annual sales in the range of $140 million today. The company's major customers include Wal-Mart, Home Depot, and Target stores. These three mega-chains accounted for 36 percent of AAON's sales in 1998.

The sprawling—and expanding—Tulsa plant and headquarters is the biggest player in a two-member team that has put AAON at the pinnacle of its business. In Longview, Texas, a plant covering 230,000 square feet builds coils that become an integral part of the AAON units produced in Tulsa.

One of AAON's biggest challenges has been to work around Tulsa's tight labor market (the city has reported one of the lowest unemployment rates in the nation for the last three or four years), even as sales and acceptance continue to increase.

With labor costs escalating and with trained or trainable job applicants increasingly

Headquarters and manufacturing facility in Tulsa— 811,000 sq. ft.

difficult to enlist, AAON spent almost $14 million on capital expenditures, mostly for automated equipment in its sheet metal fabricating operation. Consequently, a 150 percent improvement in productivity was realized—even in the face of the tightening labor market.

Meanwhile, plant expansion in Tulsa and Longview, along with the investment in automated equipment, has increased AAON's capacity for gross revenue production to a level of $200 million annually.

Meeting the Market's Evolving Needs

To succeed in the highly competitive HVAC industry requires strong new product development. That has been one of AAON's greatest assets in the company's impressive growth and improvement in earnings capacity.

In 1998 alone, AAON received patents for an improved blower housing assembly, an air conditioner with energy recovery heat wheel, and a "dimpled" heat exchanger tube. As unusual as it may sound, the "dimple" wasn't developed for its looks—it actually enhances the tube's heat exchange characteristics to eliminate the need for an internal "turbulator" and promises the buyer significantly fewer service problems in the future.

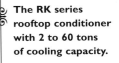

These new products were four years later, followed by the introduction of AAONAIRE®, an energy recovery system that has won customers over with its energy-saving possibilities, and a patented heat exchanger design that allows the company to increase the warranted life of this component.

Research and development are an important part of AAON's handling of the challenges it constantly faces in the HVAC market. New products in the works include an improved water chiller, as well as a redesign and enhancement of one of the company's most popular large rooftop models.

By emphasizing—and pricing for—the quality and dependability of its products, AAON at times finds itself up against competitors trying to undersell their services. But Asbjornson believes AAON's "built-in dependability" is the most important characteristic of the company's products—and is by far the best sales tool in showing customers why AAON's products not only perform beyond expectations but prove their value each and every day.

"By paying close attention to the quality of our HVAC equipment," he says, "we help build value for our customers into every owner-occupied building. The next ten years present an opportunity for us to broaden that foundation and develop new and exciting products to meet a multitude of new markets and demands." ↩

Computer controlled sheet metal fabrication equipment.

The RK series rooftop conditioner with 2 to 60 tons of cooling capacity.

The RF series rooftop conditioner with 40 to 130 tons of cooling capacity.

WHIRLPOOL CORPORATION

The coming together of Whirlpool and the City of Tulsa was more than a successful Chamber of Commerce plant acquisition—it has many of the same enviable qualities of a successful marriage.

Eileen Knecht, technician on the electric assembly team.

One has only to observe that the official mailing address of the Tulsa plant is a street called "Whirlpool Drive," or that Whirlpool invested more than $100 million in plant and equipment in a long-term commitment to the economic base of the region, to realize that both City and Corporation approached the union with something more than ordinary self-interest.

The Whirlpool plant began producing gas and electric freestanding ranges in March 1996. Since its opening in the Cherokee Industrial Park, 12 miles north of Tulsa, employment has grown from 800 to 1,400.

As the world's leading manufacturer and marketer of major home appliances, Whirlpool operations produced $10.3 billion in sales in 1998—an increase of 20 percent from the previous year. Though U.S.-based Whirlpool also has major operations in Latin America, Europe and Asia, the Tulsa plant specializes in serving the North American market.

The Whirlpool plant groundbreaking came soon after one of Tulsa's darkest periods: the dizzying drop in employment that resulted from the virtual collapse of the world's oil industry. For the City, the occasion played a symbolic role by signaling that recovery had begun—and in a field not closely related to the still important, but troublesomely changeable, oil business.

Whirlpool Corporation, Tulsa, Oklahoma.

The cooperative alliance of City and Corporation became apparent well before plant operations began. Tulsa citizens voted a special, temporary sales tax increment as an incentive for the company's location here. Once the decision was made, technical training institutions in Tulsa geared up to turn out a qualified work force from a labor base whose comprehension of kitchen ranges, up to that time, was as a vital component of the personal food chain.

"The community support has been outstanding," says Thomas J. Toth, Division Vice President in charge of the Tulsa plant. "Tulsa Technology Center has been a key partner in our hiring and training process. Tulsa Community College has helped us design and implement a technical program for the advancement of our employees."

"Through these efforts we've been able to recruit 95 percent of our workforce from the Tulsa region," he adds.

Whirlpool's response to the community shows up in the hundreds of thousands of dollars the company has settled upon a score of local institutions and causes, such as the American Red Cross, North Tulsa Heritage Foundation, Tulsa Area United Way, Philbrook Museum, Cherokee Elementary Adopt-a-school, and Youth Services of Tulsa, to name a few.

With Whirlpool's operations continuing to grow and the community enjoying the benefits of having a world-class employer right in its own backyard, the match of Tulsa and Whirlpool promises to be a long and happy one. ❖

McKissick/The Crosby Group

When companies need to lift something, they turn to the nation's most recognized name in block and tackle—longtime Tulsa company McKissick.

McKissick has been a leader in the lifting tackle business for nearly 70 years. The holder of more than 100 patents, McKissick has become the nation's leader in manufacturing blocks and sheaves for many market uses, including construction, industrial, military, energy, entertainment, and marine applications. From the many "off the shelf" items to the non-standard "special engineered" block and tackle systems, McKissick prides itself on meeting a company's every lifting need.

"If you grew up in the oil patch of Oklahoma or Texas you know McKissick," says Mike Wheeler, director of marketing for The Crosby Group, Inc., McKissick's parent company. "In addition, we serve any industry that does lifting, tying down, hauling, or suspending. McKissick products are widely used in all of these industries."

The company, which began operations as an oilfield equipment distributor, became a force in the block business after 1925, when Oklahoma passed laws requiring safety guards on the wire line entrance to oil field blocks. It was McKissick that developed and patented a wire line guard that could be opened to allow the reeving of the block without disassembly. Today the company offers a full line of block and tackle, McKissick sheaves, overhaul balls, swivels, wire rope sockets, and the Crosby wire rope clip.

In addition to being one of the world's largest producers of blocks, McKissick has also manufactured many of the world's largest block and tackle systems. For proof, look no further than the custom McKissick blocks used to set the NASA space shuttle on the back of its 747

Utilizing "state-of-the-art" robotics to fabricate sheaves.

carrier jet. The largest and most impressive example of McKissick's capabilities is the M-5000 block (6,000 metric ton capacity) for McDermott's DB-102 derrick barge, which has been used to lift a seven-story building onto an offshore oil platform.

In addition to being ISO 9001-certified, McKissick is also API Q1-certified, signifying that the company has met stringent requirements to be API certified for producing and selling equipment for use in the oilfield.

Long a force in Oklahoma's oil industry, McKissick grew beyond a regional company to national prominence when it became part of The Crosby Group in 1959. Crosby, the world's leading single source supplier of rigging hardware, is made up of six brand names that are the strongest in their respective industries throughout the country. Tulsa serves as the headquarters for Crosby U.S., and oversees worldwide operations of the company. The Crosby Group also has manufacturing facilities in Texas, Arkansas, Canada, and Belgium.

McKissick products are sold through 1,700 distributors in the United States and 500 more around the world, but all the machining and manufacturing is done here at McKissick's state-of-the-art Tulsa plant.

"At McKissick, we specialize in meeting the customer's expectations" Wheeler says. "When it comes to quality products and service, the company's reputation is second to none." ✦

Welding the hub into a sheave.

BORG COMPRESSED STEEL

Since 1946, Borg Compressed Steel has converted obsolete metal into the basic ingredient of new metal and steel. Borg has assumed a role so important to our ecological sensitivity that if it didn't exist it would have to be created.

Borg Compressed Steel corporate officers from left to right: Buddy Slemp, VP and Assistant GM; Jeffrey D. Ray, President and GM; Jane Seibert, Corporate Secretary and Transportation Manager.

Borg started business in Tulsa as a combination salvage/scrap yard at 1032 North Lewis. The modern company was launched two years later, at the same location, when Borg started serving Tulsa industries by recovering their obsolete machinery and product scrap metal.

Present owner Paul A. Schwartz purchased Borg in 1983. Jeffrey Ray, president and general manager, is in charge of local operations. Ray says he "grew up in the business" under the tutelage of his father Victor, Borg's chief operating officer and a longtime associate of Schwartz. Jeffrey Ray is a 1990 graduate of ORU.

Borg, with 75 local employees, services more than 550 industrial accounts, providing containment facilities at each customer's site to hold scrap and process residue awaiting their recovery. "We're responsible for transporting that product to our plant, where we separate and process the materials into specific sizes and shapes for foundry or steel mill consumption," Ray explains.

"Processing" seems an inadequate term to describe the high-tech transformation of the scrap into usable raw material. Borg's Vezanni 1,000-ton gravity-fed shear, for example, eats steel like a cow eats grass. It's so powerful it can cut "oversize" metal scrap to any length to meet foundry or steel mill needs.

Borg Compressed Steel's state-of-the-art steel turning facility.

Borg handles "steel turnings" for many of its customers. This product embodies a residual amount of cutting fluid from the steel machining process. With oversight by its own certified environmental manager, Borg designed a facility to house the steel turnings and capture the fluid run-off for proper disposal. This commitment to environmental awareness has strengthened Borg's relationship with its industrial customers and the local, state, and federal environmental agencies.

Its 22 trucks run six days a week collecting material from the aerospace industry, appliance, air-conditioning, heat exchanger, and oilfield equipment manufacturers and fabricators, and a host of machine shops.

But the company also serves the public. "We provide a place for residents to bring old steel appliances—and we even pay money for them," Ray explains. "It's a huge ecological benefit for Tulsa because it keeps washers, dryers, and refrigerators from going into landfill space.

"What's more," he adds, "you won't find these appliances lining the ditches in rural areas. We're a big part of keeping Green Country green."

As Tulsa and Green Country continue working to remain environmentally and economically sound for the future, you can bet Borg is going to play a major role in helping area manufacturers be a part of the solution.

"We look forward to helping Tulsa industry recycle into the 21st century and beyond." ✦

UNITED PARCEL SERVICE

Behind every package, every brown uniform, and every package car shines the faces of more than 336,000 associates around the world who make up United Parcel Service.

Delivering more than 12.4 million packages every day, UPS has gained the reputation of the leading package delivery company in the world. UPS is committed not only to delivering packages on time, but to delivering a sense of hope and help to the communities in which they live and serve.

UPS delivered its first package in Oklahoma in 1971, and now has more than 2,500 employees working in the state. With large sorting facilities in Oklahoma City and Tulsa and 16 other centers across the state, more than 700 drop box locations, and more than 700 drivers on the road each day, UPS has helped Oklahoma grow.

In 1907, when Oklahoma was celebrating its declaration of statehood, there was a great need in America for private messenger and delivery services. Few homes had telephones, so personal messages had to be carried by hand. To meet this need, enterprising 19-year-old James "Jim" Casey borrowed $100 and established American Messenger Service in Seattle, Washington. With a handful of teenagers, Jim ran his service from a small office under a sidewalk. Despite stiff competition the company did well, largely because of Jim's strict policies: customer courtesy, reliability, round-the-clock service, and low rates.

In the last 92 years, many things have changed at UPS: the buildings, the mode of transportation, the name, the face of management, the services they provide, and most definitely the technology-all adapting to remain successful in a competitive environment. One thing that has not changed is UPS's commitment to service, customers and the community.

UPS is committed to serving the needs of the global marketplace. As a worldwide carrier delivering to more than 200 countries, UPS assists global customers with Secure Document Exchange, E-Commerce, and Import Services.

As the leader in Internet and electronic deliveries as well as package delivery, UPS has been named *Fortune Magazine's* Most Admired Transportation Company for 16 years in a row.

Though UPS has given and continues to give employment and economic opportunities to thousands of Oklahomans, it may be that the greatest impact UPS is making on the culture of Oklahoma is through its community involvement.

UPS has invested millions of dollars each year in supporting community literacy, food banks, and youth programs. The company and its employees have also contributed more than $355 million to United Way since the first campaign in 1982. Oklahoma UPSers contributed more than $324,000 during the 1999/2000 campaign alone.

After seeing these programs firsthand, many UPS employees continue volunteering their time and talent through the Neighbor to Neighbor program long after the United Way campaign has ended. Corporately, employees volunteer about 30,000 hours each year, offering their time and leadership to worthy community projects across the nation.

After 92 years of building a legacy, United Parcel Service intends to spend the next century better serving customers and the community with expanded services, advanced technology, and quality service. ❖

UPS is committed to serving the needs of the global marketplace as the leader in internet and electronic deliveries as well as package delivery.

UPS Tulsa driver Valerie Tillis represents UPS's committment to the Tulsa community. After her son was murdered, Valerie created the Willis Saddler Foundation. UPS recently gave the foundation a $100,000 grant to open a safe house for kids on the street.

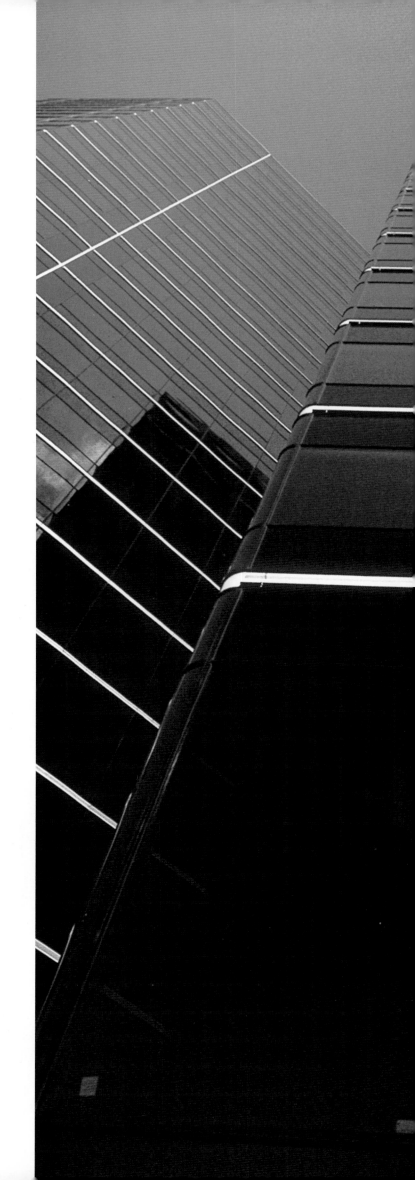

12
Chapter Twelve

THE BUSINESS COMMUNITY

Photo by Don Wheeler.

WILLIAMS

*A*sk when Tulsans forgot the shock of no longer being the "Oil Capital of the World" and were inspired to resume building the city-on-a-hill that an earlier generation set out to create in the 1920s.

There are those who say it was November 21, 1971—the day Williams announced that, in cooperation with the Tulsa Urban Renewal Authority, it would spearhead a project to convert nine square blocks of downtown's most squalid area into a national model of urban revitalization.

The public responded incredulously, but eagerly. Downtown Tulsa had changed little since World War II, and was showing its age. Once the hub of business and commercial activity, the central city was starting to suffer from the change in growth patterns. The flight to the suburbs gradually picked up speed, then began to turn into a land rush.

But the prospect of a 23-acre remake of the city's center was exciting, not just to those with property and jobs in the area. And to a majority of Tulsans who had not become acquainted with the name in a business or civic context, "Williams" took its place as a routinely invoked addition to the community's vocabulary.

Actually, Williams had been around since 1908 when two Williams brothers began a construction business. Out of that humble venture grew the world's leading pipeline engineering and construction firm. Under the Williams Brothers name, the $8 million company went public with its stock in 1957. Shareholders adopted The Williams Companies, Inc. name in 1971.

Williams' stock has delivered strong returns, especially in recent years. An investor who observed the start of 1991 by purchasing—and holding—a block of Williams stock would have celebrated a cumulative return of 826 percent on New Year's Eve 1998.

In the '90s, Williams exerted a beneficial influence in every business it entered and in every community it occupied. The result is that Williams, through its subsidiaries, today operates one of the country's largest-volume natural gas transportation systems, a leading-edge energy services company, and the nation's biggest independent single-source provider of business communications systems and international satellite and fiber-optic services. But the foundation for that preeminence was laid early in the 1970s, when Williams puts its stake in downtown.

For the city of Tulsa, Williams' leading role in the renewal of downtown was a commitment of incalculable value. Not only did it herald an upgrade of the oldest section of the city, more importantly it was a declaration that Williams was casting its lot with Tulsa, especially downtown. To undertake a major urban project was laudable; to make a clear statement that it would not be joining the exodus to newer oil patch cities, but would build its world headquarters in the new downtown development, was Tulsa's greatest news in half a century.

Joe Williams, retired president of the company, explained more than 20 years ago the decision matter-of-factly: "The easiest solution would have been to erect a headquarters building in the southeast area of Tulsa, away from the congestion of the central city and close to where many of our employees live. But we hope the new project will create a ripple effect, plus a new sense of hope and pride."

Though the rebuilt area would eventually be the site of a major hotel, the city's modern Performing Arts Center and other office buildings, the jewel of the project would be Williams' own building.

Joe Williams selected the firm of Minoru Yamasaki & Associates, designers of the New York World Trade Center among other notable engagements, to develop a plan for the area. In 1973, when Yamasaki unveiled his model of the project to Williams and city principals, it proposed one major office building for Williams and another for the National Bank of Tulsa (now Bank of Oklahoma) and general tenancy.

A former Williams executive recalls that now retired company Chairman John Williams, after long and thoughtful contemplation of Yamasaki's model, picked up one of the office buildings and placed it atop the other. "This is the way it ought to be," he announced.

And as is evident to anyone viewing the 52-story building at the northern downtown terminus of Boston Avenue, that's the way it came to be.

History, of course, has a habit of repeating itself, and February 1999 saw the introduction of the newest chapter in Williams' lasting relationship with Tulsa. Williams announced it would build a new 15-story tower, the Williams Technology Center, alongside the existing headquarters building in downtown Tulsa.

By the time Williams opens the building in mid-2001, downtown Tulsa could look much different—much of that due to the activity created by Williams. The building will accommodate 4,000 employees, with a good portion of this new growth coming in the company's communications division, according to Keith Bailey, Williams' chairman, president, and chief executive officer.

"It will be state-of-the-art in terms of technology and also will be very hospitable as a work environment," he says. "The building will reflect everything we've learned about how you put people together efficiently. Although it will be only 15 stories, it will hold roughly the same number of employees as the 52-story Bank of Oklahoma Tower."

Most importantly, the new facility will carry on Williams' long tradition of creating hope and pride—and development—in Tulsa's downtown area.

Williams in the Community

Though the Williams Center/Performing Arts Center accomplishments of the 1970s may have focused widespread attention on the company for the first time, it was just a magnification of the community service commitment that had existed in the company for decades, only in lower profile. Recently these accomplishments have served to create in the public a tendency to look to Williams for continuing civic leadership—an expectation that has proven to be well-founded.

In the 1990s, the company made monetary and in-kind donations exceeding $43 million to charitable concerns nationwide, through corporate gifts and matching grants. This, of course, is in addition to the far-reaching volunteer work of Williams employees. These efforts have taken many forms over the years, from support of countless health and community organizations to development of interactivity software for the Jason Project, which promotes the study of science to elementary through high school students around the world via the broadcast of live scientific expeditions.

Tulsa has been particularly well served by Williams' civic-mindedness, but it has not been the exclusive target of the company's support of community. With more than 23,000 employees worldwide, and other major offices in Houston, Salt Lake City and Owensboro, Kentucky, the commitment to society is widespread.

(Top) **A circa-1970s architectural model of the Williams Center.**

Williams Center construction.

The Williams trading floor in Tulsa. It is the largest trading floor west of Chicago.

Construction on Williams' fiber-optic network north of Las Vegas.

more than 260 convenience stores; and one of the nation's largest ethanol production and marketing operations.

Williams' other energy business group, gas pipeline, operates one of the nation's largest-volume systems of interstate natural gas pipelines. The network spans more than 27,000 miles from coast to coast.

The company's third group of businesses, Williams Communications, offers wholesale fiber-optic network services, North American single-source business communications systems integration, international video satellite and fiber-optic transmission, and satellite business applications.

Together, they position Williams to take advantage of great opportunities in the next millennium—both in providing customer solutions in an increasingly deregulated energy market and in meeting the surging demand for bandwidth and technology that is driving the telecommunications industry.

"Williams has never been larger, stronger, or better focused," says Williams' Bailey. "The ability to fully achieve our goals is within our grasp. Never before in our history have we been presented with more opportunity."

A Blend of Energy and Communications

Today, Williams is an energy and communications company with more than $19 billion in assets. And while Williams can mark many significant milestones in its ascendancy, one of the most notable came in 1985. That was the year the company entered the communications business, having recognized (as no one had before) that decommissioned pipelines make excellent conduits for fiber-optic cable.

The decision resulted in the creation of an 11,000-mile telecommunications network that by 1995 had become the nation's fourth largest. And it was in 1995 that Williams sold its long-distance portion of the telecommunications business for $2.5 billion—retaining a single strand of fiber, running through the entire network, making it possible for the company to concentrate on multimedia applications.

The same year it sold its long-distance business, Williams acquired Transco Energy, another major natural gas pipeline company. This paved the way for Williams to become, at the time, the largest-volume transporter of natural gas in the United States.

For most companies, such momentous changes and additions would be the crowning achievement of a lifetime. But after an absence of only three years from the long-distance industry, Williams, in 1998, re-entered the network business as a major wholesale player. Thanks to expansions and alliances, that original 11,000-mile network has just about doubled, and is scheduled to total 33,000 miles by year-end 2000.

Its acquisition of MAPCO, Inc. in a $3 billion stock-for-stock exchange in 1998, filled out Williams' energy portfolio, adding natural gas liquids, refining and propane marketing and distribution assets, and a chain of more than 250 convenience stores and travel centers.

All of these decisions have helped establish Williams as a leader in the international energy and communications scenes, a reputation Williams is continuing to solidify through the efforts of its three primary operating businesses—energy services, gas pipeline and communications.

Williams' energy services businesses include natural gas gathering and processing; gas liquids pipelines; a petroleum products pipeline; petroleum products terminaling; two refineries; an exploration and production company; a top-tier energy marketing and trading company;

The architect's original design for the Williams Center.

A Lasting Sign of Success

The head-spinning achievements of Williams' many operations have made the company a model for how-to-succeed-in-business. But surprisingly—or perhaps not surprisingly—these accomplishments are not necessarily the source of the company's greatest pride.

In 1998 Williams was selected for the United Way of America's "Spirit of America" award. It recognizes the nation's top company in all areas of corporate stewardship, and is one of the most significant accolades a corporation can receive.

Keith Bailey truly understands the heart of Williams, and he sums up the reason for and future of the company's success in this statement: "Williams and its employees strive for leadership in all endeavors, business and charitable. Its current suite of growth projects should position Williams to continue to deliver superior value to shareholders and exceptional levels of support to the communities it serves."

John and Joe Williams stand in front of the Tower shortly after its completion.

The Metropolitan Tulsa Chamber of Commerce

The Arkansas River posed a dilemma for early-day Tulsans. Ferries and even fording the river during dry spells were adequate for a sleepy cow town, but with the discovery of oil on the west bank in 1901, the pace quickened. Men and equipment needed access to the oil fields. Ignoring predictions by engineers that a bridge would inevitably sink in the Arkansas' shifting sands, enterprising Tulsans capitalized and built the 11th Street wagon bridge and linked the city to the wellsprings of its good fortune. With bravado that characterized the young city, a sign was hung above the entrance to the bridge that read simply, "They said we couldn't do it, but we did."

Business leaders and elected representatives welcome Navistar International Corporation to Tulsa. Navistar's decision to open a bus manufacturing facility at Tulsa International Airport was one of several economic development announcements that helped push business investments in Tulsa to a record $1 billion in 1999.

That same entrepreneurial spirit was in evidence when the Tulsa Commercial Club, later renamed the Metropolitan Tulsa Chamber of Commerce, hired special trains to transport city boosters on cross-country trips to promote Tulsa. Will Rogers, Oklahoma's favorite son, had the opportunity in 1908 to join one of those barnstorming sorties. He recalled his adventure 15 years later in his nationally syndicated newspaper column.

"I remember the…incident of a never-heard-of hustling little town that was hardly known as far as the county line. They…wanted to do something that would attract attention to their little town…They hired a special train for 10 days and made a trip to what to us was back East, St. Louis, Indianapolis, Chicago and Kansas City.

"Now if you are anxious to know whatever became of this tank town it's Tulsa, Oklahoma, which would have been a real town even if its people weren't greasy with oil, for it is founded on the spirit of its people."

In subsequent years, the can-do attitude behind building bridges and dispatching ambassadors across the land became known as the "Tulsa Spirit." And the embodiment of that spirit was the Tulsa

Chamber. Its role in turning a "tank town" into a real town was pivotal in remarkable projects that have earned Tulsa a reputation in boardrooms from coast to coast and, indeed, throughout the world.

Some stand out for their sheer imagination and audacity. Take, for example, the airport. Tulsans were quick to perceive the importance of aviation, but they had neither an airport nor the money to build one. Undaunted, Chamber directors and members personally signed a bank note to borrow the money and build a community airport. The Tulsa International Airport became the nucleus of an aerospace industry that now constitutes one of the city's primary economic sectors.

Nowhere is the scope of the Chamber's vision over the past century more apparent than in its support of building a navigable waterway from Tulsa to the sea. Numerous skeptics, the Great Depression, three wars, and an often-unfriendly Congress weren't enough to deter supporters from their dream, and in 1971, President Richard Nixon was on hand to dedicate the McClellan-Kerr Navigation System. America's most inland seaport originates at Tulsa's Port of Catoosa, and water-born

Chamber President Jay Clemens and Total Resource Development Campaign Co-Chairs Linda Bradshaw and T.D. "Pete" Churchwell celebrate a successful week of campaigning on behalf of the Chamber.

cargo ranging from grain to heavy equipment regularly makes its way from landlocked Oklahoma to the Gulf of Mexico.

Times have changed, and a whole new set of challenges is coming into focus. Whereas Tulsa's pioneers were concerned with the exploitation of natural resources and the development of an urban infrastructure, today's leaders are contending with a global economy and the implications of the revolution in telecommunications. Business executives, educators, elected officials, and other key stakeholders are struggling with ways to develop human potential in much the same way that our forebears harnessed the power of petroleum. Tulsa, once known worldwide as the "Oil Capitol of the World," is once again relying on the "Tulsa Spirit" to reinvent itself and prepare for the complexities of the twenty-first century.

Today, the Chamber is a primary advocate for the region's business community. Like their predecessors who sent trainloads of boosters back East to promote their city, Chamber volunteers and staff continue to provide leadership in all economic sectors. Through its Economic Development Division, the Chamber promotes economic growth and diversity by facilitating expansion of existing businesses and recruiting companies to the region. Its goals are implemented through four program areas that incorporate workforce development, existing business development, new business development and marketing, and international business. In 1999, the Chamber was instrumental in bringing over $1 billion in business investment into Tulsa and fostering the kind of balanced growth that benefits the entire metro area. Meanwhile, assistance to small and minority businesses, together with seminars, workshops, and publications, make the Chamber a one-stop-shop for businessmen and women on the road to success.

The Chamber's long-standing goal of bringing the benefits of comprehensive, publicly supported higher education to Tulsa was realized with the creation of OSU-Tulsa in early 1999. Both traditional students and adults seeking higher degrees now have the option of completing their degrees in Tulsa, and businesses can count on a steady stream of educated workers to help them prosper. Other Chamber efforts that have come to fruition and contribute to Tulsa's progressive spirit include reforms in common education, the city's designation as a disaster-resistant city, and a wide range of programs promoting healthy relationships between the public and private sectors.

Another important part of the Chamber's economic development program is the Convention and Visitors Bureau, which markets Tulsa as a destination city. Its role is crucial in a community whose tourism industry boasts a $1 billion economic impact on the area, brings in over $30 million annually in local tax collections, and generates more than 24,000 jobs. Sporting events, cultural attractions, business, and association meetings all contribute to urban vitality and an enviable quality of life for visitors and residents alike.

Today's Chamber combines one-on-one relationships with the latest in telecommunications technology. The Chamber's website includes news releases, announcements of events, and meetings, employment opportunities, and links with members' websites that enhance market penetration and help businesses grow. And special events ranging from golf tournaments to trade shows serve as constant reminders that the Chamber is nothing less than the hub of the business community—a position it's held for a century, and a position it will hold for as long as Tulsans want to make their city a better place to work, and a better place to live. ⬅

1999 Board Chair Charles E. "Chuck" Patterson presents Total Resource Development Campaign Chair T.D. "Pete" Churchwell with the 1999 Chairman's Award for his outstanding service to the Chamber.

A capacity crowd gathers at the Chamber's annual Inaugural Luncheon in downtown Tulsa.

BANK ONE

*B*ank One, Oklahoma traces its roots to one of the oldest banks in the state. Today it offers a rich tradition of banking and community excellence enhanced with national products and services. Its customers enjoy a bank with national dominance and resources that reach beyond Oklahoma's borders.

Historic Ties to Tulsa

What started as the Tulsa Banking Company in 1895 and grew to become First National Bank of Tulsa and later Liberty Tulsa, is now Bank One, Oklahoma. The employees remain committed to the growth of Tulsa and the state of Oklahoma as they have for more than a century.

National Leadership

From individual customers to small businesses and major corporations, Bank One, Oklahoma can offer customers access to national financial products and services. Bank One is the nation's leading credit card issuer. It is also the nation's second-largest lender to small business. Bank One's family of mutual funds, One Group, manages $60 billion in funds and consistently is recognized among the top mutual fund groups in the nation. All this and more are just around the corner for Bank One customers.

Local Delivery

Just around the corner means convenience to the more than 180,000 households served by Bank One in Oklahoma at its nearly 40 banking centers and 150 automated teller machines. Convenience and customer service have built customer trust. Today, nearly 15 percent of the state's total deposits are in Bank One, Oklahoma.

Bank One, Oklahoma received a "AA" rating by *Standard and Poor's* and an "Aa2" rating by *Moody Investor Service* for long-term debt. Both ratings are the highest ever achieved by a banking organization chartered in Oklahoma.

Investment Management

Banc One Investment Management Group offers clients comprehensive and professional investment and fiduciary services. With more than $125 billion in assets under management and annual revenues in excess of $1 billion, Banc One Investment Management Group is ranked among the top 25 investment managers in the United States.

The One Group Mutual Funds is the only five-star fund family with a local presence in Oklahoma. In addition to traditional investment management, BOIMG also manages real estate, oil, gas, and mineral properties. The group is one of the largest mineral property managers in the United States, with more than 60,000 properties; 20,000 in Oklahoma alone. Bank One brings all these national capabilities of professional investment management to the local customer through its local associates.

Local Decision Making

Customers will often hear Bank One employees repeat "national products with local delivery." It's a phrase that captures the essence of Bank One's promise to the state. But no factor is more critical in that pledge than the quality of the personnel who deliver it. The Bank One, Oklahoma leadership team is comprised of

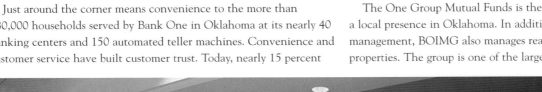

National products, local delivery.

Personalized service for walk-in customers.

individuals who have played a role in Oklahoma's banking history and its community. They have a stake in its past and its future.

Ed Keller, chairman and CEO of Bank One, Oklahoma, is among the state's most respected business leaders. His visionary leadership in the banking community, along with his active role in dozens of professional associations, has led to his appointment to premier leadership positions in the state. He served as 1998 Chairman of the Metropolitan Tulsa Chamber of Commerce and is a governor-appointed member of the Oklahoma State University-Tulsa Board of Trustees.

A Bank for All of Oklahoma

Bank One, Oklahoma is an Oklahoma bank for Oklahomans. Led by an experienced team of Oklahoma bankers with a documented record of high achievement on behalf of its customers, Bank One, Oklahoma is also a vital and growing component of the national bank.

Customers of Bank One, Oklahoma have convenient access to the world's finest banking products and services in their own communities and business centers. It's a reality many of Oklahoma's earliest bankers believed was only a dream. ⤸

Bank One employees active in the community.

Bank One, 15 East 5th Avenue, Tulsa, Oklahoma.

CITIZENS SECURITY BANK & TRUST COMPANY

In 1999, Citizens Security Bank & Trust Company of Bixby marked its 75th anniversary and the beginning of a new century with the opening of a new headquarters. The new 22,000 square-foot facility, located at 14821 South Memorial Drive, is the culmination of years of strategic planning and growth that have brought the bank's renowned personal and professional services to thousands in Bixby and South Tulsa. The new facility, along with full-service branches in South Tulsa and Glenpool, has positioned Citizens Security Bank & Trust Company to meet the needs of metropolitan Tulsa's fastest growing area.

Citizens Security Bank headquarters, located at 14821 S. Memorial in Bixby.

A History of Service

In 1924, the prominent G. A. Brown Family of Bixby founded Citizens Security Bank to serve the banking needs of the small community south of Tulsa. Primarily a rural area along the Arkansas River, Bixby residents, business owners and farmers, turned to Citizens Security for full-service banking and personal service. The bank's relationship with the community grew along with the area's population. In 1994, President Homer Paul, joined by the Carlisle Mabrey family of Okmulgee, who are prominent area community bankers, purchased majority interest of the Bank with a stated commitment of continuing local ownership and operation of Citizens Security Bank.

A Dynamic Growth Area

Although Bixby retains it's small-town charm and spirit, visionary leaders have worked to build a community prepared for the future growth of South Tulsa. As a full-service bank, Citizens Security Bank & Trust Company has played an important role in the economic development of the area by providing a myriad of products and services for hundreds of customers, new homeowners, and growing businesses.

Citizens Security is a vital part of the incredible growth and development along South Memorial Drive (U.S. 64) and U.S. 67 which intersect in Bixby and connect the area with Hwy. 75 and the Creek Turnpike. Businesses and entrepreneurs will continue to look

to Citizens Security for lending and financial services to develop this southernmost portion of metropolitan Tulsa.

Community Leadership

Citizens Security Bank & Trust Company has always played an important role as a leading corporate citizen in Bixby and surrounding communities. Whether supporting the growth of Bixby Public Schools or any number of non-profit volunteer organizations, Citizens Security has led the way. This spirit of community leadership is seen today throughout the Tulsa area. Citizens Security, its staff, and President Homer Paul have participated in leadership roles in Metropolitan Tulsa community causes. The bank is ably guided and directed by a quality Board of Directors whose members include: James W. Allison, Wanda M. Brown, W. Carlisle Mabrey, III, John Mabrey, Homer Paul, Dr. Ramona Paul, and Georgeanna Brown Thomas.

The commitment to the future of the community by Citizens Security Bank & Trust Company is evidenced by the expansion to three full-service locations and the opening of the new 22,000-square-foot headquarters. Currently with $140 million in assets and a goal of $200 million by 2003, Citizens Security has built a reputation as a strong locally-owned and managed community leader—big enough to serve every customer's banking needs and small enough to continue a tradition of personal, friendly service. ✦

An interior view of the CSB headquarters, showing the beautiful four-sided fireplace and impressive art collection.

STATE BANK AND TRUST

State Bank and Trust operates on the premise that while going with the flow may offer the least resistance, it doesn't always take you where you want to be.

State Bank has always known where it wants to be: Tulsa's favorite financial institution serving the special needs of individual customers and small- to medium-size businesses.

In 1991 the Arvest Bank Group acquired State Federal Savings, a 74-year-old thrift institution, as the nucleus of a Tulsa banking operation that has quickly grown to 16 offices across the metropolitan area.

In a strange, new banking environment where contact with customers seems to be discouraged, State Bank is taking the opposite path. "We think we need to meet and greet every customer who comes in the door," says Don Walker, president of State Bank. And that's exactly what they do!

Behind the greeting is a generous menu of services for individuals (regular and interest checking, Fifty Plus Checking, savings accounts, certificates of deposit, all types of lending, and its own ATM and Check cards), as well as for businesses (checking, including commercial NOW and money market accounts, business loans, trust services, including retirement planning and administration, cash management, and credit card services).

It may be that State Bank's customer-sensitivity goes back to the Arvest Group's entry into the banking field when, in 1961, it purchased The Bank of Bentonville (Arkansas). Thirty-eight years and several acquisitions later, Arvest had bank assets of $4 billion in Arkansas,

Oklahoma, and Missouri, and employed nearly 2,100 persons.

Again flying in the face of the conventional wisdom that seems to drive the emerging banking industry, Arvest stresses local autonomy. State Bank has its own management team, its own local board of directors, makes its own loan decisions, and sets its own deposit rates.

Having local control has led State Bank to introduce some innovative practices. "We determined that our customers need us open much later, so we decided to do something different," says Larry Choate, State Bank's executive vice president. As a result, State Bank's revolutionary "8-to-8" policy—8 a.m. to 8 p.m. business hours—was adopted to give customers the opportunity to bank when it was convenient for them.

State's mission statement is "People helping people find financial solutions for life," which explains why it's possible to find in this sophisticated institution with the small-town heritage full-service brokerage, trust services, personal financial planning, and a complete scope of home mortgage lending.

The banking landscape has certainly changed in recent years, and State has stayed on the forefront by offering on-line banking options at its web site and a large network of ATMs.

But to the gratification of those who recall nostalgically the customer-friendly banking landscape that used to be, things don't seem to have changed all that much at State Bank. ⭠

BANK OF AMERICA

*B*ank of America is the bank for business…

Fine Airport Parking Garage under construction. Financed by Bank of America.

Bank of America is a financial services organization which can meet all of a businessperson's financial needs. It offers tremendous resources to small- and mid-sized businesses, corporations, and government agencies across the nation and around the world. It is an organization that delivers capacity and product breadth, global reach, and superior execution to each client through teams of talented professionals. And it is firmly positioned at the forefront of global finance, opening doors into Asia and Europe, and southward into Latin America, helping a majority of America's leading corporations compete successfully in a burgeoning global economy.

All these accomplishments are just the beginning! Bank of America is determined to be much more. Its goal is to build a company that makes banking work as it never has before. A company reshaped around those things that matter most to both individual and business customers: convenience, simplicity, flexibility, and dependability. A company that understands and anticipates the needs of each corporate client, responding with innovative solutions and consistently delivering knowledge, creative ideas, and excellence in execution. In short, a

banking company with an outstanding global banking franchise, and the best opportunity to create greater value for its customers.

Bank of America offers many advantages its customers and clients just can't get elsewhere.

Corporate clients benefit from client teams of seasoned industry experts, product specialists, and investment bankers offering a comprehensive range of products through offices in 38 countries. Client teams can mobilize capital resources and worldwide network to deliver unmatched market perspective, transaction experience, and expertise.

Oklahoma headquarters of Bank of America, 515 S. Boulder in downtown Tulsa.

Middle-market companies realize similar benefits. A medium-sized firm with $50 million in sales appreciates working with a local client manager who fully understands it and its business. But it also appreciates access to full-service banking in Bank of America's 21 franchise states. And if the firm wants access to capital markets and transaction speed, there is no better, single bank able to address all of these issues, than Bank of America.

Small business is big business at Bank of America. As the number one small business lender in the nation, Bank of America is dedicated to enhancing the success of small business customers with products and services targeted to meet growing and changing needs.

Bank of America provides businesses with a continuum of products and services to fuel every stage of growth, whether they are just starting out, preparing for a major expansion, considering an acquisition, or taking the company public.

Bank of America approaches the 21st century with the scale and reach that its clients and customers want. It brings with it the people and the technology to create new possibilities and new solutions. Its goal is to be the most capable and responsive banking company in the country and to make banking work for its customers in ways it never has before.

Bank of America is building a bank for the future. ⬿

LOCAL OKLAHOMA BANK

From Oklahoma's oldest and second-largest thrift to its newest and fifth-largest commercial bank—all in one day, with the simple stroke of a pen.

The seemingly impossible feat has been accomplished by Local Oklahoma Bank in a conversion and name change that not only redirects its objectives, but suddenly makes it a major player in commercial lending through 50 offices in 30 communities across the state.

Actually, the conversion/name change was the culmination of a plan already in place in the mind of Chairman Edward A. Townsend and other investors when the institution, then known as Local America Bank, was acquired in 1997.

Though one of the newest banks, Local Oklahoma has a tradition and a track record going back to the beginning of Oklahoma. It was chartered in 1908 as an Oklahoma City thrift institution. In recent years, as Local Federal Bank, it has spread its influence in a broad band of office locations running from southwestern Oklahoma to the northeast corner of the state.

Jim Young, president of Local Oklahoma's Tulsa area operations, is one of those who planned the institution's transformation. "From the acquisition we have worked toward this conversion," Young explains. "Our major strategy has been to enter the market as a full-service commercial bank, aggressively seeking opportunities for commercial lending."

Savings banks' restraints on commercial lending did not match up with the goals of management. Now free to pursue its new objectives, Local Oklahoma has put together a team with proven success in commercial lending. That is especially evident in Tulsa. The bank's

headquarters are in Oklahoma City, but its commercial lending division is managed from Tulsa.

Local Oklahoma's major coverage is in Tulsa, Oklahoma City, and Lawton. There are 12 branches in the Tulsa area, including Claremore, Owasso, Sand Springs, Sapulpa, and Broken Arrow.

"With $2.1 billion in assets, we have the capacity to handle individual commercial loans up to $28 million," Young points out, "but we also can meet all the needs of small businesses."

Under the earlier savings bank charter, Local Oklahoma had to do most of its commercial lending in real estate, with little allowance provided for consumer or commercial bank-type lending. "We have a whole new philosophy now," Young says. "It is allowing us to compete with the other largest banks in the state."

But unlike many other large banks, Local Oklahoma is committed to Oklahoma. "Our size is ideal," he adds. "We have the capacity to serve large businesses in addition to the ability to offer the personal service of a community bank." ❧

Chairman Edward A. Townsend.

Local Oklahoma Bank, Tulsa, Oklahoma.

CHANDLER-FRATES & REITZ

Chandler-Frates & Reitz is a regional leader in insurance products and services, but CFR is not in business to sell insurance. CFR exists to protect clients' interests and act as a business partner.

Headquartered in Tulsa, CFR has offices in Oklahoma City and Dallas.

Protecting clients' business, home, and health, and understanding their needs has been the CFR mission for more than 50 years. CFR believes that knowledge is the key ingredient in all of their relationships. CFR professionals maintain an up-to-the-minute understanding of industry products and services and work to gain valuable insight about client needs.

CFR provides a full range of commercial, group, life, health, and personal insurance products and services through a network of professional independent insurance agents. CFR partners with clients to offer innovative solutions and comprehensive services, as well as beneficial relationships.

CFR's people are the difference. CEO Jack Allen, who joined the firm in 1976 and purchased the company in 1984, is a recognized leader in employee motivation and team building. The other members of the executive team, President Robert Gardner, Executive Vice President Glenn Day, and Vice President/Operations Sherry Burks, bring unique leadership skills to the organization.

The key to CFR's success is possessing a clear vision, having a team of people who support the vision, and establishing individual accountability for acting on the vision. With the help of CFR's goal-oriented staff, the company's independent insurance agents are among the highest producing in the industry.

Continued growth and success has led to regional expansion. CFR established offices in Oklahoma City and Dallas to expand a mission of providing the highest quality risk management and insurance services to select companies and individuals.

Success is also reflected by leadership in industry organizations such as the Council of Insurance Agents & Brokers (CIAB), Group 500, and Intersure, a professional association of leading U.S. and international independent insurance agencies. CFR has also been recognized with important industry awards, such as Marketing Agency of the Year by *Rough Notes*, the leading industry publication, and the Travelers Companies' Leadership Award for outstanding performance in representing commercial clients. Alice Mauldin, a member of the CFR family, was named 1998 Customer Service Agent of the Year for Oklahoma.

Accompanying CFR's dedication to excellence is an unwavering commitment to the community. CFR is an active corporate citizen and a long-time supporter of numerous community activities, including adoption of Sequoyah Elementary School and sponsorship of the annual Tulsa Run. Giving back in creative ways is an important aspect of this dynamic company's mission.

CFR's corporate vision is embodied in the P.S. Gordon commissioned work "Whatever you do."

What separates CFR from other insurance companies? Simply, it is a commitment to quality, a vision for the future, and a unique corporate environment that encourages growth and success. This unique culture is captured in a painting by renowned Tulsa artist P.S. Gordon which hangs in the company's headquarters. The colorful work, commissioned by CFR, shows objects which symbolize characteristics important to CFR's continuing success. ✦

SUPERIOR FEDERAL BANK

Superior Federal Bank is a fairly new face in Tulsa banking. The first Tulsa branch opened in 1998, but Superior Federal has been serving customers in other communities for more than 65 years.

Superior Federal first expanded into Oklahoma in 1993. Today, there are more than a dozen locations in the state and over 40 in Arkansas. More than 200,000 households in Arkansas and Oklahoma bank with Superior Federal.

Built on a tradition of offering the highest quality service and a variety of consumer and small business banking products, Superior Federal has carved out a niche by offering customers that special relationship they can only find in a local, community-oriented financial institution.

Superior Federal provides services such as non-interest and interest-bearing checking, ATMs, savings, money market accounts, certificates of deposit, and individual retirement accounts. Superior is well known as "The Home of Totally Free Checking." Superior Federal also offers a full array of real estate, consumer, small business, and commercial loan products. And Superior Financial Services provides access to alternative investment products such as stocks, bonds, mutual funds, and annuities.

Superior Federal's Telephone Information System allows customers 24-hour access to their accounts via Superior Touch. Superior Online provides customers with the flexibility, security, and ease of Internet banking. Customers can view their accounts, review account activity, pay bills, transfer funds, pay loans, and perform other functions with the click of a mouse, any time, from anywhere.

As part of Superior Financial Corp., Superior Federal is the major component of a $1.4 billion financial institution with nearly $1.5 billion in deposits and more than $900 million in loans. Superior Financial Corp. is publicly traded under the symbol "SUFI."

Under the leadership of Chairman and CEO C. Stanley Bailey, President Marvin Scott, and Chief Financial Officer Rick Gardner, Superior Financial Corp. and Superior Federal Bank have established a goal to continue long-term growth and increase shareholder value by expanding operations, increasing product offerings, and enhancing services utilizing available new technology.

Superior Federal Bank is pleased to offer Tulsans and thousands of Oklahoma families and small businesses a wide range of banking products and services. Oklahoma banking customers turned-off by the mega mergers of large banks, can turn to Superior Federal, famous for local and personal service. At Superior Federal Bank, customers are more than just an account number, they are friends, neighbors, and long-term relationships built on trust and uncompromising service. Superior Federal is FDIC Insured and an Equal Housing Lender.

At Superior Federal Bank, understanding your need is our focus. ❖

SAMSON INVESTMENT COMPANY/CHARLES AND LYNN SCHUSTERMAN FAMILY FOUNDATION

Charles Schusterman adds an interesting twist to his responsibilities as the co-CEO of Samson. Well-respected for his ability to generate profits and create career opportunities for the hundreds of employees of this large Tulsa-based oil, gas, real estate, and industrial distribution enterprise, Schusterman is equally admired for what he contributes back to the community through his philanthropic work as president of the Schusterman Family Foundation.

The son of immigrants, Schusterman was only 19 when his father died. Determined to make it on his own, he earned a degree in petroleum engineering from The University of Oklahoma in 1958. After a tour in the Army, he returned to Tulsa and joined his brother in the oil field salvage and marginal oil business.

Charles founded Samson (the name reflects his pride in his father, Sam, and his sense of family) in 1971. Samson is engaged in the production, development, and exploration for oil and gas reserves in the United States, Canada, Russia, and Venezuela. Samson also acquires and operates producing properties, and ranks among the 30 largest independent oil and gas companies in the United States. A subsidiary, Samson Industrial, is a leading distributor of industrial goods along the Sunbelt. Samson also develops, acquires, and manages commercial real estate in the Sunbelt through Granite Properties, an entity founded by his daughter, Stacy Schusterman.

We provide resources that help people accomplish more than they would have otherwise.

Stacy Schusterman joined Charles at Samson in 1988. After rising through various positions, she and Charles currently share the newly created office of Co-CEO of Samson with Jack Schanck.

The Schusterman Family Foundation, established by Charles and Lynn Schusterman in 1987, represents the formalization of extensive, long-time involvement of the Tulsa couple in social, civic, and Jewish causes—locally, nationally, and internationally. The Foundation's assets exceed $100 million and its reputation as a leader in the philanthropic community continues to grow.

Locally, the Foundation contributes primarily to organizations and institutions that focus on education, children, and community service—groups such as the Oklahoma School of Science and Mathematics, University of Oklahoma, Parent Child Center, and Tulsa City-County Library.

"We provide resources that help people accomplish more than they would have otherwise," says Schusterman. "We target organizations and ideas that we believe will make a significant impact on society as a whole."

The Foundation also supports programs that enhance Jewish life in the United States, Israel, and the former Soviet Union. A special interest of the Foundation is facilitating exchanges between successful projects it supports in Oklahoma and in Israel. It has brought the Discovery Program (an educational initiative for children created by the Israel Arts and Sciences Academy in Jerusalem) to Oklahoma and has sent experts in the field of child abuse to Israel to help develop a comprehensive approach to child abuse similar to a program in Tulsa.

"Some people say service to others is the rent we pay for space on this planet," Lynn reflects. "We think helping others is the down payment we make to assure a safe, secure place for our children, grandchildren, and people everywhere."

BANK OF OKLAHOMA

Given its beginnings, it's no coincidence that Bank of Oklahoma is the state's leading commercial bank. It was founded in 1910 as Exchange National Bank of Tulsa, as a way to establish financing for Oklahoma's then-new oil industry. Even then, 85 years ago, the bank was helping enterprising businesses build their city and state.

Today, that commitment is still intact. Combining sophisticated, leading-edge products with the service and responsiveness of a community bank, BOk remains dedicated to helping businesses—both large and small—prosper.

Bank of Oklahoma's lending capabilities are complemented by a unique offering of cash management, international, and investment services, plus trust, brokerage, and insurance—products that are competitive with those of the nation's largest banks.

In fact, BOk remains the clear leader in a number of business lines. In addition to being Oklahoma's leading commercial lender and cash management provider, it's the state's leader in mortgage lending and has the state's top trust company. It runs one of the region's most expansive ATM networks. And, with Internet banking, supermarket banks open evenings and weekends, and the telephone ExpressBank—open 24 hours a day—BOk is easily the most convenient bank in Oklahoma.

Yet, beyond its leadership position in the banking industry, BOk's reach goes even further. Since the mid-'90s, Bank of Oklahoma and its parent company, BOK Financial Corp., have undergone dramatic change—growing from a local bank in one state, to a regional bank with operations in Oklahoma, Texas, Arkansas, New Mexico, Kansas, and Missouri.

The result? Bank of Oklahoma's growth has helped fuel Tulsa's growth, adding jobs and capital to an already growing city. The bank's employment in Oklahoma alone has more than doubled during the 1990s. Additional employment growth is anticipated in the future as the company continues expanding in Oklahoma and the surrounding states.

Having a successful regional banking company headquartered in Tulsa benefits the community, as well. Bank of Oklahoma has been generous in sharing its good fortune with its hometown, donating millions of dollars to local charities, education, and community events. BOk's employees have also contributed, volunteering thousands of hours in the communities where they live and work.

Through its commitment to service, Bank of Oklahoma is setting the standard in providing leadership—convenience, quality, sophistication, and community involvement—that Tulsa's consumers and businesses deserve. ✦

Bank of Oklahoma's supermarket banks have redefined convenience, staying open evenings and weekends.

BOk is one of Tulsa's leading corporate philanthropists.

13
Chapter Thirteen

PROFESSIONS

❧

Photo by Don Wheeler.

DOERNER, SAUNDERS, DANIEL & ANDERSON, L.L.P.

Doerner, Saunders, Daniel & Anderson, L.L.P., is Oklahoma's oldest and one of its most respected law firms. Since its founding in 1895, Doerner Saunders has provided creative and comprehensive representation for its clients. By understanding the myriad individual needs of each client and creating innovative solutions to sensitive problems, Doerner Saunders has earned a reputation of excellence unsurpassed in the southwest.

Throughout the history of the state, Doerner Saunders' attorneys have played an important role in the growth and expansion of Oklahoma's economy by representing the legal needs of its clients in virtually every form of transaction and every kind of litigation. Multinational corporations, energy producers and suppliers, the manufacturing and construction industries, the public sector, and individuals, all rely on Doerner Saunders' expertise. The Firm serves the needs of these traditional clients as well as the changing legal needs of the business community and emerging industries by constantly adapting to meet these challenges. The Firm's clients now also include members of the telecommunications, health care, and e-commerce industries.

At the center of Doerner Saunders' ability to provide the finest service to its clients is the talent, diversity, and professional character of its attorneys. The Firm's lawyers are distinguished graduates of more than 25 colleges and universities in 20 states and have received law degrees from 17 law schools. Many of the Firm's attorneys have also distinguished themselves by serving as clerks to federal court judges prior to joining the Firm. In addition, many lawyers who began their careers with Doerner Saunders have gone on to be federal appellate and trial court judges, or have left the practice of law to become successful business leaders in the private sector. The Firm also boasts more lawyers selected by their peers as among the Best Lawyers in America than any other law firm in the Tulsa area.

Areas of Practice

Doerner Saunders' lawyers engage in virtually every area of civil practice. Although the Firm is organized into specialized practice areas, which provides in-depth expertise in each area of the law, collaboration among the various practice areas ensures that clients receive comprehensive legal services. Offering an integrated and talented team of lawyers with expertise in a broad range of legal specialties, enables Doerner Saunders to approach each client's needs with the understanding, experience, and dedication that has earned it a reputation as one of the premier multi-disciplined law firms in the southwest.

With practice areas that include Corporate, Commercial and Securities Law, Litigation, Employment and Labor, ERISA and Benefits, Creditors' Rights, Tax, Estate Planning and Probate, Real Estate, Environmental Law, Health Care Law, Family Law, and Workers' Compensation, Doerner Saunders is second to none in the breadth of services it can offer its clients.

Clients have come to rely upon Doerner Saunders' business expertise in the formation of business entities, the structuring and closing of complex transactions, and the development of investment strategies. Doerner Saunders' trial lawyers have extensive experience in state and federal courts, locally and nationally, in litigation ranging from complex commercial matters to personal injury defense. The Firm also represents clients before state and federal administrative agencies and in both state and federal appellate courts. Employers throughout

Member of the Firm's transactional practice group include (left to right) **Elise Dunitz Brennan, H. Wayne Cooper, Varley H. Taylor, Jr., Robert A. Burk** and **Kevin C. Coutant.**

The firm is led by (left to right) **Lawrence T. Chambers, Jr., Sam P. Daniel, William C. Anderson, and G. Michael Lewis.**

the southwest turn to the Firm for assistance with a broad range of employment matters, labor relations, employee benefits, ERISA, and workers' compensation issues. Business and individual clients also look to the Firm for advice on environmental concerns, business restructuring, and estate planning.

A full staff of paralegals, legal clerks, accountants, legal secretaries, librarians, and computer network administrators allows the Firm's lawyers to respond quickly and accurately to clients' needs at any time. Its investment in technology also allows the Firm to serve the needs of clients requiring representation across the nation and around the world.

The Client Comes First

The Firm is guided by a simple philosophy—the client comes first. Doerner Saunders' ability to remain a growing and dynamic firm, while maintaining long-standing relationships with clients, is the direct result of its consistent commitment to place its clients' needs first. This commitment guides the Firm from the selective recruitment and hiring of attorneys to its day to day responses to clients' opportunities and needs. While much has changed since the Firm's founding over 100 years ago, Doerner Saunders' commitment to its clients has not.

Serving the Community

Service to the client includes service to the community. Throughout its history, Doerner Saunders has committed its leadership, talent, and resources to the growth and enrichment of the many communities it serves. Doerner Saunders lawyers have been elected to boards of directors of major national and international corporations, as well as local banks. Doerner Saunders' attorneys also serve as directors of many United Way agencies, including Family and Children's Services and American Red Cross, arts and cultural organizations such as Tulsa Ballet and Tulsa Philharmonic, and a variety of other education and

Members of the Firm's litigation practice group include (seated) Tom Q. Ferguson, Gary M. McDonald, Richard P. Hix and (standing) Linda C. Martin and Lewis N. Carter.

civic organizations. Firm attorneys also provide leadership to the American, Oklahoma, and Tulsa County Bar Associations, frequently lecture and contribute to legal and professional periodicals, and assist courts by serving as settlement judges, arbitrators, and mediators.

Serving the Future

For more than a century, Doerner Saunders has given creative legal advice and been an active partner with its clients in solving problems and capitalizing on opportunities in Tulsa, throughout Oklahoma, around the nation, and abroad. That legal experience, vision, and creativity are continuing to build and protect the Firm's clients as Doerner Saunders moves into its second century of practice.

As the new century begins, the context in which legal services are provided is changing rapidly. The local, regional, and global economy are undergoing rapid change, shifting from manufacturing to service and high technology. With over a century of exceptional service in virtually every area of legal practice, Doerner Saunders has and will continue to provide its clients with the expertise, versatility, and imagination needed to successfully meet the future. ✦

Members of the Firm's labor and employment practice group include (left to right) Lynn Paul Mattson, Michael C. Redman, Shelly L. Dalrymple, Kristen L. Brightmire, and Rebecca M. Fowler.

LITTLEFIELD, INC.

What do you call a business that begins in a bedroom in 1980, then two decades later moves into its own four-story building?
A company starting over.

A Philosophy That Works

Some people would be surprised by that answer—but not David Littlefield, founder and company president. In fact, he is proud of how the company that bears his name maintains an entrepreneurial spirit.

"My goal from day one was to have an agency that would be in step with business trends, not just knowledgeable about marketing," says Littlefield. "We continue to evolve because we're passionate about offering value to our clients."

This philosophy has helped the company grow from a one person start-up to a full-service marketing communications firm offering expertise in advertising, account planning, public relations, media buying, and e-business. By offering these various disciplines, the firm offers a holistic, integrated approach to marketing—not just "advertising-only" solutions.

Littlefield Inc. understands there is no magic formula for success in this business. What clients want from an agency is a group of honest, smart people who can deliver effective results, helping to build their clients' brands and businesses. The agency's promise is to deliver marketing insight and solutions with impeccable customer service.

The Littlefield staff stays in close contact with the client throughout the process to make sure they are delivering on this promise.

Insight Leads, Solutions Follow

Agencies all know the value of learning their clients' businesses. But even more valuable to Littlefield is learning their clients' customers. After all, understanding is at the heart of any good relationship, whether it's between you and your spouse or you and your customers.

Extensive research shows that customers make buying decisions emotionally, then justify the decision rationally. That's why part of Littlefield's initial research into a client's brand experience includes account planning. With account planning, the firm not only discovers how the customers think, it also learns about their hopes and dreams, their fears and doubts. By using this exercise, Littlefield can get closer to customers' hearts, as well as their heads.

Without a doubt, the account planning process is the cornerstone of Littlefield's strategic process. Headlines for ads and message points for PR efforts have come directly from the mouths of clients' customers during account planning. This creates an emotional

The unique use of metal as the cornice, coupled with the traditional materials of brick and sandstone set off the Italian architectural design of Littlefield, Inc.'s headquarters in Tulsa's newly renovated Uptown area.

connection you can't get by relying only on traditional research.

"Account planning is an eye-opening experience for the client, the agency, and the customer," Littlefield says. "Once the analysis is complete, the client and the Littlefield team are anxious to get to work because the information is so powerful and sets a clear direction for the marketing program."

Making the Connection

The outcome of account planning gives Littlefield's staff a litmus test for the strategies and messages developed for a campaign. Armed with this valuable insight, the company's talented, knowledgeable staff comes together as a team to build the right plan—which may or may not include their particular discipline.

"One of the many virtues I admire about our staff is their desire to do the right thing for the client," Littlefield says. "They're not territorial, but rather strategic when offering ideas, so in the end our clients benefit from the agency's collective expertise."

The firm understands that people are bombarded with marketing messages and have become adept at tuning them out. But the real reason why many messages are being tuned out is not because of volume, but because they are irrelevant to the intended audience.

That's why the Littlefield team views marketing from the perspective of the client's customer—how the customer receives the messages, processes the information, then makes a buying decision. The motivation to call for more information or tell a friend about a great product or service comes from a variety of sources.

The Littlefield approach to marketing means there are no isolated incidents. Each advertisement, each media story, each contact with a salesperson is designed to build a customer's affinity for a client's brand.

"Our philosophy and work ethic has attracted seasoned marketing pros from across the country who have helped build some of the world's best known brands," says Littlefield. "We have come together in a great city like Tulsa to create the kind of agency we would want as a partner."

Commitment to Tulsa

Littlefield contributes to the Tulsa community in a variety of ways. You'll find its people sitting on the boards of great civic organizations and volunteering their time to community service.

The agency donates its marketing expertise for campaigns that make an impact on the quality of life in Tulsa. The United Way, The Susan G. Komen Race for the Cure, Citizen CPR, Catholic Charities, and Big Brothers & Big Sisters are just a few of the outstanding groups Littlefield, Inc. has assisted on a pro bono basis.

Littlefield's staff of professional strategists and creative communicators gather in the building's atrium, which, much like the piazzas or squares of Italy, serves as the agency's social foundation.

"Community service is part of our culture, because we believe in helping our employees grow as people not just professionals," says Littlefield. "Our employees care for each other and this great city, which is evident by their willingness to get involved."

Probably the most significant commitment to Tulsa is the multimillion dollar renovated, former IBM Building—now known as the Littlefield Building—located at 13th and Boulder Avenue. David Littlefield's vision helped spark interest in reinvigorating the "Uptown Tulsa" district, which has seen two other major properties experience similar makeovers.

The building has become more than just a beautiful place to work. It also serves as a venue for community events and civic meetings. The excitement surrounding the building was evident during its grand opening party that attracted more than 400 clients, friends, and local dignitaries.

"Our new facility is another extension of our agency's philosophy," says Littlefield. "It encourages people to come in, share ideas, and learn from others so we all can be successful." ←

KPMG LLP

*K*PMG *is proudly part of one of the largest international accounting organizations creating "firsts" across the globe. The ingenuity and dynamics of the firm's programs set the standard for offices in Tulsa and around the world.*

Founding partners James Marwick and Roger Mitchell recognized the value of a public accounting firm's ability to serve the worldwide needs of its clients in 1897. To solidify the emphasis, a 1987 merger of Peat, Marwick, Mitchell & Copartners, and Klynveld Main Goerdeler created a global network known internationally as KPMG.

The Tulsa office was established in 1920 and presently exceeds 50 client service and client service support personnel. Gil Van Lunsen serves as the Tulsa office's managing partner. Other Tulsa partners include Lex Anderson, Bob Dennis, and Gary Smith.

Energy and the energy service industry is still an area of major emphasis for KPMG Tulsa, along with manufacturing, health care, and public services. The firm also serves clients in the communications and entertainment industries. While audits are generally not viewed as a "value-added" service, KPMG strives to provide clients with the unique insight it obtains from providing that service. "We use the knowledge we gain from an audit to suggest new ideas and approaches to assist clients in achieving their goals," says Van Lunsen.

Clients served by KPMG Tulsa are primarily headquartered in Tulsa and northeast Oklahoma. A number of the Tulsa staff have developed unique areas of expertise and are frequently called upon to provide services to KPMG clients around the world. This specialization component is a qualitative advantage of a firm that literally operates around the world. "Just as our Tulsa staff members frequently share their special expertise with other KPMG offices, we call upon specialized knowledge located in other offices to assist Tulsa clients with their unique issues," Van Lunsen says.

Notwithstanding the firm's global view, local KPMG offices never lose sight of their primary client base—or the communities in which they live and work. KPMG Tulsa and its employees are quite active in contributing time and resources to the Tulsa community, whether that is in supporting Tulsa's arts groups, United Way, or many youth-oriented organizations such as Big Brothers and Sisters and Junior Achievement. For example, the firm was recently awarded the prestigious "Council Oaks" award for volunteer services to the City of Tulsa.

KPMG and Tulsa have undergone a sea change in the eight decades they've shared, but change has been kind to both. Both recently celebrated 100-year birthdays. Auditing and accounting has been transformed by technology and Tulsa is no longer the Oil Capital, but both city and firm have continued to grow and thrive in a diversified new economy. ✦

Partners and Management Group, KPMG LLP, Tulsa.

McGivern, Gilliard & Curthoys

The law firm of McGivern, Gilliard & Curthoys, a 34-year veteran firm in the defense of insurance litigation, maintains a premier position in Tulsa and throughout Oklahoma representing corporate clients and insurance companies.

Originally the private practice of Paul V. McGivern Jr., the firm is now comprised of more than a dozen attorneys practicing in an array of legal fields, specializing in workers' compensation defense, general civil defense, labor law, intellectual property law, and appellate practice.

McGivern, Gilliard & Curthoys is rated "AV" by Martindale-Hubbell bar register. These ratings result from confidential questionnaires sent to other practicing attorneys and members of the judiciary. The "A" rating is the highest legal ability rating, while the "V" signifies very high adherence to professional standards of conduct, ethics reliability, and diligence, and is the highest ethical rating awarded by Martindale-Hubbell.

The firm's reputation and approach to law has garnered an extensive client base across Oklahoma as well as many national insurance companies. To better serve those clients who do business throughout the state, the firm also maintains a full-service office in Oklahoma City. This office, which is linked to the Tulsa office via a state-of-the-art telecommunications network, allows the firm to provide economical service to clients on a statewide basis.

McGivern, Gilliard & Curthoys Partners (left to right) **Paul V. McGivern, Jr., Owen T. Evans, Janet Dech, Karen McGivern Curthoys, Robert Fitz-Patrick, and Michael D. Gilliard.**

Serving the Legal Needs of Clients and the Community

In addition to the customary professional services extended by the firm, all attorneys at McGivern, Gilliard & Curthoys give generously of their expertise to the community. The firm periodically offers free symposia to its clients to discuss new legislation and recent appellate decisions affecting the clients' business interests. Often, the firm's attorneys counsel with insurance companies and corporations to offer suggestions to recurring problems identified through their professional representation.

The professional staff of McGivern, Gilliard & Curthoys also has been called upon by numerous agencies and organizations to provide speakers in all the disciplines practiced by the firm. These *pro grata* presentations are an important component of the law firm, gratefully made out of the firm's recognition of its public duty to advance the general practice of law and a dedication to educate the public in important legal principles.

Clear, consistent communication between attorney and clients is a hallmark of the service provided by McGivern, Gilliard & Curthoys. The firm also prepares a periodic mailing to its clients entitled "The Update," which reports cases of interest, including unpublished cases, notices, and rule changes. From time to time, supplements are forwarded whenever case law changes and there is a need to inform clients and group representatives of an important change in the law.

Through all of these ongoing efforts, the firm of McGivern, Gilliard & Curthoys continues its long tradition of serving clients and the public by offering a wealth of experience in the field of insurance defense litigation.

14
Chapter Fourteen

HEALTH CARE, EDUCATION, AND QUALITY OF LIFE

Photo by Don Wheeler.

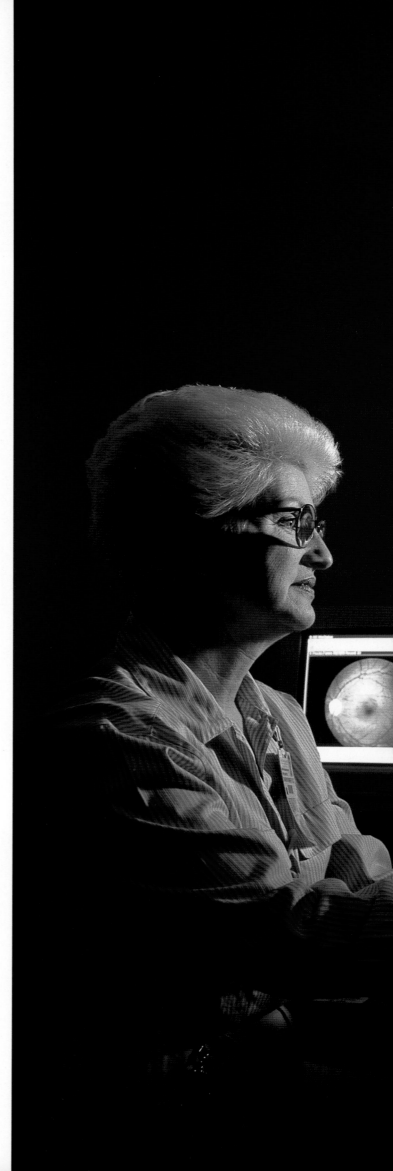

THE UNIVERSITY OF OKLAHOMA

Tulsa and the University of Oklahoma share a long history of mutual success. Since the university was founded in 1890, 17 years before Oklahoma's statehood, Tulsans have enrolled and graduated from OU's world class educational programs. The university's presence in Tulsa has consistently increased over recent years, making OU a vital component of the Tulsa community and the area's economy.

Former British Prime Minister Margaret Thatcher addresses OU's 1999 Foreign Policy Conference in Norman.

Ken Lackey, President of The University of Oklahoma—Tulsa, speaks at the announcement of the new OU Schusterman Health Sciences Center campus at 41ˢᵗ St. and Yale Ave. in Tulsa.

Since its inception, OU has had as its goal the higher education of the people of Oklahoma through quality programs. A tradition of excellence established at the end of the 19th century carries on under renewed dedication as OU offers its award-winning programs to students from around the world and boldly enters the 21st century.

The university, ranked first in the nation per capita among all public universities in the number of National Merit Scholars enrolled, is pushing the limits to offer students every opportunity to attain knowledge and improve their world. OU has the highest-academically ranked student body at a public university in the history of the state. The OU law school ranked number one among all Oklahoma law schools in overall bar exam passage rates. OU's MBA students rank in the top 18 percent nationally in GMAT scores. OU's School of Meteorology is ranked as one of the best in the world. And OU's student athletes shine academically, with more than half earning a 3.0 GPA or better.

OU's success has indeed been remarkable. Achievements in 20 colleges attended by almost 27,000 students rank the university among the best in the nation. Under the leadership of President David L. Boren, Oklahoma's former governor and U.S. senator, the University of Oklahoma is reaching for new heights that widen horizons for students and prepare them to live and compete in a global marketplace.

OU—Tulsa Connection

Currently, more than 1,700 students from the Tulsa area are enrolled at OU. Approximately 500 students from the area enroll as OU freshmen each year. More than 30 of the 200 National Merit Scholars who are enrolled as freshmen at OU are from the Tulsa area. The OU Club of Tulsa annually provides scholarships to five entering freshmen from Tulsa and one to the athletic department. And Tulsa County is home to more than 12,000 OU alumni.

Leading OU's efforts in Tulsa is Ken Lackey, former Chief of Staff for Oklahoma Governor Frank Keating, who serves as president of OU's Tulsa operations. Lackey, an active member of the Tulsa business community for 30 years, is a past chairman of the Metropolitan Tulsa Chamber of Commerce and past president of Flint Industries.

OU recently established an office of University Relations in Tulsa to serve as a liaison between the community and the offices for alumni, development, public affairs, and various colleges.

OU-Tulsa offers four undergraduate degree and 17 graduate degree programs to more than 700 Tulsa area students. OU holds an average of 70 classes in Tulsa each semester. To date, more than 1,200 students have graduated from OU programs in Tulsa.

OU-Tulsa is in the process of implementing five new master's programs and a Ph.D. program in Organizational Leadership in Tulsa. A branch of the university's renowned International Programs Center has been established. More than a dozen new resident faculty members will join OU-Tulsa in the coming years.

Research plays an important part in the success of OU. The university's Tulsa research capabilities were greatly enhanced in 1999 with the addition of the BP AMOCO Core Lab and Drilling Research Facility in mid-town Tulsa. Through a partnership with Sandia Corporation and the U.S. Department of Energy, research will be conducted in oil, gas, and geothermal energy development. The new Well Construction Technology Center will assist the medium and smaller energy-related Oklahoma businesses to compete in today's global marketplace.

University of Oklahoma Health Sciences Center-Tulsa

Teaching . . . Healing . . .Discovering. These have been the hallmarks of the University of Oklahoma Health Sciences Center-Tulsa since it was founded in 1974.

Many Tulsans, including many longtime residents, may not be aware of the vital role in our community fulfilled by the OU Health Sciences Center-Tulsa. In addition to the established tradition of educating first-class health professionals, the center provides needed medical services for thousands in the community. Established to meet the needs of Tulsa as a community-based medical school, the OU Health Sciences Center-Tulsa has become much more. The dynamic, growing institution carries out its mission of offering an uncompromising commitment to the community every day.

In the early 1970s, civic, business, and medical leaders acted upon a need within the community to locate a medical school in Tulsa. The Tulsa Medical Education Foundation was formed by a consortium of three teaching hospitals, Hillcrest Medical Center, Saint Francis Hospital, and St. John Medical Center, with that goal in mind. After the state Legislature approved the measure, a clinical branch of the University of Oklahoma College of Medicine, based in Oklahoma City, was established in Tulsa, and the first class began in 1974. In the following years, seven medical clinics were opened across the city to provide health care for thousands of Tulsa's citizens—including many who are medically needy.

In 1981, the University of Oklahoma moved administrative and academic offices and clinics to 2808 South Sheridan, where the main campus stands today. In 1989, the center's name was changed to the University of Oklahoma Health Sciences Center-Tulsa campus so that the colleges of Nursing and Public Health could create graduate programs in Tulsa. In 1998, the expansion of the Health Sciences Center continued as graduate programs in Pharmacy and Allied Health were added.

More than 825 medical students have completed their last two years of training and more than 700 physicians have fulfilled their residency requirements at the OU College of Medicine-Tulsa since it was founded. Their valuable role in our community is evident—more than 900 Tulsa graduates currently practice in Oklahoma. Each year, approximately 75 third and fourth-year medical students enroll in the medical school and approximately 160 resident physicians contract to fulfill practice requirements. Upon completion of their residency education at the Tulsa area clinics and teaching hospitals, a majority of these students become practicing physicians in Tulsa, northeast Oklahoma, and across the state. More than two-thirds of Oklahoma's physicians are graduates of the OU College of Medicine.

Medicine, nursing, pharmacy, public health, and allied health education has grown in Tulsa. Approximately 500 graduate students are enrolled in these five colleges in Tulsa. Approximately 100 full-time and more than 800 volunteer faculty provide instruction to those attending the OU Health Sciences Center-Tulsa.

The quality of education provided by the OU College of Medicine consistently ranks the system among those Top 20 Medical Schools in the nation balancing both primary care and research as reported by *U.S. News & World Report.* The Tulsa campus is an important

David L. Boren, President, The University of Oklahoma.

part of Oklahoma's response to the need to educate tomorrow's health care professionals.

The nine teaching clinics operated by OU Health Sciences Center-Tulsa comprise one of Tulsa's largest outpatient networks, providing services for 115,000 patient visits annually. The clinics focus on adult medicine, family medicine, health awareness, pediatrics and adolescent medicine, psychiatry, surgery, and women's health. OU students, resident physicians, and faculty also volunteer to provide medical services at the

Tulsa Day Center for the Homeless, Project Get Together, and other nonprofit community agencies serving those in need throughout the area.

A faculty and resident physician with the OU Health Sciences Center visit with a patient.

The Children's Justice Center, operated in conjunction with the Child Abuse Network, is located on the OU Health Sciences Center-Tulsa campus. This innovative center serves as a national model in the evaluation and treatment of child abuse and is designated as a Center of Excellence by the OU Board of Regents.

The Tulsa Health Sciences Center campus emphasizes research in the areas of pharmaceutical and medical devices, health care outcomes, health care education, and basic research. All students, residents and faculty pursue interests most compatible with their career goals and collaborate with scientists and programs at other institutions in Tulsa.

OU Health Sciences Center faculty physicians teach in small groups.

The OU Health Sciences Center-Tulsa will continue to play a vital role in the provision of health care in Tulsa and northeastern Oklahoma for years to come. In 1998, the OU Board of Regents underscored the university's commitment to health care, education, and research by approving a $55 million campus master plan that will double the size of the OU Health Sciences Center-Tulsa campus to approximately 30 acres. The five-year plan will bring all OU Health Sciences Center-Tulsa operations onto one campus with four new buildings constructed to replace current facilities.

The OU Health Sciences Center-Tulsa stays on the leading edge of health care education and services including programs in rural health education, international studies in medicine, and distance learning. Six years ago under the direction of Dean Harold Brooks, the OU Health Sciences Center-Tulsa launched a $25 million endowment campaign. We are already at $21 million with two years to go. The commitment of the students, residents, faculty, and leadership of the University of Oklahoma and the OU Health Sciences Center-Tulsa is teaching, healing, and discovering—the keys to our community's growth, health, and prosperity.

The OU Health Sciences Center-Tulsa is a vital component in the health care and health care education for the citizens in Tulsa and in northeast Oklahoma. It is a shining example of the uncompromising commitment to excellence shared by all in our community.

Future Growth

Tulsa will continue to play an important role in the future of the University of Oklahoma. Along with the growth of the OU-OSU Research and Graduate Education Center and OU Health Sciences Center-Tulsa, OU is well connected to the Tulsa area through programs such as the National Resource Center for Youth Services, the Oklahoma Geological Survey Observatory, and the Sutton Avian Research Center. OU is also moving forward with initiatives to offer on-location research and education to private companies in the Tulsa area, and the OU Office of Technology Development is serving as a contact point for private businesses in a number of enterprises.

Tulsa area alumni and donors have contributed a significant amount to OU, reaching and surpassing the goal of the Reach for Excellence fund-raising campaign. With an initial goal of raising $200 million by 2000, the campaign total is already an impressive $385 million. OU now ranks in the top 20 public universities in the nation in private endowment, the first state university to reach such levels of giving.

This fund-raising growth has spurred additional OU developments

OU's campuses are the focus of dramatic beautification projects. The South Oval gardens are among the landscaping highlights on the Norman campus.

that will benefit Tulsa and all Oklahomans. OU ranks first among Big 12 universities in research funding growth and is working with Oklahoma businesses in efforts that will benefit society and create new jobs. The $44 million Sam Noble Oklahoma Museum of Natural History, the largest natural history museum in the world associated with a university, will open in 2000. Work was recently completed on the Catlett Music Center, which features one of the finest concert halls in the Southwest. The Barry Switzer Center, a multi-purpose facility that takes OU's athletic facilities to a new level, opened in 1999.

The University of Oklahoma, like the Tulsa area, has experienced incredible growth in recent years. As the economy has diversified and as Oklahomans compete in a global economy, OU and Tulsa are poised to capitalize on a dynamic future filled with unlimited possibilities. Built on the belief that all things are possible through quality education, OU will continue to partner with Tulsa, the state of Oklahoma, and the world to open the world of possibilities for every student. ✦

Tulsa students in the College of Allied Health use the latest distance learning technologies.

Harold L. Brooks, M.D., Dean, OU College of Medicine—Tulsa.

BLUE CROSS AND BLUE SHIELD OF OKLAHOMA

ixty years. That's how long Blue Cross and Blue Shield of Oklahoma has been a leader in private health insurance in Oklahoma. Sixty years is a long time in the history of Oklahoma and the lives of those served. Times have changed, but the commitment of Oklahomans providing quality health insurance and outstanding personal service to fellow Oklahomans has remained consistent.

Ron King, President and Chief Executive Officer, Blue Cross and Blue Shield of Oklahoma.

A Strong Beginning

It all started in 1940, when civic and medical leaders in Oklahoma joined together to start one of the nation's first Blue Cross prepaid hospital plans. They needed at least $10,000. Leaders in Tulsa and Oklahoma City challenged each other—the first community to raise $5,000 would be the headquarters for the new organization. Tulsa won and became the home of Group Health Service, the forerunner of Blue Cross and Blue Shield of Oklahoma.

Today, nearly 450,000 Oklahomans are members of Blue Cross and Blue Shield of Oklahoma health insurance plans—nearly 20 percent of the state's population. The Tulsa headquarters, now employs more than 1,000 employees, and Blue Cross and Blue Shield is proud to be a corporate leader in Tulsa, just as it is in every Oklahoma community it serves.

Working for a Healthier Oklahoma

There was a time when health insurance simply protected members from unexpected health expenses. But the changing role of private health insurance has allowed Blue Cross and Blue Shield of Oklahoma to offer innovative programs and services for individuals, employee groups of all sizes, and seniors. Programs range from traditional coverage to preferred provider organization plans to BlueLincs Health Maintenance Organization, which offers the finest in managed care plans.

Blue Cross and Blue Shield of Oklahoma is committed to keeping the cost of benefits down through a number of creative programs, including:
- Preventive Care—encouraging members to be proactive with their health by getting children immunized, having women's mammograms, and other preventive measures.

- Health and Wellness—educating members about the benefits of staying healthy through classes, newsletters, and other helpful programs.
- Health Management—early identification of chronic conditions like diabetes and asthma, along with comprehensive resources encouraging self-care and regular medical care, improve the quality of life for many members.

Blue Cross and Blue Shield of Oklahoma's extensive networks of doctors, hospitals, and other health care professionals provide cost-effective, statewide access to health care.

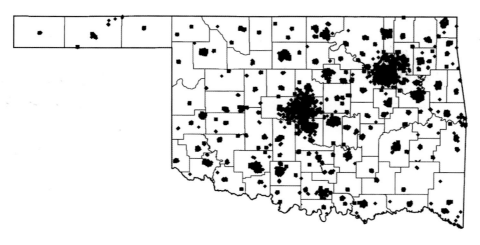

Enhancing Service for Members Through Technology

Employee group leaders and participating health care providers now have 24-hour secured Internet access to Blue Cross and Blue Shield and BlueLincs member eligibility information. Physicians, hospitals, and other health care providers now may also use the Internet site to determine which services are covered and how to bill for those services.

Finding a health care provider is also easier and more convenient for members. The company's website has the most current provider directories and is available around the clock.

Touching the Community

Blue Cross and Blue Shield's role has expanded dramatically over the years, but the uncompromising commitment to caring and personal service remains the same. As it encourages members to live healthier lives and actively participate in health care decisions, it has increased the opportunities to touch the lives of Oklahomans in the communities it serves. Blue Cross and Blue Shield has placed an added emphasis on community outreach and developed a number of exciting programs and services.

Blue Cross and Blue Shield of Oklahoma introduced the Caring Program for Children in 1995, to help families access quality health care for their children. The dynamic program benefits families of the working poor who earn too much to qualify for public assistance but not enough to afford health benefits for their families. Children in these families may see doctors for illnesses and receive regular checkups and immunizations to stay healthy. Approximately 2,000 Oklahoma children have benefited from the Caring Program for Children.

Screening for vision, high blood pressure, glaucoma, hearing, and other possible health problems has become more convenient in Oklahoma thanks to the Mobile Health Screening Unit. This ground-breaking joint venture between Blue Cross and Blue Shield of Oklahoma and Oklahoma Lions Clubs travels our state screening Oklahomans of all ages. The 30-foot mobile unit is colorfully decorated with scenes of Oklahoma history and is a popular attraction wherever it goes. Several thousand Oklahomans receive screenings in the unit each year.

Caring for the community is a hallmark of Blue Cross and Blue Shield. Giving back to the community is a point of pride and nowhere is this more evident than its involvement with the United Way. Blue Cross and Blue Shield of Oklahoma is a strong corporate supporter of the Tulsa Area United Way. Employees dedicate countless hours and personal resources to supporting the United Way's fundraising efforts.

In August 1999, the Caring Foundation launched its first Caring Van in the Tulsa area, providing free immunizations at child care centers. In the near future, a fleet of Caring Vans will provide immunizations in other communities in the state.

A Total Source

Blue Cross and Blue Shield of Oklahoma is a total source for benefits. Just as its role has evolved in the past 60 years, so too has its ability to offer solutions to individuals and group members. In addition to health insurance programs, Blue Cross and Blue Shield of Oklahoma, with its subsidiary companies Member Service Life Insurance, BlueLincs HMO, and GHS Property and Casualty, can offer individuals and companies of all sizes disability, life, Section 125, workers' compensation, auto, home, and other personal property and casualty insurance. Blue Cross and Blue Shield of Oklahoma has reduced administration costs, provided personalized customer service, and simplified benefits plans for thousands of Oklahomans. ❖

Blue Cross and Blue Shield of Oklahoma hosted the *Caring for the Human Spirit Tour* in Tulsa. The event included a mini-triathlon, health fair, and nutrition center—bringing the spirit of the Olympic Games home for Oklahomans.

The Caring Van provides free immunization for Tulsa-area children.

HILLCREST HEALTHCARE SYSTEM

Hillcrest HealthCare System's (HHS) growth has been remarkable by all standards. The organization's expansion in recent years, with the opening of SouthCrest Hospital in southeast Tulsa and the acquisition of Tulsa Regional Medical Center, Doctors Hospital, Specialty Hospital, and other healthcare facilities and physician groups, has set the pace and established a new standard in growth. Today, HHS provides quality healthcare for thousands of people in communities throughout Eastern Oklahoma and surrounding states.

Tulsa Regional Medical Center, located in the heart of downtown Tulsa, is a teaching hospital for the medical residents of Oklahoma State University College of Osteopathic Medicine.

There are countless reasons for this incredible expansion. From visionary leadership, to dedicated and caring employees, to a commitment to utilize the very latest in medical technology, HHS is a pioneer in healthcare in Eastern Oklahoma. But perhaps no reason is more important than a commitment to quality service and care which was established more than 80 years ago and is still carried on today.

Hillcrest HealthCare System

Hillcrest HealthCare System is Oklahoma's largest nonprofit, nonsectarian healthcare system, offering the services of more than 2,000 physicians, 16 acute hospitals, 48 primary care offices, 58 specialty clinics, and more than 7,200 employees. The organization is the preferred urban healthcare system for nearly 50 regional hospitals in communities through eastern Oklahoma. HHS provides acute care and specialty services previously unavailable in these communities.

Hillcrest Medical Center(HMC) is Tulsa's oldest and most established hospital; it is a 495-bed, non-governmental, not-for-profit, community-owned hospital. HMC provides a full range of diagnostic and therapeutic services for a population in excess of 1.4 million. HMC offers many specialized services including the Alexander Burn Center, Helmerich Cancer Center, Leta M. Chapman Breast Health Center and Prosthesis Salon, and the William H. Bell Heart and Lung Institute.

Kaiser Medical Center is a 112-bed hospital dedicated to providing comprehensive rehabilitative, behavioral ,and extended care services.

Children's Medical Center offers mental health, rehabilitation, and specialty pediatric services to children throughout eastern Oklahoma.

Tulsa Regional Medical Center is a nationally recognized osteopathic, acute care hospital. A close relationship with the Oklahoma State University College of Osteopathic Medicine allows this teaching hospital to provide its patients with many of the most advanced medical treatments and procedures.

Doctors Hospital is an acute care hospital that offers many senior inpatient and outpatient programs including health clinics and behavioral services. It also houses the adult and pediatric after-hour clinics.

Specialty Hospital is a unique long-term care facility. This hospital has a specialized intensive care and rehabilitation unit.

SouthCrest Hospital, which opened in May 1999, is a 153-bed acute care facility located in south Tulsa. SouthCrest is positioned to meet the needs of southeast Tulsa and Broken Arrow, two areas that have seen an explosion in population and that continue to lead metropolitan area development.

(Opposite page, top) Kaiser Medical Center opened in 1972 and it houses a unique community village, Zink Village, which allows patients to experience everyday activities such as banking, gardening and grocery shopping.

(Opposite page, bottom) Hillcrest Medical Center, which opened its doors in 1916, is a comprehensive, acute care hospital located five minutes from downtown Tulsa.

Hillcrest Medical Group and *Capstone Medical Group* joined to create the area's largest physician group. The comprehensive group has more than 100 primary care and specialty physicians offering a wide range of medical care options including family practice, internal medicine, pediatrics, dermatology, gastroenterology, neurology, rheumatology, urology, and ophthalmology.

Other HHS Tulsa metropolitan services include:

H.A. Chapman Institute for Medical Genetics—an internationally recognized center for clinical, diagnostic, and research genetics.

Tulsa Center for Fertility and Women's Health—the region's only comprehensive center providing specialized gynecology and fertility treatments with an in vitro fertilization success rate of more than 50 percent.

AirEvac of Tulsa—offers both air and ground intensive care services to residents in Tulsa and outlying communities. AirEvac features the state-of-the-art Sikorsky S-76C+ helicopter.

Community Partnerships

HHS was founded with a dedication to community involvement. Partnerships have been forged with schools, businesses, social service agencies, neighborhood groups, and other healthcare providers to continue this tradition. The goal of these relationships is to improve the health status and quality of life in every community HHS serves by working to make each community stronger. Whether developing mentoring programs for area students, adopting local elementary schools, volunteering for community projects, or providing funds for needed services, HHS plays a leadership role in the communities it serves.

The role of volunteers can not be emphasized enough at HHS. From the hundreds of hospital volunteers who provide vital patient services to employees volunteering on behalf of the Tulsa Area United Way, community service through volunteerism is a HHS priority.

Hillcrest HealthCare System's Future

Much has been said and written about the changes healthcare has seen and will see in the new millennium. Terms such as managed care, patient bill of rights, and primary care have become key words in the healthcare lexicon. HHS has led the way in marching toward progress and providing cutting edge care in Eastern Oklahoma.

The key to their incredible growth, especially in recent years, is a commitment to service, excellence, and leadership. Quality service has been the hallmark of HHS.

Whatever the future of healthcare may bring for Tulsa and Eastern Oklahoma, HHS will remain dedicated to a mission, and vision, based on service. ✧

OKLAHOMA STATE UNIVERSITY

Oklahoma State University and Tulsa have shared a unique history of teamwork and collaboration to create a better state and a brighter future.

This collaboration entered into an historic new realm in January 1999 when OSU assumed responsibility for the operations of OSU-Tulsa, formerly the University Center at Tulsa. The leadership of Tulsa's business and civic community worked to bring the highest quality public higher education to Tulsa. Now, OSU-Tulsa is a key player among the state's higher education institutions.

As the newest part of the OSU System, which includes facilities and resources across the state, OSU-Tulsa is poised to meet the public higher education needs of the Tulsa community. An aggressive 20-year plan to have 20,000 students enrolled by the year 2020 will require virtually constant expansion of services, programs, and facilities to meet the changing needs of business and industry in northeast Oklahoma.

Located just north of Tulsa's downtown business center in the historic Greenwood District, OSU-Tulsa is positioned to team with area business enterprises to offer new and exciting programs which meet the changing needs of the business landscape. OSU-Tulsa will also play a key role as a public partner in the economic, social, and cultural growth of the community.

Impressive Resources

From its beginning as the state's comprehensive land-grant university, Oklahoma State University has been among the nation's finest examples of collaboration between education and business. OSU has prepared students, from coeds to corporate professionals, to excel in life. OSU students hail from every county in Oklahoma, every state in the nation and nearly 100 countries.

With campuses in Stillwater, Tulsa, Oklahoma City, and Oklmulgee, and 66 county offices, 12 research stations, and 30 telecommunications sites, OSU's reach is impressive. OSU offers nearly 200 majors and is noted for nationally ranked programs in accounting, business administration, animal science, mathematics, chemistry, engineering, and hospitality management.

OSU meets the education needs of students at virtually every level of higher education by offering comprehensive resources. The main campus in Stillwater offers educational opportunities to more than 20,000 students. OSU-Okmulgee is a premier vocational-technical facility. Medical students from around the world attend OSU College of Osteopathic Medicine in Tulsa to become physicians. And OSU's Oklahoma City Branch provides thousands of students each year the opportunity to complete the first two years of their undergraduate studies.

Cutting-edge Research

OSU-Tulsa's new and developing research facilities join the OSU System's cutting-edge, world-renowned research capabilities. OSU's research in the areas of telecommunications, biomedicine, natural resource preservation, and product processing produces results for Oklahoma business and assists in the creation of new high-tech, high-paying jobs.

OSU teamed with Southwestern Bell, American Airlines, and Williams to bring engineering, computer, and business experience into the successful master of telecommunications program at OSU-Tulsa, preparing students for this rapidly expanding industry.

The OSU Center for Laser and Photonics Research ranks among the best in the world. OSU operates the state's only 600-MHz, high-field, nuclear magnetic resonance spectrometer, which is critical in biomedical and agriculture research. The Advanced Technology Research Center at OSU offers 165,000-square-feet of research space for the state's technology-based companies. The Food & Agricultural Products Center is developing Oklahoma's capabilities in adding value to food and raw materials through processing. And OSU delivers more than 200 business services through XTRA—eXtending Technology, Research, and Assistance.

Leadership and Teamwork

OSU-Tulsa, working with area business leaders, has identified course programs to offer and expand in the coming years. These will include many more undergraduate programs after July 2001, when all undergraduate degrees offered at OSU-Tulsa will be OSU degrees. This will require much work and increased funding through the state legislature and private sources.

The Metropolitan Tulsa Chamber of Commerce predicts the need for nearly 6,500 college-educated workers in the area within the next five years. OSU-Tulsa is working with area employers to create dynamic new methods to educate employees. New methods include distance learning, Internet-based course work, and on-site education. OSU is at the forefront of these new education technologies.

To meet the needs of every employer and every student, OSU-Tulsa has teamed with area higher education institutions to offer seamless education opportunities. The 2+2 initiative combining OSU-Tulsa with Tulsa Community College will allow Tulsa area students to follow an education track from their freshmen year, through upper division courses and graduate work. OSU and Tulsa Technology Center are developing similar education tracks.

Graduate programs and research are coordinated through the OU/OSU Research and Graduate Education Center.

Vision

The year is 2020. OSU-Tulsa is a thriving institution serving the higher education needs of more than 20,000 students and graduating nearly 4,000 students each year. The campus has expanded in size to allow for the addition of research, classroom, and housing facilities. The students and faculty of OSU-Tulsa fuel a flourishing downtown entertainment district. And more than 100,000 Tulsans participate in non-degree professional development programs and special events on campus each year. OSU-Tulsa is well on its way to becoming one of the nation's great urban universities.

This is the vision for OSU-Tulsa. Through the hard work of business, education, and community leaders, this vision will become reality. Tulsans in generations to come will look back on this time in the history in the community and remark how much was accomplished through dedication and determination.

OSU-Tulsa is the university of the future—Tulsa's future. ❖

OSU-Stillwater's 2 million volume research library.

The OSU-Tulsa vision-20,000 students by the year 2020.

ORAL ROBERTS UNIVERSITY

"Oral Roberts University is designed to be a different academic institution,"
President Richard Roberts points out proudly. And ORU is, indeed, unique.

Today, President Richard Roberts leads ORU and the largest student population in the University's history.

ORU was created in 1963 on the faith of its founder, evangelist Oral Roberts, who built this world-renowned university on one unwavering mission—to graduate integrated persons: spiritually alive, intellectually alert, and physically disciplined. Forty years later the world may have changed dramatically, but that vital spark and spirit that was the heart of ORU's founding remains as bright and strong as when ground was first broken for this south Tulsa institution.

Today the university serves more than 5,000 students enrolled in degree or continuing education programs, coming from all 50 states and 47 foreign countries. In fact, 63 percent of its students are from outside Oklahoma and represent 40 different religious denominations. The one thing they all have in common is the ability to see in ORU the promise of an extraordinary educational adventure.

Richard Roberts, son of the founder, Oral Roberts, became president of ORU in 1993. Although he was a part of his father's international evangelistic program beginning early in his life and continues to host, with his wife Lindsay, a nightly live television program, his selection to fill that enormous role may have been one of the wisest in the university's history. In Richard Roberts' first six years as president, enrollment has gone up by more than 60 percent. On-campus dorms are nearing capacity, and renovation of the school's 24 famous futuristic buildings, spread over a campus of 263 acres, are just some of the visible signs that Roberts is taking the university to new heights.

Past and present presidents— Richard and Oral Roberts.

"God opened a door for me a few years ago," Roberts says. "I'm grateful and thankful for my father, who has built a tremendous base."

Mind, Body, and Spirit

According to Roberts, ORU was built with the purpose of training students in Mind, Body, and Spirit to develop the whole person.

Indicative of the effectiveness of the ORU intellectual, spiritual, and physical regimen are these figures: its graduates have an 80 percent acceptance rate at graduate schools across the country; and at law schools the acceptance rate for ORU graduates is 90 percent. Graduates of ORU's Mass Media Communications program are highly sought after by major networks and production studios.

Oral Roberts University is accredited by the North Central Association of Colleges and Schools and offers 67 undergraduate majors, 10 master's degrees, and two doctoral degrees. In addition, its schools of Music, Nursing, Theology and Missions, and Education hold national and regional accreditation, as do its Social Work and Engineering Departments.

Because of the changing face of education, ORU offers a number of delivery options for delivering that quality education. In addition to the full-time residential students, ORU has a large population of "adult learners" living across the country and overseas. To meet this need, ORU offers a wide choice of distance education programs via mail and the Internet. As the on-campus population continues to grow, school officials have set a 10,000-student goal for the near future—5,500 students on campus, 4,500 off campus.

ORU students engage in a program to produce a high level of fitness and health as well. For many who make up the NCAA Division I Golden Eagles sports teams at ORU, the expectations are higher. In its first two years as a member of the Mid-Continent conference, ORU has captured 15 conference championships, and made NCAA post-season appearances in women's volleyball, tennis, and basketball, and men's baseball, and track and field.

And finally, ORU helps its students to succeed in whatever discipline they choose and to be effective witnesses for Christ. In the summer, hundreds of students travel the world as part of ORU's missions program. During the school year, students are active in all parts of the community through volunteering at over 40 different organizations, as well as being involved in numerous music ministries and churches.

"ORU is a university designed to prepare you to be a top individual in whatever field you decide to enter," says Roberts. "And we're seeing the results—in business, education, ministry, everywhere our students are. Our graduates are making an impact."

Staying the Course

A university with ORU's mission must be independent to survive and grow. Its curriculum, though clearly capable of producing graduates strongly competitive in any field, is distinguished by nuances that public universities would not dare invoke and that many other private schools no longer enforce. The ORU administration believes they are the subtleties that set ORU apart and that mark its graduates for distinction in the after-college world.

These differences, combined with demanding admission standards, high intellectual expectations, and the spiritual commitment that accompany them, create an atmosphere that draws students to ORU for a one-of-a-kind college experience, one that will have an effect on them for the rest of their lives.

For all the success the University has enjoyed under his leadership, Roberts is determined to make sure ORU continues its original course.

"My father was, and is, a visionary and a builder," Richard Roberts says. "While I have some visions and dreams of my own for the university, my calling is to see ORU stay true to its founding purpose. We're continually re-examining our values to make sure we're in harmony with how the university was founded. We may change methods, but we will not change the principles behind them." ❖

 The $250 million dollar campus encompasses 263 acres of rolling hills in south Tulsa.

THE UNIVERSITY OF TULSA

"We are what we repeatedly do. Excellence, then, is not an act, but a habit."

Aristotle

University of Tulsa senior Starr Horne is a chemistry whiz, a community volunteer, and a class leader. In 1998, as a sophomore, he won a Goldwater Scholarship. In 1999, as a junior, he won a Truman Scholarship. When he graduates from TU in 2000, he is bound for graduate school and a career as a chemistry professor with a focus on public policy and chemical and biological terrorism.

In the meantime, Starr is teaching atomic structure to first graders at a Tulsa elementary school. The program he developed bears his name "Starr Science," and he is busy writing a textbook to support the curriculum.

No doubt this University of Tulsa student is a star, and TU is proud to be the school that encouraged him to shine.

Individual attention has long been a strength at TU, where small classes and close faculty interaction encourage students to reach for the stars. This commitment to cultivating excellence has garnered impressive results.

In the past five years, TU has produced 15 Goldwater Scholars—plus the recipients of seven National Science Foundation Awards, three Truman Scholarships, three Department of Defense Fellowships, four Fulbright Fellowships, and two British Marshall Scholarships, the first of which was the first Marshall Scholarship awarded in Oklahoma in 27 years.

"We are proud that these young scholars have chosen to call The University of Tulsa home," says TU President Bob Lawless. "The accomplishments of our national scholarship winners are a testament to what sets TU apart—a commitment to the individual attention that fosters excellence."

Continuing the Legacy

The University of Tulsa is a private, comprehensive, doctoral-degree-granting university affiliated with the Presbyterian Church (USA). TU provides a personal education for each of its nearly 4,200 students. With a low student-to-faculty ratio of 11 to 1, an average undergraduate class size of 20, a distinguished faculty, the extensive resources of a residential campus, and the excitement of NCAA Division I athletics, The University of Tulsa is ranked among the top 150 national universities out of the 1,400 colleges and universities surveyed by *U.S. News & World Report*.

Situated on a 200-acre campus in the heart of Tulsa, the university traces its roots to Indian Territory, where the school was founded more than 100 years ago as a mission school for Indian girls. From these territorial roots grew Henry Kendall College, a Presbyterian-affiliated school that moved from Muskogee to Tulsa in 1907, in the early days of the oil boom.

Renamed The University of Tulsa in 1920, the school established its course early in the city's history thanks to the pioneer oilmen and civic leaders who were determined that their boomtown should have an institution of higher education.

The university flourished with the city, and through a series of trusts established by Tulsa families, TU has attracted a distinguished faculty, created a residential campus, established a national reputation, and built an endowment that ranks among the 60 largest college and university endowments in the United States. This firm footing is a testament to the generosity of the Tulsa civic leaders whose names grace many of the buildings across campus.

Cultivating Academic Excellence

At the heart of The University of Tulsa's reputation for academic excellence is the Tulsa Curriculum, a nationally recognized foundation of study. In addition to instilling a core knowledge of the sciences, humanities, and arts in all undergraduates, the Tulsa Curriculum teaches students to think critically and communicate clearly.

"We believe there is a foundation of knowledge all students should acquire, whether they choose to study biology or business," says

President Lawless. "The ability to reason, write, and communicate is a crucial career and life skill in any field of endeavor."

Just as the Tulsa Curriculum has received recognition for its emphasis on "the basics," so TU faculty members have won acclaim for their commitment to teaching.

There is no higher honor in college teaching than the Professor of the Year Award bestowed by the Carnegie Foundation for the Advancement of Teaching. In 1998, University of Tulsa Professor Sujeet Shenoi received this award, selected from a field of distinguished candidates at research and doctoral universities nationwide. Professor Shenoi is the only Oklahoma educator ever to be so recognized.

The Carnegie Foundation recognized Shenoi, a professor of computer science, for his "extraordinary dedication to undergraduate teaching, commitment to students, and innovative teaching methods." In particular, the foundation was referring to the Tulsa Undergraduate Research Challenge (TURC), a program Shenoi founded at TU in 1992.

Today, many of the students in the TURC program—such as Starr Horne—are winning national recognition for their scholarship and leadership. There is perhaps no greater example of this achievement than this fact: In the past five years, The University of Tulsa, MIT, and Stanford produced an equal number of Goldwater Scholars, tying for seventh place in the nation.

"These national honors awarded both to faculty and students testify to The University of Tulsa's academic excellence," says President Lawless. "There is no stronger proof that a distinguished faculty working closely with talented young students produces the scholars and leaders of tomorrow."

Looking to the Future

Although The University of Tulsa's international reputation in engineering—particularly petroleum engineering—has been one of its enduring legacies, the university also is known today for outstanding programs in arts and sciences, business administration, engineering and natural sciences, and law.

In 1999, internationally acclaimed writer V.S. Naipaul visited The University of Tulsa to conduct research in his literary archive, which

has been housed in McFarlin Library's Special Collections since 1995. Naipaul is one of many distinguished writers, including James Joyce and Jean Rhys, whose papers are part of the permanent holdings in Special Collections.

In addition to its strength in 20th-century literature, the university offers innovations such as its new master's degree in museum anthropology, the result of a partnership with Gilcrease Museum. This collaboration unites the vast resources of the museum and TU's nationally known anthropology faculty.

Although cultivating the life of the mind remains The University of Tulsa's primary mission, the university also provides students with a well-rounded residential campus experience.

In 1998 The University of Tulsa dedicated its $28-million Donald W. Reynolds Center, home to Golden Hurricane NCAA Division I athletics, as well as to academic programs in athletic training and sports medicine.

Across campus, The University of Tulsa College of Law will dedicate its new Mabee Legal Information Center in March 2000. This $11.6-million facility is equipped with "smart" classrooms, more than 200 wired study spaces, and research resources serving students, alumni, legal professionals, and the greater community.

Finally, on the west side of campus, work is under way on a major development that will include track and soccer fields, an intramural football field, a women's softball facility, a tennis center, and a student recreation center.

The expansion evident across campus owes much to the alumni, supporters, foundations, corporations, and city leaders who have given generously of their time, money, and talent. Among many examples of this generosity, one stands out: The University of Tulsa's five-year New Century Campaign. This centennial "celebration" raised a record $108.5 million for the university and set the strategic course for The University of Tulsa's next 100 years and beyond. ✦

"Starr Science," taught by 1999 Truman Scholar Starr Horne, was one of the children's favorite classes at Saints Peter and Paul School in Tulsa.

The university's $28-million Donald W. Reynolds Center provides a home court advantage for Golden Hurricane athletics and a showcase for commencement, concerts, and other campus and community events.

CANCER CARE ASSOCIATES

People with cancer deserve access to high quality care, interdisciplinary oncology specialists, the latest drugs available, and the opportunity to participate in clinical trials...

William D. Burleson, M.D., (left), radiation oncologist at the Mingo Valley Campus, and Demetri Ingram, dosimetrist, (right), treat patients with a linear accelerator, which precisely targets cancerous tumors with high velocity X-rays and electrons to stop the spread of cancer.

The 3-D treatment planning systems at Cancer Care Associates' three radiation facilities reconstruct the exact dimensional shape of a patient's tumor, enabling radiation teams to plan treatment fields. The system ensures full coverage of a patient's tumor while sparing normal healthy tissue.

For the last 25 years, Cancer Care Associates has delivered that care with determination and compassion to their patients and families, providing the best, most advanced treatments and therapies available.

Cancer Care Associates has grown from the sole practice of Dr. George Schnetzer III in Tulsa into a statewide network of more than 40 board-certified physicians, specially trained in Hematology, Medical Oncology, Radiation Oncology, and Gynecologic Oncology Surgery.

Whether it's applying the most precise 3-D conformal treatment or participating as a national leader in clinical research, Cancer Care Associates sets itself apart in its ability to anticipate the future of rapid change in healthcare and to develop an unequaled statewide delivery system for providing comprehensive cancer care. Highlights of this care include:

Cancer Care Associates' "Firsts"

- Cancer Care Associates launched the oncology profession's first comprehensive electronic information system that fully integrates patient information directly with internal business and scheduling systems.
- Cancer Care Associates has Oklahoma's only freestanding, multi-disciplinary treatment facilities with radiation therapy alongside chemotherapy in three major population centers across the state.
- Cancer Care Associates' well established peripheral blood stem cell transplantation programs in Tulsa and Oklahoma City are the state's only outpatient programs, which allow patients greatly reduced risks of infection at one-third the cost of inpatient treatment. Through early use of transplant treatment, some types of cancers have shown significantly improved outcomes.
- Cancer Care Associates serves patients' needs throughout Oklahoma, with four locations in Tulsa, four in Oklahoma City, and offices in Stillwater, Norman, Bartlesville, Enid, Duncan, Shawnee, Claremore, and Ardmore.

For several years Cancer Care Associates has been planning and developing sites where patients can easily access a broad range of cancer-related services at a single location. The current practice offices are the culmination of studying patterns and trends in providing care to patients with cancer and reviewing patient satisfaction surveys and focus group studies, along with information published by national patient advocacy groups. Now, Cancer Care Associates patients who need both chemotherapy and radiation therapy can get their treatments from a unified provider at one location.

The Bright Future of Cancer Care Associates

Through its affiliation with US Oncology, a national physician management organization exclusively for oncologists, Cancer Care Associates has the advantage of remaining a private practice, while benefiting from comprehensive management services that provide for hundreds of oncologists across the United States. This relationship benefits patients in several important ways: lower healthcare costs and better quality of care with the latest therapies and drugs available.

Today, there is a need to control healthcare costs, to reduce waste and inefficiency in the provision of healthcare, and to develop new, creative ways to allow collaboration rather than competition among providers— that is where Cancer Care Associates is headed for the future. ⬑

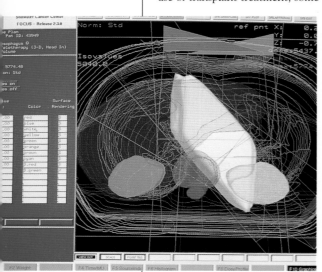

NORTHEASTERN STATE UNIVERSITY

With a grand 90-year tradition of providing a quality education, Northeastern State University (NSU) continues to play a vital role in northeastern Oklahoma's growth and development.

NSU serves as the only four-year public university for most of the eastern third of Oklahoma. It's a setting where teaching is a priority, professors are accessible, and students receive hands-on experience and a quality education they can put to use immediately.

"We want people to be aware of the role Northeastern State University has played in the growth and development of this area," says NSU President Larry Williams. "This institution impacts the quality of life among citizens throughout northeastern Oklahoma, whether they choose to pursue a degree, participate in continuing education classes, or attend sporting events, cultural programs, or entertainment shows that fill our calendar. Northeastern draws thousands of visitors to this area every year and, in turn, has a vital impact on the economy as well. Without a doubt, we are a living, breathing institution that plays a crucial role in many areas, both in the classroom and beyond."

Northeastern State University has served Oklahoma as a state institution of higher learning for 90 years, but the school's roots go back even further. The university can trace its history back to the state's first female Cherokee seminary that opened at Park Hill in 1851. As such, the school is the second oldest institution of higher education west of the Mississippi.

A Quality Education

NSU provides undergraduate and graduate education leading to bachelor's degrees, master's degrees in selected fields, and a doctoral degree in Oklahoma's only school of optometry. Programs are offered on the main campus at Tahlequah, as well as on the Muskogee, Broken Arrow and OSU-Tulsa campuses.

-Tahlequah. This tree-lined campus in the historic capital of the Cherokee Nation serves as home to nearly 6,000 students and the university's six major academic colleges: Arts & Letters; Business & Industry; Education; Mathematics, Science & Nursing; Social & Behavioral Sciences; and Optometry.

-Muskogee. NSU's branch campus in Muskogee has more than 1,500 students enrolled in upper level and graduate courses in such areas as education, business, nursing, and industrial management.

-Tulsa. For more than 18 years, the University has been a part of a four-university consortium providing higher educational opportunities in the Tulsa metropolitan area. NSU offers more than 26 degree programs at OSU-Tulsa.

-Broken Arrow. Broken Arrow voters in 1998 overwhelmingly approved two measures that have paved the way for construction of a new NSU branch campus in southeast Broken Arrow. Classes are scheduled to open in the fall of 2001.

"Our success and growth are due in large part to a strong sense of traditionalism among those we serve and a commitment among our faculty and staff to maintain the standards that originated with our roots more than 148 years ago," says NSU President Williams. ❖

Students at Northeastern have the opportunity to pursue 60 under-graduate degree programs, 13 master's programs, and 14 pre-professional programs in an environment that inspires friendships and personal growth.

Historic Seminary Hall, completed in 1889, is the center-piece of NSU's main campus in Tahlequah. The building underwent extensive renovation in the mid-1990s and is technologically equipped for the demands of the 21st century.

TULSA TECHNOLOGY CENTER

At Tulsa Technology Center students master the skills and knowledge it takes to succeed in today's work place.

Tulsa Technology Center offers a wide variety of programs for high school students and adults designed to prepare them for success in the workplace.

Tulsa Technology Center is the oldest and largest area vo-tech school in Oklahoma and is dedicated to the mission of preparing people for success in the workplace by providing quality education, training and services.

Tulsa Tech is recognized as a leader, statewide and nationally, in providing innovative, cutting-edge vocational-educational training programs. That's because students are given the unique opportunity to gain valuable job expertise before they ever enter the business world.

TTC's major instructional program areas include: Aviation Maintenance, Business Technology, Computer Technology, Construction, Electronics, Graphic Arts, Health, Manufacturing, the Service Industry, and Transportation. The courses are taught at Tulsa's four campuses: Lemley, Peoria, Broken Arrow, and TTC's newest addition, the Riverside Campus for Applied Science, Technology and Research, which opened in fall 1999.

A Practical Approach to Learning

In 1965, the state legislature passed a constitutional amendment creating a new vocational-technical system. From 1965-1973, the Tulsa Vo-Tech Center was a part of the Tulsa Public Schools system. In 1973, TTC became a stand-alone system through legislative enactment.

Today, TTC serves approximately 1,500 secondary students from 14 public school districts throughout Tulsa County, as well as private, parochial, and home-schooled students. There are approximately 800 adults in full-time programs and approximately 15,000 adults in short-term training classes annually.

"We've seen a lot of change over the years," says Dr. Gene Callahan, TTC's superintendent and CEO. "The economy really drives what we do. When Tulsa's aviation industry took off, we created programs to prepare students in that field. The most recent change is the growth in telecommunications—it's a huge industry in Tulsa now. We're moving into that arena as well, so we can deliver students who are knowledgeable and ready to make a difference at companies like Williams and MCI WorldCom."

Tulsa Tech provides meaningful education and technical training for high school and adult students through a variety of programs:

Full-time programs: These extensive programs, designed for high school students and adults, prepare students for entry-level jobs or help them update their skills. Most of the full-time students continue their education through Tulsa Community College or OSU-Okmulgee while still at TTC.

Adult & Continuing Education: Most of the 15,000 adults who participate in TTC's part-time programs through the year do so to upgrade their job skills or acquire new ones to help with job advancement. These courses, held on evenings and weekends, feature flexible schedules at sites located throughout Tulsa County and are taught by instructors who work in the business and industry areas they teach.

Business and Industry Training Services: Both the Business & Industry Training Services (BITS) and the Business Assistance Center (BAC) programs support public and private sector companies by providing a variety of programs and services to help with their training and development needs.

As Tulsa's economy continues to grow and evolve, Tulsa Technology Center is dedicated to preparing Tulsa students for success in the work place by providing quality education, training and services. ✦

TULSA COMMUNITY COLLEGE

Tulsa Community College is the entry point for public higher education for hundreds of thousands of Northeast Oklahoma residents. Each year, approximately 20,000 students of all ages enroll in TCC credit programs to begin their dream of attaining higher education, renew their professional talents, or simply expand their knowledge of the world around them.

As one of the premier two-year community colleges in the nation, TCC has pioneered innovative teaching methods and alternative modes of learning such as partnering with business to offer corporate contract training in the workplace, satellite classes, telecourses, and Internet courses.

TCC offers 69 associate of arts and associate of science degree paths, 52 associate in applied science degrees, and dozens of certificate programs with specialized educational training.

TCC's goal is to offer seamless education. More than half of Tulsa area higher education students begin at TCC. TCC offers comprehensive two-year programs which prepare individuals to continue their education or immediately enter the workforce. Alliances with other higher education institutions, such as the 2 + 2 relationship with OSU-Tulsa and the long-standing partnership with Tulsa Technology Center, provide students the opportunity to complete their degree path within a virtual college system.

TCC utilizes all available technology to offer students comprehensive training in highly sought after skills. Computer and information technology education is a TCC specialty. And TCC's excellent faculty has been recognized as among the finest in the nation.

The winner of countless awards for excellence in education, TCC was one of only 11 community colleges in the nation recognized by the National Science Foundation for the preparation of science and mathematics teachers. Three TCC faculty members have been named

Oklahoma Professors of the Year by the Carnegie Foundation for the Advancement of Teaching in recent years.

TCC's Phi Theta Kappa Student Honor Society was recently named the number one chapter out of 1,400 international chapters. Stephanie Wright, a Northeast Campus student, served as Phi Theta Kappa International President in 1999-2000.

Quality facilities are a TCC hallmark. With four campuses located throughout Tulsa, TCC offers convenience and availability. Recent additions include the outstanding Performing Arts Center for Education (PACE) at the Southeast Campus and the new Student Center at the Metro Campus. In 1999, the community approved an $18.3-million capital bond program to develop new facilities and technical programs at all college locations.

As a vital institution supporting community and cultural development, TCC presents the TCC Performing Arts Institute, Tulsa Fest—Festival of the Arts, and the ever-popular College for Kids and Teens each summer, along with thousands of hours of continuing education programs.

Tulsa Community College believes in the growth and worth of the person as an individual and as a member of society. The college believes that education is a lifelong process that contributes to an enriched human experience and career development. At Tulsa Community College, "Your Success is Our Business." ✦

International language instruction at Tulsa Community College includes 14 languages. Here, students sharpen their skills in one of TCC's fully equipped language labs.

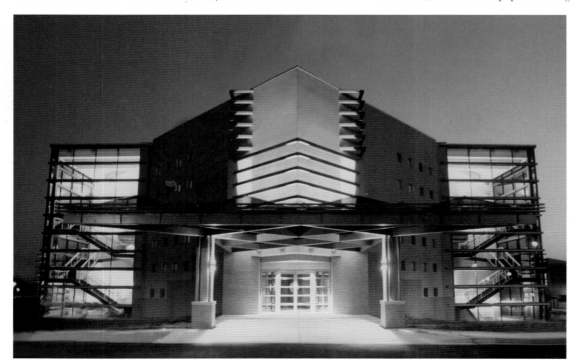

Performing Arts Center for Education, Tulsa Community College Southeast Campus.

HOLLAND HALL SCHOOL

Educating, nurturing, and empowering students for lifelong learning are at the heart of an exceptional academic experience for more than 1,000 children from PreSchool through Grade 12 at Holland Hall School.

Holland Hall emphasizes value and character for children in all three divisions.

Founded in 1922 as a college-preparatory, Episcopal day school, Holland Hall is Tulsa's oldest independent school and a member of the National Association of Independent Schools. Holland Hall enjoys a national reputation for a rigorous academic program grounded in core values that include intellectual and open inquiry; inspiring and innovative teaching; mental, physical, and spiritual growth; appreciation of diversity; and responsibility to self and others.

"Our faculty meticulously prepare our children for the academic challenges they will face beyond Holland Hall," says Robert E. Graves, Head of School. "At the same time, our teachers recognize the importance of motivating their students to become enlightened, articulate, compassionate, and contributing citizens of the world."

Thus, with outstanding teachers, an innovative curriculum, and unparalleled facilities, the school teaches the essential foundation of education and much more. Science, mathematics, technology, humanities, and the arts are at the core of the curriculum, while stimulating academic projects, outdoor education, creative electives, community service, and other meaningful experiences are woven through an overall program that emphasizes excellence at all levels.

Middle school science students and their teacher make discoveries during an outdoor lesson.

The academic program features a flexible modular schedule for the Upper School (Grades 9-12), an interdisciplinary program in the Middle School (Grades 4-8), and an open classroom/team teaching approach in the Primary School (PreSchool through Grade 3).

Holland Hall's affiliation with the Episcopal Church is reflected in religious studies and chapel services administered by resident chaplains. All Saints Chapel serves students regardless of their religious affiliation.

Located on a 162-acre campus in a wooded area of south Tulsa, Holland Hall's impressive facilities include seven science labs, three computer labs, three libraries containing 60,000 volumes and extensive Internet capabilities, and the 70,000-square-foot Walter Arts Center that supports programs in music, visual arts, and dance.

The Kistler-Gilliland Center for the Advancement of Learning promotes faculty study and the application of learning, particularly in relation to the unique development of the individual learner.

Holland Hall recently completed a successful capital campaign that raised nearly $9 million toward faculty endowment, student financial aid, and the new 18,000-square-foot Duenner Family Science, Mathematics, and Technology Center.

Scheduled for completion in fall 2000, the Center will be a state-of-the-art addition to the Upper School that complements Holland Hall's science, math, and technology curriculum.

Headmaster Graves notes that the campaign's success demonstrates extraordinary commitment by parents and alumni.

"Our children and their families forge a meaningful partnership with Holland Hall," says Graves. "This unique relationship between school and families results in a strong school community that is a Holland Hall tradition." ❖

SOUTHCREST HOSPITAL

In SouthCrest, Tulsa's newest hospital, patients and their families find a high-tech departure from what the public has come to expect hospitals to be. But at the same time it offers simple reminders, all but forgotten in current hospital fashion, of the traditions of care giving.

SouthCrest, a joint project of Triad Hospitals, Inc. and Hillcrest Healthcare System, is a 153-bed facility that offers a glimpse into the future of hospital systems. The 50-acre campus, at 91st Street and Highway 169, is located in south Tulsa but serves all of northeastern Oklahoma. In an area that is booming with new residences, it was a natural conclusion that a hospital was needed to serve the growing population. It's expected that the 2000 Census will show nearly 33 percent of Tulsa's population is located within a five-mile radius of SouthCrest.

The goal of SouthCrest is "to provide the highest quality healthcare for patients and their families and to be a valuable addition to our community," explains Anthony Young, president and CEO.

The hospital does that by providing its special mix of traditional and cutting-edge healthcare. Walk down the halls and you'll see nurses wearing traditional white uniforms and nursing caps, a practice that has disappeared from most hospitals. At the same time, the technology in the hospital is so advanced it allows nurses to observe patients via special devices built into the beds and to monitor the heart rate of patients walking down the halls.

SouthCrest offers a full range of ancillary services, including a full-service emergency room with 15 exam areas, a complete outpatient diagnostic center, a cardiovascular center with cardiac catheterization and open-heart surgery capabilities, inpatient care, neurosciences, orthopedics, primary care, and the Women's Pavilion.

Within the Women's Pavilion is a birthing center, a well baby and special care nursery with the latest in security systems to protect new mothers and their newborns.

Modern diagnostic equipment includes MRI, CT scans, diagnostic X-ray, ultrasound, nuclear medicine, stress testing, interventional/diagnostic procedures, angiography, and cardiac imaging. The Breast Center offers mammography.

There are many unique aspects to the new facility. SouthCrest's emergency room, for example, was designed so that patients seeking after-hours care and those with life-threatening situations are treated in separate areas. Another amenity is that each of the 153 patient rooms is private—with windows that actually open. The rooms are also equipped with two phone jacks—one for a telephone, the other for a laptop computer. The first floor features an atrium, a gift shop, and the wonderful food served to patients is also available in Michael's Café.

A three-story, 120,000-square-foot Physician's Medical Plaza adjoins the hospital.

"We are a community hospital," says Young, "and our mission is bringing quality to life through people caring for people." ✦

Anthony R. Young, President and CEO.

SouthCrest Hospital.

SouthCrest Medical Plaza.

CASCIA HALL PREPARATORY SCHOOL

Cascia Hall Preparatory School provides an educational experience rich in tradition. Founded by the Order of Saint Augustine in 1926, Cascia Hall gives students the opportunity to excel and become an important part of the Tulsa community.

A Catholic school, Cascia Hall educates the whole person physically, emotionally, psychologically, spiritually, and intellectually. Emphasis is placed on self-motivation, self-discipline, and self-responsibility, traits necessary for success in education and life.

The school operated as a boys' school for grades 7-12 until 1986. That year, Cascia Hall added a middle school and became a coeducational day school for grades 6-12. The total enrollment is restricted to 575 students. The Middle School emphasizes the intellectual and human skills necessary for future studies. The Upper School program is college preparatory, emphasizing the liberal arts.

Excellence in educational achievement at all levels is a goal of every student. Cascia Hall consistently produces National Merit Scholars and Finalists. Fifteen percent of the class of 2000 was recognized by the National Merit Corporation. College counseling is an integral part of the educational sequence. Ninety-nine percent of graduates enter colleges and universities across the country.

Athletics play a major role in student development. Sports competition is an important part of the Cascia Hall heritage, and winning teams are a school tradition. Student athletes have won state championships in tennis, football, golf, basketball, track, and volleyball. In 1999 alone, Cascia varsity teams won four state championship titles.

The performing and visual arts have become an integral part of the curriculum, which has an outstanding reputation for its strong math, science, literature, and language courses. A wide variety of extracurricular activities offer students the opportunity to broaden their horizons through academics, fellowship, community service, journalism, and dozens of other programs.

The Cascia Community is comprised of thousands of individuals and families who come together to share in and work toward the success of students. Parents, Augustinians, faculty, and staff join in furthering the educational mission of the school.

Cascia Hall has continually built for the future. Construction on the 40-acre, $15-million campus and physical plant has been a virtual constant over the years. The school recently marked the completion of the Cascia Connection, a $3-million addition connecting the Upper and Middle Schools, as well as other improvements of facilities. The Connection brought together the Upper and Middle Schools to form "one community with two levels of education."

Under the leadership of Reverend Bernard Scianna, o.s.a. and the Board of Directors, emphasis for the near future will be building the school's endowment. Alumni, parents, and other generous supporters will work to expand the school's $3-million endowment and grow the Cascia Hall Foundation, established in 1999.

The Cascia family will come together in Fall of 2000-Spring of 2001 to celebrate the school's 75th anniversary. This "school year of excellence" will offer many opportunities for alumni, family, and friends to reminisce on the achievements of the past and build for the future.

For generations of Tulsans, Cascia Hall has played an important part in forming a community of faith, love, and work, based on the teachings of Saint Augustine. Cascia Hall has served the educational needs of Catholics and other faiths by producing well-rounded graduates prepared for success in life. Alumni have advanced to become business and community leaders in Tulsa and around the world—taking with them the lessons learned about their God, themselves, their friends, and the glorious world around them. ❖

The Augustinian values of Truth, Unity and Charity are imparted to the Cascia Hall students. Photograph courtesy of Brandi Stafford, *Tulsa World*.

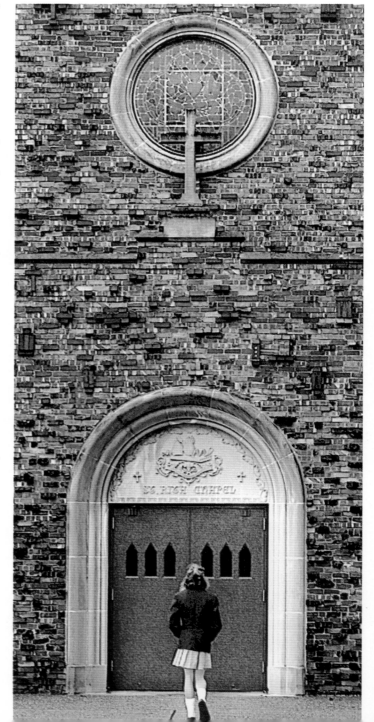

MED-X CORPORATION

"Tulsans serving Tulsans." For more than three decades, Med-X Corporation has done just that... and more. Today, Med-X and Drug Mart stores can be found throughout Tulsa and in neighboring communities in the metropolitan area. Yet the service philosophy of the neighborhood drug store that was practiced when Med-X began business, holds true for each store today.

Founded in 1967, Med-X Corporation has expanded to serve Tulsa's growing population and changing lifestyles. As outlying communities have experienced rapid growth in recent years, new locations and store concepts have been introduced.

New residents to the Tulsa area, as well as second and third generation customers, find friendly professional pharmacists, a great selection of drugs and merchandise, and competitive prices at every Med-X and Drug Mart store. Customers have the choice of shopping at their neighborhood Med-X, where the emphasis is on convenience, or they can visit one of the Drug Mart stores for expanded product selection and every day low prices. With continued growth expected in the metropolitan area, people in the community can expect additional expansion from Med-X Corporation.

Few relationships in retail are based on the level of trust that customers have for their pharmacist. At Med-X Corporation, such relationships established with families decades ago continue today. Offering expert advise based on years of professional training and experience in practice, Med-X and Drug Mart pharmacists work closely with area health care specialists to provide proper prescription services. Their pharmacy computer system is at the leading edge of pharmacy technology, which helps to assure that pharmacists provide accurate and efficient processing of all prescriptions. Med-X and Drug Mart accept most health insurance programs

As an important member in the regional healthcare community, Med-X Corporation provides products and services for thousands of area families and individuals. As full-service drug stores, Med-X and Drug Mart offer a wide variety of other products and services for customers, including film processing and photographic supplies, over the counter drugs and remedies, cosmetics and fragrances, greeting cards, gifts, snacks, and literally thousands of other items.

Med-X Corporation is proud to be a corporate citizen of the Tulsa metropolitan area. With several hundred full and part-time employees, the company is a major employer and is committed to the continued growth and prosperity of the community. Med-X Corporation is active in community service, with special interest in organizations that support the elderly and attend to their special needs.

For three generations of Tulsans, either Med-X or Drug Mart has been the drug store of choice. Their goal, as Tulsans serving Tulsans, it to continue those relationships for generations to come. ❖

15
Chapter Fifteen

REAL ESTATE & DEVELOPMENT

❀

Photo by Don Wheeler.

WILLBROS GROUP, INC.

Willbros has built an enviable reputation over the last 90 years by designing and constructing pipelines and facilities around the world. It has brought energy supplies and technology to the farthest reaches of the world, including nearly every Middle Eastern country, the swamps of Indonesia and Nigeria, the wetlands and mountains of the United States, the frozen tundra of the former Soviet Union, and the Andes Mountains of South America.

A ditcher built by Willbros at work on 54 miles of 20-inch pipeline laid for Manufacturer's Light & Heat in Pennsylvania, 1946.

The Company traces its roots back to 1908, when David R. and S. Miller Williams founded the Williams Brothers Company in Fort Smith, Arkansas, building their first pipeline in 1915. Responding to the demand for pipeline construction contractors when oil was discovered in Oklahoma, the brothers soon moved the company to Tulsa. In 1939, when the Company entered the international market with the construction of a pipeline in Venezuela, this small construction company quickly became synonymous with pipelines everywhere in the world.

When the growing company (then named The Williams Companies) sold its construction unit to key employees in 1975, Willbros was formed to continue the Company's pipeline construction business. To expand its overall capabilities, Willbros acquired the engineering firm Butler & Associates, Inc. in 1981. Since then, Willbros has evolved into one of the world's leading independent contractors serving the oil and gas industry, providing construction, engineering and specialty services to major oil companies and government entities.

Willbros has designed and constructed many challenging pipelines that have often become milestones for the entire industry. Over the years, Willbros' achievements have opened energy corridors, strengthened economies, and played a pivotal role in the development of new energy resources and the growth of many countries. A few of Willbros' significant projects include:

- Constructing the 253-mile, Clayton, New Mexico, to Denver, Colorado, section of Colorado Interstate's 1927 Amarillo-to-Denver natural gas pipeline which, in addition to significant rock and mountain content, crossed the 900-foot wide, 500-foot deep Purgatoire Canyon and was probably the first suspension crossing of this magnitude
- Constructing the Big-Inch crude oil and Little Big-Inch refined petroleum products War Emergency Pipelines built in the United States during World War II, which moved 250,000 barrels a day from Texas and the Gulf Coast to the northeast seaboard for U.S. military operations, known as the longest and largest-diameter pipelines of their time
- Constructing the 194-mile Trans-Andean crude oil pipeline which crossed the Andes Mountains in 1969, climbing to a peak altitude of 10,540 feet, then plunging 7,500 feet and rising to nearly 10,000 feet once more within the next 23 miles, before dropping to sea level
- Designing and furnishing a rapid deployment fuel pipeline distribution and storage system for the US Army which was used extensively and successfully in Saudi Arabia during Operation Desert Shield/Desert Storm in 1990-1991 and in Somalia during 1993.

The Importance of People

With offices and work sites around the globe, Willbros and its employees are involved in a wide range of community projects. In Nigeria, for example, the Company undertakes a variety of projects, including delivering needed medical immunizations to infants in remote areas and donating books in the region. Willbros is also an active participant in Tulsa causes ranging from United Way to Habitat for Humanity. These contributions are one of the many ways that Willbros gives back to the communities in which it works.

Tie-in of large-diameter pipeline in the Niger Delta.

With administrative and engineering offices in Tulsa, Willbros has relied upon Tulsa for a skilled workforce and remains one of the city's major employers. "We are fortunate that we have ample resources to provide the high level of service our clients have come to expect of us," says Larry J. Bump, Chairman and CEO of Willbros Group, Inc. "I believe, however, that Willbros' most important assets cannot be found on our balance sheet, but rather in our good reputation and our people. These cannot, in fact, be separated because our good name has been earned through over 90 years of capable and dedicated performance by Willbros people."

Delivering Solutions

From its earliest years, Willbros' focus has always been on the needs of its customers. As the world becomes more sophisticated, Willbros' clients demand more with every project—and Willbros rises to each and every challenge. "Sometimes the challenge may be difficult terrain, harsh climatic conditions, an unreasonable time schedule, or a combination of the above," says Bump. "Whatever the cause, Willbros has always answered the challenge."

During the early years when pipelines were constructed with general equipment, Willbros knew that equipment designed specifically for pipeline construction would allow faster installation and ultimately save clients money. Its spirit of innovation and drive to meet its customers' needs led Willbros to the forefront of developing some of the world's best-known heavy equipment including the design of the first ditch trencher, modification of a crawler crane into a backhoe, engineering the sideboom, and creation of the bulldozer by simply placing a blade on a farm tractor.

To successfully complete some of the biggest and toughest construction jobs in the world on time and within budget, Willbros has developed a reputation for logistical planning and management. An illustrative example of this expertise is the support Willbros provided to Ecuador when earthquakes devastated the country in 1987. Having built the original Trans-Ecuadorian Pipeline in 1970-72, Willbros was called in to repair the earthquake damage on an urgent basis. Within 30 days of the contract award, Willbros had several hundred pieces of major equipment and hundreds of people on the scene rebuilding the pipeline and designing bridges.

Tape and Wrap Coating Crew.

While many contractors move from project to project, Willbros has recognized its clients' needs for ongoing, reliable support and specialty services. Since the 1960s, Willbros has expanded its role to that of a full-service provider who offers continuous, area-specific services such as pipe coating, dredging, marine heavy lifting services, pipeline rehabilitation, rig moving, and concrete piling fabrication in remote areas such as Nigeria, Oman, and Venezuela.

As Willbros plans for the energy industry of the future, the company remains committed to its objective—furthering the growth of its clients by meeting their challenges with innovative solutions. ❖

Willbros USA, Inc., Tulsa, Oklahoma.

MANHATTAN CONSTRUCTION COMPANY

Manhattan Construction Company has been part of the Oklahoma experience since its beginning, having been established 11 years before statehood—so well established, in fact, that it was the clear and logical choice to build Oklahoma's original State Capitol Building.

Brighton Gardens of Tulsa.

Manhattan quickly became a pace-setter when L.H. Rooney and some associates started the company in Indian Territory in 1896, in what was to become Oklahoma. As a growing force through the entire 20th century, Manhattan has achieved an extraordinary record of stability and success across North America, literally helping to mold the face of the nation with construction projects that already have become landmarks and newer structures destined to become landmarks.

Notably, this record of success built on L.H. Rooney's vision has been achieved by the three generations of family succeeding him. Leadership of the company passed from the founder to his son, L.F. Rooney, then from him to his son, L.F. Rooney, Jr. Manhattan presently is directed by L.F. Rooney III, chairman, and his brother, Timothy P. Rooney, president.

Continuity of leadership for more than a century probably explains the unique characteristics that set Manhattan apart in an era when management and employees often seem to be reading from different scripts. "My brother and I have a good work ethic," says President Timothy Rooney. "We actively manage the company, rather than it

being led from afar by people that nobody knows." The average tenure of senior management is more than 20 years.

"We have a highly skilled team of people at Manhattan, who deliver quality construction services at the optimum cost, resulting in a positive experience for the building team and retention of our valued clients," says John Snyder, vice president of the Oklahoma Division. "In retaining clients, our people have created the opportunity to develop market niches."

Those "market niches" have expanded significantly over time, and claims on new and different markets are being staked every year. The singularity and magnitude of many of its projects underscore the company's willingness to take on complex projects with confidence.

Recent projects in Oklahoma include the Tulsa Technology Center at R.L. Jones Airport in Tulsa, the award winning MCI/WorldCom Module 5 in Tulsa, and two Brighton Gardens Marriott assisted living facilities, one in Tulsa and one in Oklahoma City. Projects in progress in Oklahoma include expansion of the St. John Medical Center campus in Tulsa, the Williams Technology Center in downtown Tulsa, and the Gallagher-Iba Arena renovation at Oklahoma State University in Stillwater. In other areas, Manhattan has completed the Ballpark in Arlington, home field of the Texas Rangers baseball team, the George

Cascia Hall middle school addition, Tulsa, Oklahoma.

Bush Presidential Library Center at Texas A&M University, the Santa Fe Opera House reconstruction, and the Brooke Army Medical Center Hospital in San Antonio—replacing the original historic Army facility with a model for the 21st century.

Not all of Manhattan's work is in the "mega" class; at any given time each division may be working on projects in the $5-million to $10-million contract range.

The company's Oklahoma Division office is based in Tulsa, as are the human resources, accounting, and IS departments for the entire company, nationally and internationally. Tulsa is one of the four division offices, the others being Dallas, Houston, and Washington, D.C.

The Washington office, opened in 1983, is Manhattan's newest (Houston was added in 1946 and Dallas in 1965). The company has successfully transported its success record from the Southwest to the nation's capital, building significant projects in the area like the Walter Reed Army Institute of Research. In addition to the four division offices, Manhattan serves clients from area offices in Oklahoma City, Mobile, New Orleans, and Mexico City.

The company is licensed in 16 states, starting in the District of Columbia and extending through the South into the Southwest. In all its markets Manhattan strives for a balance between public and private projects, and even more precisely, between business and industrial projects, to insulate it from market fluctuations.

The strategy has worked for more than a hundred years. Considered a "large" general contracting company, Manhattan employs over 1,200 people.

Aware that "being big" provides no assurance of market success, Manhattan has adopted the latest technology to create operating efficiencies as well as to bolster construction quality. "We have invested a significant sum in technology to network all of our people in order to be more efficient," says President Timothy Rooney. "All offices are on-line full time."

The ability of offices to communicate constantly by e-mail is an important development, he points out, but the real technological payoff comes with the ability to deliver drawings and specifications among the offices electronically. "Paperless projects— that's where we think we're going," Rooney says. The company has put the network to great use by installing a software system able to electronically review Manhattan's historical project cost data, then project them into estimates for jobs that still are in the conceptual stage.

But Manhattan's success was neither built on, nor depends on, technological magic. "We continue to do what we've been doing for over a hundred years," says Oklahoma Operations Manager Dewey Davis. "We still rely on our construction experience to build projects on time and on budget—we just do it with new tools." ⋖

Tulsa Technology Center at R.L. Jones Airport, Tulsa, Oklahoma.

Hotel Ambassador, Tulsa, Oklahoma.

SUITE OPTIONS CORPORATE APARTMENTS

Suite Options is a growing business built on the belief that a home is better than a hotel. The temporary housing industry's leading company, Suite Options has operated in Tulsa since 1996. Hundreds of business executives, consultants, relocating employees, and families moving into the area have discovered the Suite Options difference.

Suite Options corporate apartments are located in exclusive apartment communities throughout the Tulsa metro area.

Suite Beginnings

Suite Options was founded in Wichita, Kansas, in 1990, to provide temporary lodging for corporate executives coming to the area to conduct business. As a leading-edge temporary housing company, Suite Options set the industry standard for customer service and value by offering a variety of suite locations and options. The company quickly expanded and now has operations in Tulsa, Des Moines, Little Rock, Wichita, Kansas City, and Oklahoma City. The company's dynamic business practices have been featured in local, regional, and the national media, including CNN.

The Suite Choice

The reasons why people in transition are choosing Suite Options over hotels are many. Suite Options customers get more furnishings, amenities, square footage, location choices, and the feel of home while saving up to 50 percent when compared to hotels. The traditional hotel room is approximately 280-square feet. A Suite Options corporate apartment is at least 700-square feet and features a full kitchen, one, two, or three bedrooms, all utilities paid, and more.

The Vice President Suite is the most popular Suite Options apartment.

How does Suite Options do it? Simply, by providing a variety of locations in the finest apartment communities in all areas of Tulsa. Suite Options contracts with the apartment community, relieving customers of the need of signing leases. Whether clients want to be close to work, close to the airport, or in a specific school district, Suite Options will provide the perfect location at a price much less than a traditional hotel or even an extended-stay hotel.

Then they furnish and decorate each suite to meet the everyday living or working requirements of our customers. All that is required is a minimum seven day stay. It's that simple. Suite Options will take care of all the rest, including complete linen supplies and weekly cleaning service. All the comforts of home, plus a few extras.

A Variety of Options

Customers choose the location and price range at Suite Options. Because the living needs of each person or family differ, Suite Options has a series of suites from which to choose.

The Accountant Suite: The Economy Suite includes the basics, including a queen "poly-down" bed, sofa, chair,

television, fully equipped kitchen, microwave, dresser, security alarm, free local telephone service, and answering machine.

The Vice President Suite: The Signature Suite contains all the basics with upgraded furniture quality and additional items such as a loveseat, a 25" television with VCR and expanded cable, the decor package, and deluxe home accessories.

The CEO Suite: The top-of-the-line Suite includes all the finest basics with the addition of a recliner, king size bed, 32" television, stereo system, and the complete decor package.

Most of the apartment communities Suite Options contracts with offer luxuries such as swimming pools, hot tubs, tennis courts, and athletic/fitness facilities. And just in case our customers need extra items to make their Suite more homelike or like their office, we can also provide extras such as VCRs, Fax machines, stereo systems, computer desks, washers and dryers, cribs, high chairs, roll-away beds, and sofa sleepers.

Suite Relationships

Suite Options has developed solid working relationships with many corporations, the government, entrepreneurs, families, and even travel agents. Suite Options offers corporate discounts and discounts for extended stays of six months or more. Some Suite Options customers come back to Tulsa year after year to vacation or visit relatives. Providing quality temporary housing for all of our clients' needs is a hallmark of Suite Options. Service before, during, and after staying with Suite Options is our pleasure and your satisfaction is always unconditionally guaranteed.

Suite Options is proud to provide temporary housing for people coming to Tulsa to conduct business or for individuals and families relocating to the community. Tulsa has experienced incredible growth in recent years. Suite Options is a strong supporter of the continued growth of Tulsa and is pleased to be able to provide quality temporary housing for visitors or new residents.

We invite you to try Suite Options. Stay a week, a month, or longer. Suite Options is dedicated to serving all of our customers' temporary housing needs. Suite Options—enjoy your stay, make yourself at home. ❖

Fitness centers are available at most apartment communities as well as many other amenities not normally found at hotels.

Completely furnished kitchens allow Suite Options guests to cook meals during their temporary stay in Tulsa.

FIRST COMMERCIAL REAL ESTATE SERVICES CORP.

First Commercial Real Estate Corporation is a full service commercial real estate company with specialization in the sales and leasing of office, retail, industrial and general commercial, and the sale of multi-family real estate and land.

Weekly associate meeting for new listing presentations.

In addition to complete commercial brokerage and leasing services, the company offers services in site selection, site analysis, build-to-suit, lease analysis, property tax analysis, project feasibility studies, broker price opinions, property research, site planning, interior design, and a variety of related services.

The company was formed in 1995 when four associates, with a shared vision of providing superior quality service incorporating cutting edge technology and research, left a national brokerage company. First Commercial provides property information, statistical information, history, and financial analysis with the touch of a button in a conference room presentation environment. By being on the cutting edge of technology and armed with the most complete information in the market, First Commercial's brokers and associates can provide clients with information on the entire market without leaving the office. This ability allows the client to review many properties in a comfortable environment before choosing a property to personally tour. The process saves the client a great deal of time and limits nonproductive driving time.

Brokers and associates are supported by a custom-designed brokerage, leasing database and operating system written exclusively for First Commercial. This system is one of the most advanced and comprehensive systems in the United States. The Gateway Destination 2000 computer presentation system allows brokers and associates to do on-screen presentations of properties, the market, and city information. The staff is equipped with individual Pentium computers and a full menu of software including Microsoft Professional Office. All staff and associates are networked using Windows NT Server.

First Commercial is one of only a few commercial real estate firms its size to have a full commercial closing department, including an in-house closing coordinator, who tracks transactions from contract to closing and coordinates daily with due diligence service providers, lenders, appraisers, surveyors, and Title companies. First Commercial is totally committed to the highest level of service possible, believing that being focused on a long term client relationship, rather than a single transaction, is the key to the client receiving the highest level of service possible.

First Commercial has been fortunate in achieving a high degree of success in its first five years. The company is noted for closing more than $100,000,000 in a single year with only four associates. The Apartment Group was honored by NAIOP with the apartment "Deal of the Year" for three consecutive years, 1997 - 1999. The company has grown to include 12 brokers and associates with more then 140 years of combined brokerage experience providing specialization in all commercial real estate disciplines.

In 1998, the First Commercial Network was formed, allowing an expansion of the company into select United States markets. The first network office, located in Oklahoma City, has proven successful by closing more than 40 properties in its first year. ✦

First Commercial staff and associates from left to right: Susan Watkinson, Karla Berry, Worden Parrish, Bob Meyer, Leola Farmer, Pam Avison, Dick Sudduth, Peggy Kahler, Max Heidenreich, Bruce Locke, Sara Dwyer, (not pictured Raymond Lord and Ray Canfield).

Photo by Don Sibley.

16
Chapter Sixteen

MARKETPLACE & ATTRACTIONS

Photo by Don Sibley.

DOUBLETREE HOTEL AT WARREN PLACE

Comfort. Peace and quiet. Elegant surroundings. For business people who travel 200-300 days a year, these are things to be cherished. That's why the Doubletree Hotel at Warren Place has built its reputation on delivering all that and more to guests every day.

Guests are greeted with warm Doubletree cookies on arrival.

Nestled in a quiet corner of south Tulsa, the Doubletree Hotel offers unparalleled service with its variety of restaurants, ballrooms, and business facilities. But it's the special things that truly set the Doubletree at Warren Place apart: warm chocolate chip cookies, the kind your mother had waiting for you after school, a walk along a quiet tree-lined path on the hotel grounds, a meal to remember in the Warren Duck Club. It all comes together to create an unforgettable experience for corporate and leisure travelers.

Catering to the Business Person

In the midst of today's frenzied business world, the Doubletree Hotel at Warren Place stands as a welcome oasis for business travelers. The hotel is equipped to handle large-scale conventions, but specializes in meeting the business needs of smaller groups. This puts the focus more on personalized service for the individual.

"A small group can get lost with the many activities at a convention hotel," says Bill Mink, the hotel's Director of Marketing. "At the Doubletree, we may have two or three board meetings coming in from several Fortune 500 companies. They may only have 15 guest rooms each, but every one of them needs to receive special treatment."

All 370 guest rooms are designed for today's busy traveler. Guests who are constantly on the road appreciate the welcoming touches of a king size bed or two over-sized doubles and a sumptuous overstuffed chair, complete with a footstool and reading lamp. Each room also features a large, solid worktable with plenty of room to spread things around. And there are the added conveniences that business travelers

rely on, from in-room irons and boards to coffee makers and hair dryers.

The Doubletree's typical business meeting is a very professional group of business people who need to have a perfect meeting so they can achieve a specific objective. The hotel is a popular destination for national board meetings, and has long catered to the oil & gas industry and top-level business executives of Tulsa's leading corporations.

To meet the needs of these business organizations, the Doubletree at Warren Place offers a wide selection of impressive facilities. The Grand Ballroom can be divided into smaller rooms for business breakout sessions or left intact for large plenary sessions and elaborate social events. A smaller ballroom, the Warren Ballroom, is located on the adjacent high rise's top floor and offers a breathtaking view of Tulsa through its floor-to-ceiling windows. Because of its striking setting, this ballroom has become a Tulsa favorite for weddings and private dinners for companies and families.

The Tulsa Learning Theater.

A Technology-Friendly Atmosphere

Today's business travelers need more than a place to meet. They need fast, convenient access to technology, and the Doubletree at Warren Place is wired and ready to go.

The hotel is equipped with the latest in communications for fast connection to the Internet in each guest room, and has the unique ability to provide groups up to 100 phone lines for corporate meetings.

In the Ballroom area, the Doubletree offers its corporate guests an "office away from their office" with its one of two Business Centers. Guests can prepare work for their meetings at the hotel or just catch up while they're away with access to computers, printers, scanners, copiers—everything they need to conduct business. Corporate guests staying on the hotel's

"Executive Level" also have access to that floor's 24-hour Business Center, which provides the same business amenities. Each Executive Level guest enjoys a complimentary continental breakfast, business periodicals, even a comfortable lounging robe. Just as important, they also have use of the exclusive Executive Level lounge after a long day with complimentary cocktails and hors d'oeuvres.

Next door to the meeting rooms guests also can take advantage of the Doubletree's Tulsa Learning Theater, a 56-person auditorium with theater seating and an audio/visual booth for technology oriented presentations. In fact, the Doubletree at Warren Place has its own in-house audio/visual company to help guests coordinate and make presentations.

A Quiet Place to Reconnect

While the Doubletree at Warren Place has become Tulsa's top location for business professionals, it also caters to leisure guests looking for that special night or weekend escape.

"Most of our leisure customers are local to Tulsa," says Mink. "They are trying to find an escape from the business world or life at home. For them, it's a way to refocus. You can see couples wander through the park after dinner. It's a perfect chance to reconnect with each other."

In addition to fine dining and a chance to relax on the hotel's grounds, leisure guests can enjoy a swim in the pool, time in the sauna or steam room, even get a good workout in the state-of-the-art fitness center.

There are all the makings of a perfect getaway weekend: check into a comfortable room, experience dinner at the Warren Duck Club, enjoy live entertainment in Encounters, take a quick walk through the park, and then head back to your room for a quiet night's rest. After sleeping in the next morning, start the day with breakfast in bed from room service, enjoy the pool and sauna, then stroll beside the stream that runs through the park.

A Taste of Elegance

The Doubletree Hotel at Warren Place has built an outstanding reputation by offering innovative cuisine prepared and served by culinary experts. The Warren Duck Club offers guests a true culinary adventure, from the wonderful appetizer bar to an extraordinary dessert buffet.

As the city's many food aficionados and critics will point out, the Warren Duck Club is not merely the finest hotel restaurant in town—it is the state's finest restaurant, period. For further proof look no further than AAA, which has named the Warren Duck Club one of only two restaurants in Oklahoma deserving of the AAA Four Diamond Award.

The restaurant's award-winning "signature items" are themselves famous in Tulsa—blackened tenderloin and rotisserie duck. The restaurant is equally well known for its highly attentive servers, who are always mindful that diners may be conducting business or enjoying romance for the weekend. It's an elegant atmosphere for enjoying a special lunch or evening on the town.

If you're looking for distinctive dining in a more relaxed environment, the Doubletree offers Greenleaf's on the Park with a spectacular view of nature. This sidewalk cafe is a great spot to enjoy your morning coffee, grab a quick bite for lunch, or indulge yourself with dinner in a relaxed atmosphere.

Choose from prime rib on Friday or Saturday night, a Wok in the Park, the pasta bar, or the full self-serve deli. Greenleaf's also offers one of Tulsa's most elaborate Sunday brunches, featuring such choices as an Eggs Benedict station that offers "customized" variations with salmon or blackened tenderloin.

And when evening comes, Encounters is the place to dance the night away. Or, after a long day of meetings, it's an inviting atmosphere that provides a place to unwind and celebrate a successful day of business over a friendly cocktail.

The AAA Four Diamond rated Warren Duck Club.

Romantic setting on the grounds of the Doubletree Hotel at Warren Place.

In fact, the entire dining lineup at the Doubletree— from restaurant to business and social catering—is well known throughout the region.

"Our reputation for food and beverage quality and service is particularly strong in this market," explains Mink. Whether it's the introduction of a new chef or expansion of one of the area's finest wine collections, the Doubletree At Warren Place has firmly established itself in Tulsa's social catering circles—to the point where the hotel is now recognized as *the* place to have social benefits and fundraisers. The Doubletree at Warren Place coordinates five or six such social events every month, each one a masterpiece.

Mink is quick to point out that some venues around the city are larger and can host bigger events. "But we don't want to be the biggest. Instead, we try to be the best. Our goal is to provide the customer greater value by hosting a very unique and special event."

A Partner With the Community

The Doubletree at Warren Place is very active in the community, for a simple reason: "we feel we're supported by the community, so it's fitting that we do everything we can to support it," Michael Hughes, General Manager.

An example of this can be found just down the street at Saint Francis Hospital, one of the region's leading medical centers and one of the top children's hospitals in this part of the country.

When young patients are brought in from outlying areas to the children's hospital for tests and treatment, their parents sometimes don't have much money for an extended stay. So the Doubletree puts the family up for free. "It's one small way we can pay back the community," says Hughes.

Likewise, various Tulsa charitable organizations request and receive rooms to give away as gifts and prizes to donors. Overall, the hotel returns approximately $80,000 in services to the community each year—not including the hotel's support of United Way, which tripled last year.

A Relaxing Stay

Words like "calm" and "peaceful" really don't do justice to the beautiful grounds located behind the Doubletree at Warren Place.

The park and its design have won awards for landscape architecture. Hotel guests take walks down the lit footpath, past rows of azalea bushes that explode in pinks, reds, and white every spring. Ducks are regular visitors on the park's stream.

Even Greenleaf's on the Park restaurant carries through this theme, with a gradual transition from the green of the park to the hanging plants and relaxed atmosphere of the restaurant.

This emphasis on a relaxing stay carries through the entire hotel. At one time or another, most travelers are inconvenienced by hotels conducting major renovations. But you won't hear about the Doubletree at Warren Place having to shut down or expose guests to inconvenient construction. The hotel staff prides itself on never letting the hotel deteriorate to the point where it needs a major renovation. Last year, for instance, guests probably were never aware that all the rooms systematically received new drapes, upholstery and bedspreads.

"We're continually spending significant

The Grand Ballroom offers elegance and style.

amounts of money to keep our hotel in peak condition, constantly reinvesting in our hotel for our visitors," says Hughes.

So whether you're looking for the perfect business facility, the tastiest blackened tenderloin or the ideal location for a get-away weekend, the Doubletree Hotel at Warren Place is ready to meet your needs—and do it with a grace and style unlike any other hotel in Oklahoma. ✧

Indoor pool, whirlpool, steam and sauna rooms.

The Doubletree Hotel at Warren Place.

CROWN AUTO WORLD

There was a time when Henry Primeaux racked up more than 250,000 frequent flyer miles each year. He was very successful as a sales consultant, primarily for the auto industry in the U.S. and internationally. But the miles took their toll on him and his family. The New Orleans native decided to settle down and take a shot at putting his popular sales techniques and world-class motivational skills to the test at his own dealership.

Henry Primeaux and son Henry Joseph Primeaux on site at the new Crown Auto World dealership in Bristow, Oklahoma.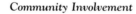

He looked around the country at the many cities he had done business in, but really knew from the start that Tulsa would be the place he, his business, and his family would call home. He had visited Tulsa a number of times, especially during the oil-boom years of the late 70s and early 80s. He put a lot of faith in the belief that Tulsa would recover from the oil bust and see unparalleled growth as it headed for a new millennium. He was right.

Coming to Tulsa

In 1991, Primeaux, and wife Jane, purchased Crown Auto World and immediately instilled in their 100-plus employees his belief in hard work, service, compassion, and most of all dedication. He ignored the marketing experts' advice and did his own radio and television commercials with his heavy Louisiana accent. His down-home pronunciation of the dealership's location at "4444 South Sheridan" was an immediate hit and his nod to Sam's Warehouse next door was a brand marketing coupe. His honesty, humor, and genuine love and excitement for his new home caught on quickly and business has grown at a remarkable pace each year.

Crown Auto World is built upon Primeaux's creed of "the value always exceeds the price." Every employee works to exceed each customer's expectations every time—whether making that late-night service call or working to make a sale to a customer for the first time—there is almost no limit to the value placed on customer relationships.

The dealership has been recognized as one of the finest in the nation and received national sales and service awards from all three of its auto lines— BMW, Jeep, and Buick. Primeaux has opened Crown Bristow in Bristow, Oklahoma, selling Dodge, Chrysler, and Jeep.

Community Involvement

The business of selling cars has really never been Primeaux's sole focus. His belief that strong community support and involvement are the finest practices any business can endeavor to do has proven correct. Dozens of nonprofit community service, sports, and cultural organizations have benefited from Primeaux's commitment to community. His support, in the form of donations, promotion, serving as board member, and most importantly time, have made him one of Tulsa's most respected citizens.

Support for the community doesn't stop at Tulsa's city limits. Primeaux is active in many statewide organizations. Like many Oklahomans, he puts a great amount of faith in the belief that every community wins when we all work together.

"We all live here and taking care of the community is everyone's responsibility," Primeaux often says.

Building for the Future

Crown Auto World is a prime example of challenging employees to strive for their best. Personal goals, vision, and mission statements are as much a part of employee performance as a commitment to outstanding sales and service.

Henry with "Automotive YES" board members. Left to right- William Boyd- Daimler Chrysler, Jack Smith- Chairman and CEO of General Motors, Henry Primeaux-Crown Auto World, Jim Willingham- Chairman NADA, Frank McCarthy- President NADA.

Giving individuals the opportunity to improve themselves is another Primeaux hallmark. Crown Auto World was a pilot dealership in the Automotive YES program to train high school students to become skilled technicians. The program uses mentor relationships to build strong individuals and a stronger dealership.

"There is nothing that cannot be accomplished with education," Primeaux adds. "We are committed to providing the best education possible for all of our citizens."

The Primeaux Family Foundation has made a multi year major financial commitment to AYES. Inspiring and motivating people is a personal crusade for Primeaux. Not a week goes by that he is not asked to speak to area students or community groups to tell his personal success story and motivate others to reach for their goals.

Family Business

A commitment to community is not something Henry Primeaux or the Primeaux family takes lightly. He is very proud that each of his children has relocated to Tulsa to become a part of the business and active participants in the community. Henry Joseph has become the dealer of The Crown Bristow Dealership, a new Primeaux business venture; daughter Lisa Lotz is the dealership's finance manager; son-in-law Steve Longa is a sales manager; and his brother Robert manages the make ready department. Primeaux is also quick to point out that three of his grandchildren are native Tulsans. This is where they will call home.

The Crown Auto World group is the centerpiece of several businesses Primeaux will pass to children in the coming years. Along with the dealership, he is a partner in the popular Flavors restaurant, and president of Primeaux Marketing. Additionally, the Primeaux Family Foundation, run by daughter Joann Longa, was founded in 1998.

There is no secret to the success of Henry Primeaux and Crown Auto World. Dedication, commitment, ethics, and compassion are the reasons for the continued growth of the dealership. Exceeding expectations and placing the highest value on customer relationships are the driving force behind the dealership's remarkable accomplishments. Giving people the opportunity to excel and challenge themselves is the key to the Crown's future. And of course, no mention of Henry Primeaux's Crown Auto World is complete without pointing out that, "Sam's is still next door." ⬸

Service mentor Mark Maroney instructs AYES student Sarah Stiles. Left to right- Mark Maroney, Henry Primeaux, Sarah Stiles.

The Henry and Jane Primeaux family. Left to right, front row- Michael Longa, Lisa Primeaux Lotz, Nichole Lotz, Joann Primeaux Longa, Brian Longa. Back row- Edward Lotz, Henry Primeaux, Jane Primeaux, Henry Joseph Primeaux, Steve Longa, Jeff Longa.

DOLLAR THRIFTY AUTOMOTIVE GROUP, INC.

If you have frequent opportunities to travel for fun, you probably are familiar with the names of Dollar Rent A Car and Thrifty, Inc. What you may not know, though, is that the international headquarters for each of these powerful vehicle rental brands is located in Tulsa. In fact, the two businesses are sister companies, and they are owned by Tulsa-based Dollar Thrifty Automotive Group, Inc. (NYSE:DTG). Combined under the DTG umbrella, the two create the world's fourth-largest publicly traded car rental company.

Dollar Thrifty Automotive Group's worldwide headquarters is located at Dollar Thrifty Plaza in Tulsa.

While Dollar and Thrifty both primarily serve value-conscious travelers, each operates independently and has its own business approach. Dollar is a retail operation that focuses on company-owned locations in the top 50 U.S. markets. From predominately on-airport locations, it targets domestic, leisure travelers. It also receives a high volume of business from international tour operators. Thrifty, predominantly a franchise operation, derives one-half of its revenue from airport markets, and the balance from local (downtown and neighborhood) markets. Dollar and Thrifty have operations in about 75 countries throughout the world, including 900 corporate and franchised locations in the United States and Canada.

Steady Growth

Dollar and Thrifty provide customers excellent service and competitively priced vehicles. Both consistently go the extra mile to perform efficiently and cost-effectively for customers. As a result, DTG has carved out its own niche in the $16-billion-plus rental-car industry. Dollar and Thrifty have established reputations as best-value links in the industry chain and have earned a presence as serious competitors.

Joe Cappy, DTG's chairman, chief executive officer, and president, is proud of the company's success. "We have an excellent management team that takes calculated risks, moves forward with confidence, and follows its business intuition," he says. "Our reward is strong transaction volume growth, solid returns for our shareholders, and exciting company-wide growth."

That success has translated into a constantly building employment bonanza for Tulsa. To keep pace with accelerating rental volumes, Dollar and Thrifty have increased their corporate office staffs substantially. By mid-1999, approximately 1,100 employees occupied the three buildings located near 31st Street and Darlington Avenue. In October 1999, the complex was renamed "Dollar Thrifty Plaza" in honor of DTG's growth and dominant presence.

"Dollar and Thrifty employees increase our value by discovering savings opportunities, identifying new streams of revenue, and displaying an extraordinary work ethic," Cappy says. "They think

Dollar Rent A Car, with locations at most major U.S. airports, has approximately 430 worldwide locations in 26 countries.

creatively, exercise initiative, and take appropriate risks." But their commitment to excellence doesn't stop at work. Employees from Dollar and Thrifty are immersed in community activities—from coaching Little League teams to working with the elderly. Corporately, DTG makes huge financial commitments to enhance life in the Tulsa area by supporting organizations such as United Way, Adopt-A-School, and Boy Scouts of America.

Beyond Tulsa

In order for Dollar and Thrifty to efficiently handle the sizable gains in vehicle bookings that each has experienced during the past few years, DTG recently opened two additional state-of-the-art reservations centers to supplement their Tulsa operations.

Thrifty's new call center in Okmulgee, Oklahoma, came on line in September 1998 with a staff of 80. In December 1998, Dollar opened the doors to a $2.5-million worldwide reservation and telecommunications center staffed by 250 in Tahlequah, Oklahoma. Together, the centers respond to more than 12 million calls annually.

Dollar's fleet utilization of about 85 percent continues to set a benchmark for the industry. And, it expects that standard to continue in all regions, with particular strength in Hawaii, Florida, California, and Nevada. Of note is Dollar's unique operation at the Sanford International Airport, near Orlando, Florida, which caters to international charter-tour flights. Often, Dollar's rental volumes there exceed 700 vehicles within three hours.

Successful franchising of Thrifty's brand also sets enviable standards. For example, Thrifty added 70 new locations during 1999 and franchised several new countries. *Entrepreneur* magazine's Annual Franchise 500 ranking, which is considered the world's best and most comprehensive franchise ranking, recently named Thrifty the #1 Franchiser in its Auto Rentals and Sales category. Thrifty also has received the magazine's Business Travel Award for five consecutive years.

Dollar and Thrifty work aggressively to take their brands to the worldwide community. At the beginning of 1999, more than 430 Dollar locations could be found in 26 countries outside the United States. Thrifty's operations have a strong presence in 67 nations where more than 1,200 locations display its logo. Thrifty also has a dominant position in three of the four largest car rental markets in Europe, and it is poised for further expansion.

In a move to capture a growing share of the international market, Dollar recently established an alliance with Sixt, AG, the largest car rental agency in Germany. "Our combined capacity will serve the global market at more than 1,000 locations in 49 countries, with a fleet of more than 140,000 vehicles," says Gary L. Paxton, Dollar Rent A Car president and chief executive officer.

Creative Thinking

Successfully rotating used vehicles out of inventory is a challenge that all car rental companies face, and the used car auction has been the industry's traditional method to do so. In February 1999, however, DTG entered the $1-trillion auto retailing business with Thrifty Car Sales, a used-car franchise system. This new business is the first nationwide, entrepreneur-owned, non-manufacturer branded used-car operation. "We're leveraging our expertise in franchising, vehicle acquisition, and disposal to create a parallel franchise system," explains Don Himelfarb, Thrifty, Inc., president and chief executive officer. As of December 31, 1999, this new business had eight locations in operation and another four signed—pending facility completion.

Performance commitment

Dollar and Thrifty continue to introduce additional service enhancements and improvements that add to the value of their brands. Cappy notes, "DTG will continue to demonstrate sound management, and grow revenues and profits. By going the extra mile in all that we do, DTG will continue to seize opportunities that allow us to continue excelling in Tulsa, the United States, and in our worldwide markets." ❖

Thrifty Car Rental is one of the world's largest international car rental franchise networks, with over 1,200 locations in 67 countries.

QUIKTRIP

Of the thousands of businesses headquartered in Tulsa, perhaps none touches the lives of more people everyday than QuikTrip.

State-of-the-art facilities are a QuikTrip trademark.

QuikTrip is the most respected convenience store operation in the nation. With over 330 stores in nine states, QuikTrip plays a part in the daily lives of millions of Americans. Whether in need of a snack, a morning cup of coffee or cappuccino, a tank of gas, or any of thousands of products carried by the stores, millions turn to QuikTrip every day.

There is no secret to QuikTrip's remarkable success. Every customer knows the key—QuikTrip employees. Behind every QuikTrip counter are employees who work to make the QuikTrip experience head and shoulders above any similar experience. QuikTrip's people make the difference every day.

The first QuikTrip store opened just south of 51st Street and Peoria in 1958. Co-founders Chester Cadieux and Burt Holmes had a dream of someday operating 10 stores throughout Tulsa. Through the early lean years, the company learned from mistakes and capitalized on its strengths. The original dream of 10 stores was soon realized and surpassed as Tulsans flocked to these "new" convenience stores.

After more than a dozen stores were opened in the Tulsa area in the 1960s, QuikTrip expanded into new markets. QuikTrips opened in small Oklahoma communities and then expanded into Kansas City, Wichita, and Des Moines. The growth required the company to reevaluate its strategy. Although its main selling point was convenience, gasoline sales would lead to record growth. New stores were designed to feature more gas pumps and existing stores were either retrofitted or relocated to meet this new standard. QuikTrip credit cards were introduced to offer customers another level of convenience.

A commitment to gasoline sales, backed up by an unconditional guarantee of every gallon of QuikTrip gasoline sold, pushed the company to new levels of sales growth. Today, QuikTrip sells more than 1.2 billion gallons of gasoline each year—nearly one percent of all gasoline sold in the U.S.

In the 1980s, QuikTrip developed the Travel Center concept, which combines QuikTrip convenience with the amenities of large truck stops. Today, more than 14 travel centers serve customers traveling interstate highways for business or pleasure.

To facilitate the highest level of operations and growth into new markets, QuikTrip founded Quik'n Tasty foods, the corporation's distribution arm. Each week, Quik'n Tasty trucks travel more than 300,000 miles delivering products, including QuikTrip's own Quik'n Tasty products.

QuikTrip stores traditionally have sales volume in excess of 2 1/2 times the national average. Deciding where the stores will be located has changed incredibly since the first stores were erected. Today, nearly two years of research goes into each location. The standards QuikTrip has set require the work of a team of Store Development professionals.

QuikTrip successfully expanded into the St. Louis and Atlanta markets in the 1980s. In 1999, QuikTrip expanded into Dallas and in 2000, into Phoenix. The new divisions were chosen for their strong economies and growth potential.

The company recently completed an aggressive project to remodel 250 stores and close or move dozens of outdated locations opened before 1986. The average age of a QuikTrip store is 8.2 years. Just as the community changes, QuikTrip adapts its locations to meet the needs of the communities it serves.

Customers can walk into a QuikTrip in Tulsa, Des Moines, Atlanta, or Dallas and find the same look and feel. QuikTrip doesn't just open a new location when it moves into a new city. The key to success is the ability to infuse the company's culture. This is done by transferring experienced personnel to open the first 10 stores in any new city.

Yet, no matter where QuikTrip expands, it is the company's people that set it apart. Just as QuikTrip spends more than the industry average on developing every location, the company invests more to hire, train, and retain the finest staff in the

Ask many customers what they enjoy most about their favorite QuikTrip they'll say it's the quality service and smiles they receive from the company's extraordinary employees.

industry. Hiring is done at division headquarters and training follows a strict program. The company proudly maintains a record of promoting managers from within. Every store manager, just as every division manager and most people in upper management, served customers at the store level before moving up in the company.

At QuikTrip, employees are empowered to make sure each customer receives the finest service and the highest quality products. If a customer is unhappy, every attempt is made to satisfy the customer immediately. If customers need further assistance, QuikTrip maintains a 1-800 telephone number that is personally answered by QuikTrip corporate management personnel. QuikTrip employees work hard to establish relationships with customers. Customers may visit "their" neighborhood store daily, several times a week, or even several times each day.

A long-standing aspect of QuikTrip's community relationships is a dedication to community service. QuikTrip is a longtime supporter of many community organizations, especially the United Way. Every employee is invited to participate in the United Way's annual campaign and QuikTrip matches every dollar pledged. QuikTrip contributes five percent of corporate profit to charitable causes in the communities it serves. And in established divisions, every QuikTrip location is designated a Safe Place, where children can turn for help when they are in need.

At QuikTrip, the numbers truly speak for themselves—more than 50 million fountain drinks and 40 million cups of coffee are sold annually; more than 25 million Quick'n Tasty sandwiches are manufactured and sold each year; and more than 1.2 billion gallons of gasoline are pumped each year. There are more than 330 stores in nine states and the company is listed among the top 100 privately-owned businesses in the U.S.

For more than 40 years, QuikTrip has been a part of the Tulsa community. QuikTrip and its 700 Tulsa-area employees are proud to call Tulsa home. Tulsans making their commute to work in the morning or visiting a city far from home can take pride whenever they step into a QuikTrip. This is "their" store, wherever they go. ⤴

QuikTrip included self-serve fountain drinks years ago and still maintains the highest quality fountain offer in the industry.

A strong commitment to gasoline sales—backed by guaranteeing every drop it sells—has spurred QuikTrip to become a leading gasoline retailer.

THE TULSA ZOO AND LIVING MUSEUM

𝒫olar bears swim and play. Cheetahs lope through tall grass. Jaguars peer from the shadows of a tropical rain forest.

The endangered golden-headed lion tamarin resides in Tulsa Zoo's lush Tropical American Rain Forest.

It could take years of traveling the globe to glimpse these wild animals. Or, one can easily drive just eight miles northeast of downtown Tulsa to experience the same thrills and excitement—all courtesy of the Tulsa Zoo and Living Museum.

Tulsa Zoo is one of the nation's top zoological parks and consistently one of the top tourist attractions in northeast Oklahoma, averaging more than 600,000 visitors each year. Whether you're taking in the sights of the African Savanna or pressing your nose against the glass inside the Chimpanzee Connection, the Tulsa Zoo provides an enjoyable experience—and a better understanding of the role of wildlife in the natural world—by immersing visitors in each exhibit.

The idea of a zoo for Tulsa was first introduced to the Park Board in May 1927, and the Zoo officially opened in 1928 with 35 animals. Today, the Tulsa Zoo manages over 4,500 animals representing approximately 500 different species. Of that number, 19 are threatened or endangered and 17 are managed by Species Survival Plans (SSP), a vital conservation program supported by the Tulsa Zoo.

Since 1975, the Tulsa Zoo has set itself apart from other zoos in the United States by positioning itself as a "living museum," where animals are not the sole focus of attention. Instead, they are a component of an overall collection that offers the community a zoo, natural history museum, aquarium, and botanical garden—all integrated into one unifying theme. The Tulsa Zoo is a nationally recognized leader in the

Living Museum philosophy, having achieved accreditation as a zoo, a museum, and a botanical garden.

"Conservation, education, and recreation are major responsibilities of every accredited zoo," explains Larry Nunley, Tulsa Zoo director. "By taking a holistic approach, our mission is to educate visitors of all ages on the importance of conserving our natural world through a fun and exciting visit to the zoo. We call it 'keeping the wonder alive.'"

The zoo is able to accomplish its mission through the unique partnership it has with the City of Tulsa and Tulsa Zoo Friends, the official development and promotional organization of the Tulsa Zoo. This non-profit group was formed in 1971 to foster the growth and development of the zoo. Tulsa Zoo Friends helps the zoo reach its goals by hosting annual fundraisers such as *WALTZ on the Wild Side* and bringing in special exhibits, as well as operating food and gift concessions and overseeing admissions, development, promotions, and marketing. In the last 10 years, Tulsa Zoo Friends has been responsible for more than $10 million in capital improvements to the Zoo.

With the development of a new strategic Master Plan, the Tulsa Zoo is preparing to take visitors into the next century by expanding current exhibits and adding several new animals—including penguins, gorillas, and orangutans. Some things will never change, however, and after more than 70 years the Tulsa Zoo continues its role of delighting and educating visitors about the natural world around us—and how humans fit in as a piece of the world's puzzle. ⮜

Siberian tigers enjoy water sports at the Tulsa Zoo.

MAY'S DRUG STORES, INC.

The May's Drug / Drug Warehouse organization has carefully defined the market it chooses to dominate in the next century. It's all within a comfortable drive of Tulsa, and the competition is invited to take note, and get ready.

From its start in Joplin, Missouri more than 60 years ago, this dynamic chain—still owned and operated by the same family—stays focused on the communities it serves. Now headquartered in Tulsa, May's Drug and companion Drug Warehouse stores are staking claim on a market comprised of much of the Sooner state, plus those sections of Missouri, Kansas, and Arkansas that meet at a four-corners' conjunction with Oklahoma.

It's a thoroughly familiar market for this long-time retail leader, with 39 May's Drug or Drug Warehouse outlets in Missouri and Oklahoma. The company will expand to 45 stores in the next two years.

"One of the reasons we've been successful over the last 63 years is that we've had a localized focus on the community," says Gerald Heller, CEO. "We operate within a 165-mile radius of Tulsa, so we have a good feel for what people want in a drug store, and we cater to their expectations."

May's sets "the standard for pharmacy excellence," through emphasis on communities and by using the latest technological advances. It is one of only two privately owned drug store chains in the U.S. that hold the number one share in a significant retail market. Tulsa is the 87th largest retail market in the nation.

Both May's Drug and Drug Warehouse walk the walk of community service, by providing flu shots and other healthcare services, by donating money to the communities in which its stores are located, and by encouraging associates to participate in community service projects.

More than 55 percent of May's business involves filling prescriptions. Staffed with knowledgeable, dedicated, friendly, family pharmacists working with the latest technology and the best staff assistance, May's emphasizes a patient/pharmacist relationship built on trust.

"Our customer commitment is not only to provide fast, accurate, prescription service, but to ensure that all patients understand how and when to take their medication," says Heller.

In addition to its pharmacy services, the May's Drug / Drug Warehouse chain includes 19 one-hour photo labs and 15 food marts. The company operates its own distribution center in Tulsa.

May's has long been a leader in technology in the drug store industry. "We were the first drug chain in the country to be completely computerized," says Heller. The company adopted computers in 1975.

That spirit of innovation will help the company retain its industry leadership role in the 21st century as well. Soon, May's customers will order refills over the Web, and its site will provide information about medications, helpful health tips, and money-saving specials. And among its plans for the new millenium is a system that allows customers to call in and automatically access their prescription information. ❖

President and CEO of the largest independent drug chain in Oklahoma, Gerald Heller says May's Drug and Drug Warehouse set the standard for pharmacy excellence in the state.

JAVA DAVE'S EXECUTIVE COFFEE SERVICE

Success has been brewing for more than two decades for Java Dave's Executive Coffee Service.

A Java Dave's patron enjoys a delicious coffee drink at one of the many coffee houses located in Oklahoma.

In 1980, soon after graduating high school, Dave Neighbors moved to Tulsa from Oklahoma City to expand the family business—Executive Coffee Service. He, along with his brother Stan, had learned all aspects of the coffee business, from sales and service to distribution, from their mother and father, Lorena and Earl Neighbors. The family's success in Oklahoma City was soon realized in Tulsa.

Executive Coffee Service saw rapid growth, expanding from two employees and a 400 square-foot warehouse to become the largest coffee service in Tulsa. In 1988, the company opened the first Neighbors Quality Coffee House to capitalize on the gourmet coffee niche. The concept proved to be a success and after purchasing several locations in Oklahoma City in 1993, the name of the retail coffee houses was changed to Java Dave's.

Along with the expansion into retail, came the opportunity to offer more Java Dave's brand name products. The retail locations offer a variety of products, ranging from gift baskets to specialty coffee flavors and espresso, and have become the place to stop for a morning cup of coffee or cappuccino to go or quiet evening gatherings with friends.

In 1995, Java Dave's Executive Coffee Service built a state-of-the-art coffee roasting/manufacturing facility which enabled the company to blend, roast, grind, and package their own line of coffees, teas, cocoa, and cappuccino mixes. Today, there are more than 200 Java Dave's manufactured products available for purchase in retail stores, the office coffee service, the Java Dave's mail order catalogs, or over the Internet.

Founders of Java Dave's Executive Coffee include from left to right: Earl Neighbors, Stan Neighbors, Dave Neighbors, and (center) Lorena Neighbors.

Franchising has become a company emphasis in recent years. There are now more than a dozen Java Dave's franchise locations in Oklahoma. The Neighbors family goal is to expand to 40 franchises throughout the region by 2005 by offering new concepts and opportunities for entrepreneurs. Strict franchise requirements and the highest quality of products and service guarantees that when a customer walks into a Java Dave's in Tulsa, Oklahoma City, or any other city, they can expect the same quality products and personal service the company is famous for.

Java Dave's Executive Coffee Service continues to expand into new markets. By maintaining an industry leading level of service and offering unique Java Dave's products, Executive Coffee Service continues to see strong growth in Tulsa and communities throughout the region.

Java Dave's Executive Coffee Service takes great pride in serving thousands of Oklahomans every day. Java Dave's celebrated its special relationship with Tulsa by developing "Black Gold" a special blend that was the official coffee of the Tulsa Centennial.

Java Dave's Executive Coffee Service looks forward to meeting all of their customers' coffee needs. Coffee is not just their business; it is their life. They are pleased to give the very best service to their customers. ❖

ENTERPRISE INDEX

AAON, Inc.
2425 South Yukon
Tulsa, Oklahoma 74107
Phone: 918-583-2266
Fax: 918-583-6094
E-mail: aaon@aaon.com
www.aaon.com
Pages 192-193

The Bama Companies
PO Box 4829
Tulsa, Oklahoma 74159
Phone: 918-732-2020
Fax: 918-585-5484
E-mail: pmarshal@bama.com
http://bamanet.bama.com
Pages 186-187

Bank of America
515 South Boulder
Tulsa, Oklahoma 74103
Phone: 918-591-8577
Fax: 918-591-8375
E-mail: ed.fariss@bankofamerica.com
www.bankofamerica.com
Page 210

Bank of Oklahoma
PO Box 2300
Tulsa, Oklahoma 74192
Phone: 918-588-6348
Fax: 918-588-6853
www.bankofoklahoma.com
Page 215

Bank One
15 East 5th Street
PO Box One
Tulsa, Oklahoma 74102
Phone: 918-586-1000
Fax: 918-586-5606
www.bankone.com
Pages 206-207

Blue Cross and Blue Shield of Oklahoma
1215 South Boulder
PO Box 3283
Tulsa, Oklahoma 74102-3283
Phone: 918-560-3500
www.bcbsok.com
Pages 232-233

Borg Compressed Steel
1032 North Lewis
Tulsa, Oklahoma 74110
Phone: 918-587-2511
Fax: 918-587-2520
E-mail: borg@galstar.com
Page 196

Cancer Care Associates
6151 South Yale Avenue, Suite 100
Tulsa, Oklahoma 74136-1902
Phone: 918-499-2060
Fax: 918-499-2160
www.cancercareassoc.com
Page 242

Cascia Hall Preparatory School
2520 South Yorktown Avenue
Tulsa, Oklahoma 74114
Phone: 918-746-2600
Fax: 918-746-2636
E-mail: info@casciahall.tulsa.ok.us
www.casciahall.tulsa.ok.us
Page 248

Chandler-Frates & Reitz
4501 East 31st Street
Tulsa, Oklahoma 74135
Phone: 918-747-8631
Fax: 918-747-8619
www.cfr-ins.com
Page 212

Charles and Lynn Schusterman Family Foundation
Two West Second Street
Tulsa, Oklahoma 74103-3103
Phone: 918-591-1090
Fax: 918-591-1758
E-mail: clsff@ionet.net
www.schusterman.org
Page 214

Citizens Security Bank & Trust Company
14821 South Memorial
Bixby, Oklahoma 74008
Phone: 918-366-4000
888-272-8866
Fax: 918-366-1437
E-mail: citizens@ionet.net
Page 208

Crown Auto World
4444 South Sheridan
Tulsa, Oklahoma 74145
Phone: 918-663-4444
Fax: 918-628-1478
www.crownautoworld.com
Pages 266-267

Doerner, Saunders, Daniel & Anderson, L.L.P.
320 South Boston Avenue, Suite 500
Tulsa, Oklahoma 74103
Phone: 918-582-1211
Fax: 918-591-5360
E-mail: postmaster@dsda.com
www.dsda.com
Pages 218-219

Dollar Thrifty Automotive Group, Inc.
5330 East 31st Street
Tulsa, Oklahoma 74135
Phone: 918-660-7700
Fax: 918-669-3912
www.dtag.com
Pages 268-269

Doubletree Hotel at Warren Place
6110 South Yale
Tulsa, Oklahoma 74136
Phone: 918-495-1000
Fax: 918-495-1090
www.doubletreehotels.com
Pages 262-265

**First Commercial Real Estate
Services Corp.**
7134 South Yale, Suite 500
Tulsa, Oklahoma 74136
Phone: 918-495-1551
Fax: 918-481-8404
E-mail: peggyk@first-commercial.com
www.first-commercial.com
Page 258

Hillcrest HealthCare System
110 West Seventh Street, Suite 2700
Tulsa, Oklahoma 74119
Phone: 918-579-1000
www.hillcrest.com
Pages 234-235

Hilti, Inc.
5400 South 122nd East Avenue
Tulsa, Oklahoma 74146
Phone: 918-252-6000
800-879-8000
Fax: call for number
E-mail: call for department
www.us.hilti.com
Pages 178-181

Holland Hall School
5666 East 81st Street
Tulsa, Oklahoma 74137-2099
Phone: 918-481-1111
Fax: 918-481-1145
E-mail: mcruncleton@hollandhall.org
www.hollandhall.org
Page 246

**Honeywell Aerospace Services,
Tulsa Heat Transfer Operations**
6930 North Lakewood
Tulsa, Oklahmoma 74117
Phone: 918-272-8000
Fax: 918-272-2462
E-mail: angie.repsher@honeywell.com
www.lori-ht.com
Pages 190-191

Java Dave's Executive Coffee Service
6239 East 15th Street
Tulsa, Oklahoma 74112
Phone: 918-836-5570
Fax: 918-835-4348
E-mail: davebeans@aol.com
www.javadavescoffee.com
Page 274

KPMG LLP
100 West Fifth Street, Suite 310
Tulsa, Oklahoma 74103
Phone: 918-560-2813
Fax: 918-560-2868
E-mail: gjvanlunsen@kpmg.com
www.kpmg.com
Page 222

Littlefield, Inc.
1307 South Boulder Avenue
Tulsa, Oklahoma 74119-3215
Phone: 918-295-1000
Fax: 918-295-1001
E-mail: info@littlefieldinc.com
www.littlefieldinc.com
Pages 220-221

Local Oklahoma Bank
2250 East 73rd Street, Suite 200
Tulsa, Oklahoma 74136
Phone: 918-494-2863
Fax: 918-495-1284
Page 211

Manhattan Construction Company
5601 South 122nd East Avenue
Tulsa, Oklahoma 74146
Phone: 918-583-6900
Fax: 918-592-4334
E-mail: jssnyder@mccmail.com
www.mccbuilds.com
Pages 254-255

May's Drug Stores, Inc.
1437 South Boulder, Suite 1100
Tulsa, Oklahoma 74119
Phone: 918-592-6297
Fax: 918-592-4545
www.maysdrug.com
Page 273

McGivern, Gilliard & Curthoys
1515 South Boulder
Tulsa, Oklahoma 74119
Phone: 918-584-3391
Fax: 918-592-2416
E-mail: mcgivern@ionet.net
Page 223

MCI WorldCom
6929 North Lakewood Avenue
Tulsa, Oklahoma 74117
Phone: 918-590-1000
www.wcom.com
Pages 162-163

McKissick/The Crosby Group
2801 Dawson Road
Tulsa, Oklahoma 74110
Phone: 918-834-4611
Fax: 918-832-0940
E-mail: crosbygroup@thecrosbygroup.com
www.thecrosbygroup.com
Page 195

Med-X Corporation
7130 South Lewis, Suite 520
Tulsa, Oklahoma 74136
Phone: 918-497-1400
Fax: 918-497-1492
Page 249

Metropolitan Tulsa Chamber of Commerce
616 Boston, Suite 100
Tulsa, Oklahoma 74119-1298
Phone: 918-585-1201
Fax: 918-585-8016
E-mail: webmaster@tulsachamber.com
www.tulsachamber.com
Pages 204-205

Photo on Page 275
by Don Wheeler.

MiraTech Consulting Group
6709 East 81st Street, Suite G
Tulsa, Oklahoma 74133
Phone: 918-495-0507
Fax: 918-495-0533
E-mail: davidg@miratechconsulting.com
www.miratechconsulting.com
Page 169

The NORDAM Group
510 South Lansing
Tulsa, Oklahoma 74120
Phone: 918-587-4105
Fax: 918-560-8535
www.nordam.com
Pages 174-177

Northeastern State University
600 North Grand
Tahlequah, Oklahoma 74464
Phone: 918-456-5511
Fax: 918-458-2320
E-mail: webmaster@cherokee.nsuok.edu
www.nsuok.edu
Page 243

Oklahoma State University
Tulsa:
700 North Greenwood Avenue
Tulsa, Oklahoma 74106
Phone: 918-594-8223
Fax: 918-594-8007
E-mail: mdruumo@osu-tulsa.okstate.edu
www.tulsa.okstate.edu
Stillwater:
219 PIO
Stillwater, Oklahoma 74078
Phone: 405-744-6260
Fax: 405-744-9073
E-mail: natalea@okstate.edu
www.okstate.edu
Pages 236-237

ONEOK, Inc.
100 West Fifth Street
Tulsa, Oklahoma 74103
Phone: 918-591-5000
Fax: 918-588-7273
www.oneok.com
Page 168

Oral Roberts University
7777 South Lewis Avenue
Tulsa, Oklahoma 74171
Phone: 918-495-6161
Fax: 918-495-6033
E-mail: publicrelations@oru.edu
www.oru.edu
Pages 238-239

Paragon Films, Inc.
3500 West Tacoma
Broken Arrow, Oklahoma 74012
Phone: 918-250-3456
Fax: 918-254-9676
E-mail: mjh@paragon-films.com
www.paragon-films.com
Pages 182-185

Public Service Company of Oklahoma
PO Box 201
Tulsa, Oklahoma 74102
Phone: 918-599-2000
E-mail: corpcom@csw.com
www.csw.com
Page 166

QuikTrip
901 North Mingo
Tulsa, Oklahoma 74119
Phone: 918-836-8551
Fax: 918-836-7000
E-mail: dgraham@quiktrip.com
www.quiktrip.com
Pages 270-271

Samson Investment Company
Two West Second Street
Tulsa, Oklahoma 74103-3103
Phone: 918-583-1791
Fax: 918-583-9096
E-mail: webmaster@samson.com
www.samson.com
Page 214

SouthCrest Hospital
8801 South 101st East Avenue
Tulsa, Oklahoma 74133
Phone: 918-294-4000
Fax: 918-294-4809
E-mail: pamela.weldon@triadhospitals.com
www.southcresthospital.com
Page 247

State Bank and Trust
502 South Main Mall
Tulsa, Oklahoma 74103
Phone: 918-631-1000
Fax: 918-631-1183
www.statebank.arvest.com
Page 209

Suite Options Corporate Apartments
9435 East 51st Street, Suite J
Tulsa, Oklahoma 74145
Phone: 918-663-5000
Fax: 918-663-4938
E-mail: tulsa@suiteoptions.com
www.suiteoptions.com
Pages 256-257

Superior Federal Bank
Loan Production Office:
7633 East 63rd, Suite 255
Tulsa, Oklahoma 74133
Phone: 918-294-8694
Fax: 918-294-1810
Corporate Office:
5000 Rogers Avenue
Fort Smith, Arkansas 72903
Phone: 501-452-8900
Fax: 501-484-8543
www.superiorfederal.com
Page 213

T.D. Williamson, Inc.
8506 East 61 Street
Tulsa, Oklahoma 74133-1919
Phone: 918-447-5001
Fax: 918-447-5050
E-mail: info@tdwilliamson.com
www.tdwilliamson.com
Pages 188-189

Tulsa Community College
6111 East Skelly Drive, Suite 415
Tulsa, Oklahoma 74136-6198
Phone: 918-595-7884
Fax: 918-595-7929
E-mail: sbrown3@tulsa.cc.ok.us
www.tulsa.cc.ok.us
Page 245

Tulsa Technology Center
6111 East Skelly Drive
PO Box 477200
Tulsa, Oklahoma 74147-7200
Phone: 918-828-5000
Fax: 918-828-5059
E-mail: jkeim@tulsatech.org
www.tulsatech.com
Page 244

The *Tulsa World*
PO Box 1770
315 South Boulder Avenue
Tulsa, Oklahoma 74103
Phone: 918-581-8400
Fax: 918-581-8353
E-mail: tulsaworld@tulsaworld.com
www.tulsaworld.com
Pages 158-161

The Tulsa Zoo and Living Museum
5701 East 36th Street North
Tulsa, Oklahoma 74115
Phone: 918-669-6600
Fax: 918-669-6260
www.tulsazoo.org
Page 272

TV Guide
7140 South Lewis Avenue
Tulsa, Oklahoma 74136
Phone: 918-488-4450
Fax: 918-488-4637
www.tvguideinc.com
Pages 164-165

United Parcel Service
5805 South 118th, East Avenue
Tulsa, Oklahoma 74145
Phone: 800-PICK-UPS
Fax: 405-948-3800
www.ups.com
Page 197

The University of Oklahoma
Tulsa:
5310 East 31st Street, Suite 301
Tulsa, Oklahoma 74135
Phone: 918-838-4777
Fax: 918-838-4700
E-mail: jmabrey@ou.edu
Norman:
660 Parrington Oval
Norman, Oklahoma 73019
Phone: 405-325-3916
Fax: 405-325-7605
E-mail: dboren@ou.edu
www.ou.edu
Pages 228-231

The University of Tulsa
600 South College Avenue
Tulsa, Oklahoma 74104-3189
Phone: 918-631-2000
Fax: 918-631-2033
www.utulsa.edu
Pages 240-241

VoiceStream® Wireless
4200 East Skelly Drive, Suite 100
Tulsa, Oklahoma 74135
Phone: 918-523-8600
Fax: 918-523-8650
E-mail: jay.gibbon@voicestream.com
www.voicestream.com
Page 167

Whirlpool Corporation
7301 Whirlpool Drive
Tulsa, Oklahoma 74117
Phone: 918-274-6000
Fax: 918-274-6900
www.whirlpool.com
Page 194

Willbros Group, Inc.
c/o Willbros USA, Inc.
600 Willbros Place
2431 East 61st Street
Tulsa, Oklahoma 74136
Phone: 918-748-7000
Fax: 918-748-7087
E-mail: sales@willbros.com
www.willbros.com
Pages 252-253

Williams
One Williams Center
Tulsa, Oklahoma 74172
Phone: 800-Williams
www.williams.com
Pages 200-203

BIBLIOGRAPHY

Blakey, Ellen Sue; Bowman, Robbie; Downing, Jim; Hall, Ina; Hamill, John; Ridgway, Peggi. *The Tulsa Spirit*, Continental Heritage Press, 1979.

Butler, William. *Tulsa 75: A History of Tulsa*, Metropolitan Tulsa Chamber of Commerce. 1974.

Basie, William "Count," as told to Albert Murray. *Good Morning Blues*, Paladin Books, 1987.

Debo, Angie. *Tulsa: From Creek Town to Oil Capital*, University of Oklahoma Press, 1943.

Goble, Danney. *Tulsa! Biography of the American City*, Council Oaks Books, 1997.

Gregory, Robert. *Oil in Oklahoma*, Leake Industries Inc., 1976.

Herndon, V.E. *The Story of Tulsa: From an Indian Village to a Modern Metropolis*, Tulsa Public Schools, 1950.

The Junior League of Tulsa, The Tulsa Historical Society, The Tulsa Preservation Commission. *Tulsa History, A to Z: A Primer on Tulsa*, The Junior League of Tulsa, 1997.

Walton, John Brooks. *One Hundred Historic Tulsa Homes*, HCE Publications, 2000.

The author also wishes to acknowledge information gleaned from *Agenda* magazine, *Inside Tulsa*, *Tulsa Economic Profile*, *Tulsa Guide to Education*, *Tulsa Lifestyle*, *TulsaPeople Magazine*, *Tulsa Magazine*, *Tulsa Relocation Guide*, *Tulsa Visitors Guide*, and *Tulsa, The Annual Report*.

INDEX